THE PLACE OF REASON

D0209011

THE PLACE OF
REASON
INETHICS
❀❀*❀*

STEPHEN TOULMIN

WITH A NEW PREFACE

THE UNIVERSITY OF CHICAGO PRESS * CHICAGO & LONDON

An Examination of the Place of Reason in Ethics
was first published in 1950 by Cambridge
University Press.

The University of Chicago Press, Chicago 60637
The University of Chicago Press, Ltd., London

Preface © 1986 by The University of Chicago
All rights reserved. Published 1950
University of Chicago Press edition 1986
Printed in the United States of America

95 94 93 92 91 90 89 88 87 86   5 4 3 2 1

Library of Congress Cataloging in Publication Data

Toulmin, Stephen Edelston.
  An examination of the place of reason in ethics.

  Reprint. Originally published: Cambridge : Cambridge
University Press, 1950. With new pref.
  1. Ethics.   2. Reason.   I. Title.
BJ1031.T68   1986   170   86–16187
ISBN 0–226–80843–2
ISBN 0–226–80844–0 (pbk.)

πολλά τά δεινά κούδὲν ἀνθρώπου δεινότερον πέλει·
...καὶ φθέγμα καὶ ἀνεμόεν
φρόνημα καὶ ἀστυνόμους ὀργὰς ἐδιδάξατο....

Of all the many wonders, none is more wonderful than
Man...who has learnt the arts of Speech, of wind-swift
Thought, and of living in Neighbourliness....

SOPHOCLES, *Antigone*

PREFACE, 1986

I BEGAN work on *Reason in Ethics* forty years ago, in summer 1946. The first draft was submitted as a fellowship thesis at King's College, Cambridge in the bitter winter of 1947, and I learned of its success on returning from a day trip across the flooded Fens during the sudden March thaw. The final text was written in my rooms at King's during the dry summer of that year, and is entangled in memory not just with the heat, but with the sound of J. S. Bach's *St. Anne Fugue* coming through my window from the organ of the nearby chapel. So looking back from 1986 and asking what gave my thesis its unforeseen longevity awakens unavoidable nostalgia. In this preface, therefore, I shall put the book in a historical context, and ask how it addressed the central questions of moral philosophy as seen by British analytical philosophers just after the Second World War. But I shall add some personal remarks which help pinpoint the things that gave it a position independent of the current orthodoxies, and enabled it to point ahead to intellectual issues that have come into sharp focus only recently.

The Place of Reason in Ethics was the work of a philosophical tyro. This fact explains both its strengths and its weaknesses. Having done undergraduate work in mathematics and physics from 1940 to '42, I came back from war service in 1946 and was allowed to start research in the Cambridge Faculty of Moral Sciences without ever having taken a course or examination in philosophy. By then G. E. Moore had retired; C. D. Broad and A. C. Ewing were teaching from their published works; Wittgenstein's classes foreshadowed the *Philosophical Investigations*, and were no more concerned with ethics than those of John Wisdom. Of the active faculty members only Richard Braithwaite was working on ethics, and he was using mathematical "game theory" to analyze moral issues, a line of inquiry that I personally found questionable. Thus the chief stimulus to my thinking was in part my own private reading, in part discussions with my fellow students, notably Camo Jackson from Melbourne.

One weakness of my book is its limited documentation.[1] It did not address the theoretical preoccupations of current analytical philosophy directly, but came at them from an angle that reflected my eccentric background. Yet this fact also gives the book some of its merits. Having been trained as a natural scientist, I had always hoped to relate philosophical issues to practical experience, and could never wholly side with Hume the philosopher against Hume the backgammon player.[2] In departing from the deliverances of common sense[3] (I thought) the philosophers' analytic arguments undercut themselves; to ignore the accepted "good reasons" of everyday life was not to discredit them. After hearing Wittgenstein's skeptical arguments[4] several hours a week for eighteen months, I could not just take the accepted program of "metaethics" on trust. Instead, I looked for a way of moving beyond the problems to which that program gave rise (discussed in my initial chapters on the objective, subjective, and imperative theories) into the realm of practical moral reasoning.

In doing so, I now see, I was reversing the step by which the modern tradition in English moral philosophy was established a century ago. Until the 1860s, the standard text on ethics at Cambridge University was William Whewell's book, *The Elements of Morality*.[5] In style and content, that book had been a secular version of a classical moral theology text. It did not start from general abstract theories, but focused on specific concrete problems of different kinds (such as Cicero's case of the corn merchant who conceals news of the approach of fresh supplies to a starving city so as to profit from the shortage while he can), and treated duties of distinct kinds—such as those arising from family relationships, promises, or the claims of general benevolence—under separate headings. Whewell's *Elements* did not present all these obligations as the formal consequences of a single universal principle any more than Aristotle's *Nichomachean Ethics* treated all kinds of *philia* as carrying the same moral claims.[6] Different considerations impose different demands; and these can often be squared with one another, in practice, only by the exercise of moral perception and discernment.[7]

Whewell did not despise more general and abstract ethical issues. Indeed, the name of the Cambridge ethics chair was changed during his tenure so that the Knightbridge Professorship of Casuistical Divinity became (as it now is) the Knightbridge Professorship of Moral Philosophy. Still, his theoretical interest in abstract issues of philosophical ethics never destroyed his feeling for the variety and complexity of practical moral issues and concrete human problems. The man who changed the focus of moral philosophy and revived the more universal, theoretical ambitions for ethics about which Aristotle had always been skeptical[8] was Henry Sidgwick, who succeeded Whewell in the Knightbridge Chair. Sidgwick found Whewell's account of morality sloppy. Put off by the seeming untidiness of everyday moral reasoning, he looked for methods of argument in ethics more rigorous than those that Whewell's *Elements* had relied on. As he wrote in his old age:

My first adhesion to a definite Ethical system was to the Utilitarianism of Mill: I found in this relief from the apparently external and arbitrary pressure of moral rules which I had been educated to obey, and which presented themselves to me as to some extent doubtful and confused; and sometimes, even when clear, as merely dogmatic, unreasoned, incoherent. My antagonism to this was intensified by the study of Whewell's *Elements* which was prescribed for the study of undergraduates in Trinity. It was from that book that I derived the impression—which long remained uneffaced—that intuitional moralists [e.g. Whewell himself] were hopelessly loose (as compared to mathematicians) in their definitions and axioms.[9]

By contrast, Sidgwick's own book, *The Methods of Ethics*, set out to correct the logical deficiencies of practical moral argument, and give back to ethical reasoning abstract theoretical foundations of a kind the concrete pragmatic procedures of case morality lacked. Not that Henry Sidgwick despised case reasoning about particular moral issues. As a young Cambridge don he was required to take Holy Orders, which went against his personal beliefs; to resolve his quandary, he wrote out a careful analysis of the resulting *casus conscientiae*.[10] Still, his basic conviction remained that moral philosophy must rise above the level of specific practical cases and become a critical debate about general abstract principles, and the theoretical investigations that he initiated dominated English moral philosophy at least until the Second World War.

Sidgwick's distaste for the messiness of practical moral arguments is still alive today. Little more than a dozen years ago Jonathan Glover criticized the "baroque complexity" of moral practice, and justified the moral philosophers' preoccupation with abstract theory by appealing to "the aesthetic preferences most of us have for economy of principles, the preference for ethical systems in the style of the Bauhaus rather than the Baroque."[11]

Still, aesthetic preferences can be allowed to operate safely only on an intellectual level. Permitting a passion for simplicity or elegance to influence moral decisions in actual practice risks errors of judgment similar to the medical errors that Bernard Shaw pilloried in his play, *The Doctors' Dilemma*. Shaw's medical specialists based their clinical judgments not on what they found out about a patient's illness by open-minded examination, but on prior assumptions that his condition was one that they specialized in and were equipped to treat. Of course, anyone with a serious and complex illness should trust a physician who takes his clinical condition as he finds it—"baroque complexities" and all—more than one who oversimplifies his diagnoses to serve his own theoretical preoccupations; and a parallel problem arises in ethics, too. If we are to pursue elegance and logical rigor, as Sidgwick proposes, we must not allow abstract theoretical considerations to blind us to the circumstances of actual concrete cases, however messy and complex.

Since Sidgwick, English moral philosophy has gone through three phases. In the late nineteenth century, the general programme was to take as a starting point the moral judgments ("intuitions") of educated common sense, and look for the systematic procedure of theoretical analysis—in Sidgwick's terms, the "method" of ethics—that best rationalized those practical judgments and tidied up the associated patterns of arguments. At the outset, this did not rule out the possibility that different kinds of situations and obligations (e.g., promises, professional duties, and acts of benevolence) might need to be accounted for in different terms. For instance, F. H. Bradley's essay on "My Station and its Duties"[12] allowed for kinds of obligations as varied and diverse as Aristotle's types of *philia*. Still, as time went on, the drive toward generality and universality led philosophers to make more comprehensive claims on behalf of ethical theories. Ethical arguments should be not just tidy and rigorous; but also consistent: you could not properly claim to be a "utilitarian" one day, in one context, and a "deontologist" the next day, and for another purpose. The "methods" of ethics should no longer be viewed as complementary:

they now aimed at a uniqueness and universality that (Aristotle argued) was not available in the realm of *phronesis*.

The second phase was part of the wider revolt against nineteenth century (especially idealist) philosophical ideas, that launched British analytical philosophy. The key document is G. E. Moore's *Principia Ethica* (1903). Moore presents his argument as a dispassionate analysis of the *meaning* of our basic moral terms; but his analysis is directed by underlying passions, and ends with the famous chapter in which he calls on us to organize our lives around the appreciation of beautiful objects and the enjoyment of personal friendships. His Bloomsbury associates took this chapter as gospel: Roy Harrod's biography of John Maynard Keynes, for instance, finds one of the prime sources of Keynes's early thought in the "flaming advocacy" of Moore's book.

After the carnage of World War I, G. E. Moore's "ideal utilitarianism" lost its earlier charm, and moral philosophers tried harder to separate analysis from advocacy. In *The Right and the Good* and *Five Types of Ethical Theory*, for instance, W. D. Ross and C. D. Broad respect Sidgwick's goals of tidiness, consistency, and universality, and play down their own personal attitudes; the example of these books set the ground rules for the research program that was current when I began my own work—commonly referred to by the term "metaethics." Metaethical analysis had one purpose only: to give formally accurate accounts of the meanings of moral terms, to the exclusion of advocating any substantive positions. By the 1950s, the program was so entrenched that serious Oxford moral philosophers could claim that *any* course of action was a subject for a genuinely "moral" decision: what color tie to wear, quite as much as whether or not to hit a defenseless child.[13] The *meaning* of ethical terms was neutral as between all substantive applications: statements about meanings were "analytic" products of logical inquiry, substantive moral judgments "synthetic" expressions of actual people's personal attitudes.

The later history of English ethical theory reflects the impact of outside events. Despite their vast scale and brutal effects, the two world wars were not seen as raising novel issues for ethics. But after Hiroshima and the medical horrors of the German concentration camps, the situation changed. With the 1960s and the Viet-

nam War, practical concerns forced themselves anew on the attention of moral philosophers. Given the governmental double-talk
of the '60s and '70s, in particular, there was a widespread inclination to "question authority" and challenge earlier complacencies.
Beginning in medicine, matters of professional ethics became issues
of public concern, and there arose a new field of "bioethics": this
differed from earlier metaethics in being, first and foremost, more
practical than theoretical, and in being concerned with the detailed
circumstances of specific clinical and social situations.

The formal, abstract analysis of the meanings of moral terms
now yielded to substantive issues of (e.g.) human experimentation
and clinical practice: "advocacy" was no longer rejected as inconsistent with ethical theory proper.[14] Just as the work of the analytical moral philosophers threatened to run into the sand, Medicine came along and saved the life of ethics.[15] So today few moral
philosophers *either* dismiss substantive judgments as expressing
personal attitudes, irrelevant to the properly "logical" concerns of
philosophy, *or* refuse to discuss the substantive differences between
practical cases of different kinds. After being set aside for a century, the methods of "case morality" are coming back into fashion,
and we are back where we started with Whewell.

Viewed against this background, *Reason in Ethics* illustrates three
historical points:

(1) It was written at a transition point in the evolution of analytical philosophy, when the focus of analysis was moving from
"logic and language" to "concepts and practical procedures."

(2) By questioning the universality of moral rules it pointed
ahead, implicitly, to the revival of "casuistry."

(3) It also hinted at the need to "historicize" moral philosophy,
which happened to philosophy of science during the same period.

To comment briefly on each of these points: (1) In the years
around 1900, Bertrand Russell and G. E. Moore launched analytical philosophy by proposing two related yet distinct modes of
analysis. They agreed that the confused language in which late
nineteenth century philosophy had been presented deprived it of
any clear meaning, and advocated a program of intellectual
clarification designed (in Locke's phrase) to "clear away the under-
brush that stands in the way of knowledge." How was this to be
achieved? The two men answered that question differently.

Given his mathematical preoccupation with propositional logic, Russell favored adopting the logical symbolism of *Principia Mathematica* as the instrument of philosophical analysis also, and used it to design an "artificial language" (what Leibniz called a *characteristica universalis*) more exact and less misleading than the familiar "natural languages."[16] G. E. Moore, for his part, stayed with everyday English. He, too, aimed at weeding out the confusing and ill-conceived modes of expression with which philosophers had been misled into making grandly impressive assertions (e.g., "time is unreal") that proved on closer examination to lack solid meaning. But, in Moore's view, this could be done without any need to use mathematical symbolism, by redefining the problematic terms involved in the manner of a first-rate lexicographer. For purposes of philosophical analysis, the key question about everyday terms like *good, exists,* and *desirable* will then be, "If *brother* means 'male child of the same parents', what then does *so-and-so* mean?"[17]

Despite these technical differences, Russell and Moore agreed on one other basic point: whether formal or verbal, the results of philosophical analysis all take the form of *necessary* statements. My brother does not *just happen* to be "a male child of my parents," in the way that we just happen to have the same color of hair. Being brothers, the fact that we share the same parents is not *contingent:* it cannot help being so. The best method of analysis may be quasi-mathematical, or quasi-lexicographic: in either case, the products of analysis are open to philosophers' direct insight, not to empirical (let alone scientific) investigations.

In the 1930s, few analytical philosophers in England questioned this shared position. From 1945 on, as Wittgenstein became more influential, people began to look behind these "necessary" truths, and ask on what presuppositions they in turn rested. Instead of taking philosophical analysis as defining a self-subsistent world of necessary relations to which philosophical reflection gave one access, it was now recognized that shared concepts, meanings, and utterances ("language games") are embedded in, and depend for a sense on, the larger, more-than-linguistic world of human activities, purposes, and procedures ("forms of life"). On that deeper level of analysis, the outcome of philosophical reflection is no longer a separate collection of "necessary truths": instead, it requires a discursive account of our "meanings," which places these linguistic items in the larger context of human history, culture, and conduct. Going to and fro between Wittgenstein's rooms in Whewell's Court at Trinity and my desk at King's, I moved in the direction indicated by the idea of "forms of life." *The Place of Reason in Ethics* did not add to the existing corpus yet one more formal or lexicographical analysis of ethical language. It discussed the "functions" of ethical thought, language, and reasoning, leaving open the possibility that, within their own forms of life, people of different cultures and periods might develop overlapping but distinct traditions of moral belief.

At the time, it did not occur to me to pursue questions about the *historical evolution* of our moral concepts and modes of thought. This issue was never far below the surface of *Reason in Ethics*, but it became an active problem for me personally only after I worked my way through R. G. Collingwood's *Essay on Metaphysics* in the mid-1950s. In retrospect, my manifesto on the need to supplement informal logic with conceptual history, which I included at the end of *The Uses of Argument* (1958), was as relevant to ethics as it was to epistemology or philosophy of science. But it took me a long time to recognize this point, and to make a great deal of it now would be pure hindsight.

(2) In 1948, when I finished *Reason in Ethics*, some readers saw more clearly than I the implications of my position, and the directions in which I was pointing. Notably, my argument had placed limits on the universalizability of moral concepts and arguments, and so opened up the possibility of reviving older traditions of practical moral reasoning; especially, the much despised tradition of "casuistry," or case morality. Indeed, it came as a shock when, in the 1970s, I read Benjamin Nelson's article on "Casuistry" in the 14th edition of the *Encyclopedia Britannica*, and found him citing *Reason in Ethics* as an early forerunner of renewed interest in the subject.

Recent British moral philosophers had shared Sidgwick's distaste for the messiness and complexity of everyday moral ideas and intuitions, and had framed their theories of morality in abstract, universal terms, with all-embracing principles. In extreme cases, they still dreamed of generalizations (such as Alan Gewirth's "principle of generic consistency"[18]) which might serve as the axioms of complete ethical systems. Ideally, such principles "entailed" substantively correct answers to the moral questions arising in any conceivable situation. Even those philosophers whose theoretical ambitions were more modest tended to delimit the field of moral judgments and concepts (the "moral point of view") with a single comprehensive formula. *Reason in Ethics*, by contrast, placed limits on the scope of ethical theory. It did not seek to define the field of "ethics" by a general formula; still less, to offer a body of universal principles ("ethical axioms") for settling substantive moral problems in practice. Like "rules of law" in the common law tradition, general rules of argument in *practical* morality carried more or less weight—had more or less force—depending on the specific nature and circumstances of the current problems and cases. While general in form, they gave us guidance only "on the whole" about what holds good in any relevant class of cases; and it was not crucial to construe these rules as claiming an invariable and universal "essence" for morality.

In this respect, *The Place of Reason in Ethics* was already edging toward Aristotle's account of moral wisdom as "practical prudence" or *phronesis:* the power to discern not just common features in different instances, but also those aspects that make particular cases unique.[19] As in Whewell's *Elements*, such things as family ties and promises, general benevolence, and fairness define separate kinds of moral claims, duties, and obligations; and there is no reason to demand that they all be illustrations of the same universal principle. The assumption that moral claims of all kinds spring from a single, all-embracing principle need be no more plausible than the assumption that legal doctrines of all kinds—whether in tort or contract, agency or personal status, international or criminal, admiralty or testamentary law—are just so many parallel deductions from a common set of jurisprudential axioms. In either law or morality, the philosopher's task is not to find an underlying principle that binds all obligations and claims together: rather, it is to develop a sufficiently varied taxonomy of cases, circumstances, and considerations, allowing for (and doing justice to) the differences between them.

This point had long since been accepted in jurisprudence and legal philosophy. Eighteenth-century German rationalists like C. F. Wolff might dream of systematizing the entire code of civil and criminal law under a single, comprehensive set of axioms; but, by

1800, Savigny had shown the irrelevance of this notion to the actual historical practice of law. During the next 150 years, both legal philosophy in the German historical tradition and sociological jurisprudence, its American offspring, set aside all *a priori* systematicity in favor of a historically and socially informed pragmatism.[20] Indeed, given the historically-evolving common law tradition as a standing example, it is curious that so many English moral philosophers of the nineteenth and early twentieth centuries still aimed at developing universal and ahistorical accounts of ethics.

Only during the last twenty years has that redemption of casuistry for which Benjamin Nelson was looking begun to make serious progress.[21] It has done so in part because some fine scholars who are not accredited moral philosophers have written about general ethical issues: Michael Walzer and Sissela Bok spring to mind.[22] This change has also been a by-product of the bioethics movement and medical ethics in general. Recognizing that ethics plays a part in actual clinical practice brings moral issues to the patient's bedside, and there questions arise about the specific moral considerations that are relevant to this particular patient or that, and to these specific circumstances or those. As a result, the practical task of developing an adequate taxonomy of significant moral considerations—by *genus* and *species*—has been tackled more explicitly and carried further in medicine than in most other areas of moral practice.[23]

(3) Finally, the problems about "limiting questions" posed in the last chapter of *Reason in Ethics* have had their own independent history over the last 30–40 years, and merit a comment. This phrase has become a focus of debate (e.g.) among theologians of hermeneutic tendencies. As time passed, the *paralogistic* nature of these questions—their tendency to generate insoluble problems—faded into the background. Instead, they became seen as bringing back to the surface the presuppositions underlying our modes of thought and argument.[24]

That development, too, is one I could not foresee in the late 1940s, and it reflects a shift in philosophy as well as theology. As the term "paralogistic" indicates, the notion of limiting questions had a source in Kant as filtered through Wittgenstein, and was an attempt to locate the boundary between the meaningful and the meaningless, the functional and the nonfunctional use of terms in any field of discourse. This was one of the central goals of *Sprach-kritik* ("critique of language") in Wittgenstein, and in Mauthner before him.[25] Both writers formed their views before 1914. They hoped to map this boundary *here and now*, for the purpose of intellectual sanitation; and neither man asked whether its location may not itself be a historical variable. By the mid-1980s that possibility is one that we all take seriously. Seeing what statements and questions *make sense* in the context of any practical enterprise requires us to reflect on that enterprise's *current* "language games" and "forms of life." It did not suit Wittgenstein's purpose to explore the historical changes in human practices and procedures—let alone the implication that questions and statements that were meaningful or nonsensical at one time might change places—so that meaningful statements were deprived of sense by historical changes in our intellectual or practical procedures, while meaningless ones acquired a sense they never had before.[26]

In this way, room has opened up for a fresh "research program" for philosophers, theologians, and intellectual historians to collaborate on. The dominantly *theoretical* character of the seventeenth and eighteenth centuries' debate in philosophy meant that all questions about the dividing line between meaningful and meaningless ideas were handled in timeless, unhistorical terms. When Leibniz attacked the account of Creation implicit in Newton's cosmology as meaningless, he did not assume that our approach to such questions was open to revision in the light of changed intellectual or practical methods. Instead, he appealed to considerations which were meant to rule out any such theory *forever*.[27]

To the extent that we now recognize that the assumptions which underlie our basic patterns of thought (or "conceptual frameworks") are something less than *a priori* necessary truths, the history of scientific and philosophical ideas must seek, among other things, to decipher the processes by which those assumptions evolve historically, along with our language games and forms of life. And that is precisely the link between philosophy and conceptual history which I first found in Collingwood's *Essay on Metaphysics*, and advocated at the end of *The Uses of Argument*. The case I made out in 1958 for a more historical approach to questions about "the bounds of sense"[28] has evoked little response from English and

American philosophers; but a similar move by more recent West German historians and philosophers—under the title of *Begriffs-geschichte* or "history of concepts"—has had more notable results.[29] With the prospect of a reëmergence among English-speaking philosophers of Aristotle's "practical philosophy" and the *phronesis* tradition, this line of inquiry may take root among them also. In that case, the union of history and philosophy for which Collingwood always hoped may finally realize its full potential.

THE GETTY CENTER   STEPHEN TOULMIN
SANTA MONICA, CALIFORNIA
April–May, 1986

Notes

1. On reading my fellowship thesis, George Rylands (the English tutor and theatrical producer at King's) commented unkindly, but not without some basis, "Ah, all your goods in the shop window, I see!"

2. Recall Hume's contrast between the way he understood philosophical arguments when alone in his study, and when dining with friends.

3. I might have used the word "intuitions" here as a shorthand. This is not a term I welcome, but it has relevance to my paper, "Knowledge of Right and Wrong" (*Proc. Arist. Soc.* [1949–50]), which defends two ideas: (1) that there are some things that we "just know," without any need to point to further "grounds" in their support, and (2) that these things include some elementary moral truths.

4. I do not imply that Wittgenstein was a skeptic of the *modern* sort, like René Descartes with his "method of systematic doubt," Hume in his study, or Russell in *The Problems of Philosophy*. Wittgenstein no more *doubted* philosophical statements than he *asserted* them. But conversations with Avner Cohen and Phillip Hallie showed me how close Wittgenstein was to the *classical* skepticism of Pyrrho, Sextus Empiricus, and Montaigne, all of whom challenged philosophy because its statements were too general and remote from experience to be intelligible as they stood. Rather than *assert or deny* these statements, we should wean ourselves from the temptation to accept such questions at all. See Hallie's book, *The Scar of Montaigne* (Middletown, Conn., 1966), chap. 2.

5. Whewell, *The Elements of Morality Including Polity* (Cambridge, 1846).

6. See *Ethica Nicomachaea*, bks. 7 and 8: W. D. Ross's Greek edition of the *Ethics* actually describes these books as "a casuistry of friendship."

7. See James Gustafson, *Ethics from a Theocentric Point of View*, 2 vols. (Chicago, 1981, 1983), *passim*.

8. *Eth. Nic.* 2.2.3, 1104a and 6.5.3, 1139b.

9. From a personal memoir found among Sidgwick's papers after his death and published by Constance Jones, in the preface to the 6th edition of *The Methods of Ethics* (1901).

10. Cf. J. B. Schneewind, *Sidgwick's Ethics and Victorian Moral Philosophy* (Oxford, 1977).

11. See his paper, "It makes no difference whether I do it or not," in the *Proc. Aristot. Soc.* supp. vol. 49 (1975):183.

12. F. H. Bradley, "My Station and its Duties," in *Ethical Studies* (London, 1876; 2d. ed. Oxford, 1927).

13. I recall leading a graduate seminar at Oxford in the early 1950s in which discussion focused precisely on the question of what made any issue a "moral" issue, and under what conditions the question of wearing a wrong-colored tie could become genuinely *moral*. The matter aroused a serious division of opinion, with Kurt Baier on the "substantive" side, Philippa Foot on the "formalist" side.

14. The journal *Philosophy and Public Policy* is one vehicle for essays in "applied philosophy"; see also the reports of the National Commission for the Protection of Human Subjects (Washington, D.C., 1975–79).

15. Cf. my article "How Medicine Saved the Life of Ethics," *Perspectives in Biology and Medicine* 25 (1982):736–50.

16. The problems that Russell found in (e.g.) "definite descriptions," he dealt with by spelling out the meaning of such statements in logical symbolism. As a result, he analyzed "The King of France is bald" as "There exists one and only one thing x, such that, both x is King of France, and x is bald," or, in symbolism, "$\exists! x$: (x is King of France). (x is bald)." What makes this form less problematic and more perspicuous than the original? The answer to that question was clear only to those who had tried to incorporate definite descriptions into propositional logic, and had run into difficulties as a result.

17. Even so, some key terms proved to be "unanalyzable": no simpler terms were available by which to define them, and so clarify their meanings. The classic instance, for Moore, was the term *good* itself. This gave rise to one of the central doctrines of *Principia Ethica*, viz. that good is an "unanalysable, non-natural predicate"—see the discussion in my chapter on objectivism below.

18. See Alan Gewirth, *Reason and Morality* (Chicago, 1978).

19. *Eth. Nic.* 5.10.2ff, 1137b. Aristotle's word for "universal" is just the colloquial Greek phrase for "on the whole" (*kat'holou* or *katholou*), and it applies equally to arguments that do, and do not, depend for their force on the existence of "essences."

20. Dr. Roger Michener wrote a fascinating Ph.D. thesis on Savigny for the University of Chicago. See also Edward H. Levi, *An Introduction to Legal Reasoning* (Chicago, 1949).

21. Alan Donagan drew my attention to "common morality" as long ago as 1974; see also his book, *The Theory of Morality* (Chicago, 1977). For a full-scale modern reappraisal of the relationship between the casuistical tradition and moral philosophy, see the forthcoming book by A. R. Jonsen and S. E. Toulmin, *The Abuse of Casuistry* (Berkeley, 1987).

22. See Michael Walzer, *Just and Unjust Wars: A Moral Argument*

with Historical Illustrations (New York, 1977), and Sissela Bok, *Lying* (New York, 1978).

23. See A. R. Jonsen, M. Siegler and W. Winslade, *Clinical Ethics,* 2d. ed., (New York, 1986) and the *Hastings Center Reports,* notably the cases about transsexuality and marriage in the August 1981 issue, pp. 8–13.

24. See David Tracy, *The Analogical Imagination* (New York, 1981).

25. Ludwig Wittgenstein, *Tractatus Logico-Philosophicus* (London, 1921); Fritz Mauthner, *Beiträge zu einer Kritik der Sprache* (Stuttgart, 1906–13), etc. See also the discussion of this topic in A. S. Janik and S. E. Toulmin, *Wittgenstein's Vienna* (New York, 1973).

26. My favorite example comes from a competition of French Academy of Sciences "to determine the weight of fire." It seems nowadays sheer common sense to know that fire is not massive and has no measurable weight, but this became obvious only after John Dalton. E. M. Forster wrote a charming essay about the summer Voltaire spent at Mme. du Chatelet's chateau, while they were both trying to win this competition.

27. In his correspondence with Clarke, Leibniz complains about Newton's view that God might create the world wherever and whenever He chose. That, he argued, is nonsense. In his view, Space and Time were defined by relation to the objects of the world, so that there was no perceptible (or meaningful) difference between God's creating the world where He did, and His creating it (say) 200 miles to the left.

28. This phrase is, of course, Peter Strawson's. See the linguistic reading of Kant's critiques in his book, *The Bounds of Sense* (London, 1966).

29. I have in mind the work of Reinhardt Kosellek, for example.

PREFACE

Francis Bacon is remembered nowadays among philosophers as the first man to give a systematic account of the logic of induction, and so as the spiritual father of modern science. Yet his interests were wider, and comparatively early in his career (in 1597, along with the early version of his *Essays*) he published his first discussion of the logic of evaluation—the fragmentary study *Of the Coulers of Good and Evill*, which he later revised and expanded for its place in Book VI of the *Advancement of Learning*.

This early interest in the notions of ethics failed to keep the same place in his thoughts as did his passion for the possibilities of science. And this is perhaps a pity, for certainly few since his time have brought to the study of ethics quite the lucidity and straightforwardness which mark his work. The obscurity from which he rescued inductive reasoning still envelops evaluation.

In this book, I have taken up the discussion where Bacon left off. But I have also extended its range for, where he confined himself to pointing out the limitations of some of the more common ethical arguments, I have tried to discover, more generally, what it is that gives these arguments such value and scope as they possess. This has meant going at considerable length into the nature of reasoning and the foundations of logic; and here I have run up against a difficulty. Recent advances in the understanding of these subjects have never been coherently expounded, and there is no book to which readers can be referred. I have therefore had to sketch in as I went along descriptions of such logical methods as are necessary tools for my argument: this accounts in particular for the length of Part II, which might seem over-elaborate if one considered only its immediate purpose.

However, patience with these excursions is not, I hope, too much to ask of my readers, considering the nature of the subject. (Those who want to skip will in any case find a summary of the argument in the Epilogue.) For, as Francis Bacon himself wrote, in his early examination of the arguments used to give colour to ethical conclusions,

> To make a true and safe iudgement, nothing can be of greater use and defence to the minde, than the discovering and reprehension of these coulers, shewing in what cases they hold, and in what they deceive....

This confidence has at any rate encouraged me in the belief that the work was worth pursuing, and that the result was worth publishing despite its shortcomings. May these spur others to do the work better!

STEPHEN TOULMIN

KING'S COLLEGE
CAMBRIDGE
February 1948

CONTENTS

I
THE PROBLEM, *page* I

PART I. THE TRADITIONAL APPROACHES

2
THE OBJECTIVE APPROACH, *page* 9

3
THE SUBJECTIVE APPROACH, *page* 29

4
THE IMPERATIVE APPROACH, *page* 46

5

INTERLUDE: A CHANGE OF METHOD, *page* 61

PART II. LOGIC AND LIFE

6

REASONING AND ITS USES, *page* 67

7

EXPERIENCE AND EXPLANATION, *page* 86

8

REASONING AND REALITY, *page* 102

PART III. THE NATURE OF ETHICS

9

INTRODUCTION: IS ETHICS A SCIENCE? *page* 121

10

THE FUNCTION AND DEVELOPMENT OF ETHICS, *page* 130

11

THE LOGIC OF MORAL REASONING, *page* 144

12

ETHICS AND SOCIETY, *page* 166

PART IV. THE BOUNDARIES OF REASON

13

PHILOSOPHICAL ETHICS, *page* 185

14

REASON AND FAITH, *page* 202

15

SUMMARY AND EPILOGUE, *page* 222

ACKNOWLEDGEMENTS

It will be obvious how much I owe in my general approach to the philosophical tradition of Cambridge; but there are some particular debts, which could not be covered in the references and must be acknowledged here. At all stages in the preparation of this book, I have turned to Mr R. B. Braithwaite and Mr A. C. Jackson for help over points of difficulty; many of the problems would have been beyond my power but for the light which I have derived from the lectures of Dr Ludwig Wittgenstein and Mr John Wisdom; I have discussed parts of Chapters 3 and 4 with Prof. G. E. Moore; Prof. L. J. Russell has read the completed manuscript and has made detailed and helpful comments; and my wife has been indefatigable throughout in the defence of good sense and good style. Where I have persevered in error in spite of their help and advice, I alone am to blame.

It is a pleasure to thank the Electors to the Harold Fry Studentships at King's College, the Managers of the Arnold Gerstenberg Studentship in the University of Cambridge, and the Ministry of Education, for that financial help without which I should not have had the leisure to study, far less to write.

I must also thank those publishers who have given me permission to make use of passages from their books: Messrs George Allen and Unwin for the passage from Goldsworthy Lowes Dickinson's *The Meaning of Good*; Messrs Wm Heinemann for passages from Mrs Garnett's translation of *The Brothers Karamazov*, by Dostoevsky; the Yale University Press, and their agents in this country, the Oxford University Press, for a number of passages from Charles L. Stevenson's *Ethics and Language*; the Oxford University Press for a passage from the late Aylmer Maude's translation of *War and Peace*, by Tolstoy; and Messrs Longmans, Green and Co. for the passage from Dr G. M. Trevelyan's *English Social History*.

One last remark, in place of a dedication: although I have grown up in the precincts (as it were) of John Maynard Keynes, I never had an opportunity of knowing him personally. Still I think, from all that I have been told about him, that the writing of this book is an enterprise in which he would have been interested and, had he lived, it would have been to him that I should have wished to dedicate it.

S. E. T.

I

THE PROBLEM

ETHICS is everybody's concern. Scientific problems and scientific theories may from time to time intrigue or arrest all of us, but they are of immediate, practical importance to only a few. Everyone, on the other hand, is faced with moral problems—problems about which, after more or less reflection, a decision must be reached. So everybody talks about values.

This does not mean that the principles of right action or the nature of goodness are perennial topics of conversation—far from it; often the discussion is anything but explicit. Still, as 'Liberty', 'Progress' or 'Education' (which Chesterton called 'the three dodges to avoid the discussion of the Good');[1] as 'Democracy', 'Self-Determination' or 'the Four Freedoms'; or simply as the number of calories needed to prevent starvation; openly or under some alias, ethical concepts find their way into our thoughts and into our speech.

This universal interest in ethics creates a number of special difficulties. At all times, a steady stream of ethical literature, some of it cool, rational, detached, some of it passionate and hortatory, pours into the world—in books and learned periodicals, from newspaper offices and pulpits. And what a variety of arguments is presented! One man claims self-evidence in support of his view—'Common Decency', he declares, 'forbids any other course.' Another proclaims that his suggestion is 'in the National Interest', and regards any further justification as unnecessary. A third is interested only in the results of an action; while a fourth pays more attention to 'rights' and 'responsibilities'. A fifth excuses—'A little of what you fancy does you good'. A sixth warns—'You never know what may happen!' At one church door the Wayside Pulpit wakes the hidden chords of sympathy in our hearts, but the next church, round the corner, rejects both reason and sympathy in favour of theological authority—'Why did God give us Sunday?', it imperiously enquires (begging what many

[1] G. K. Chesterton, *Heretics* (1928), pp. 25–6.

would regard as the most important question); 'For Rest and Worship', it declares (for the question was rhetorical); 'Therefore, Vote A G A I N S T Sunday Cinemas'.

Even in normal times, ethical arguments tend to be vaster in bulk, more varied in character and more confused than other kinds of discussion—and we all know how a pinch of righteous indignation can set two disputants at cross-purposes, making their speculations appear to them (to use Hume's phrase) 'unduly real and solid'.[1] But at times of crisis, when problems of particular complexity and importance are to be considered, the volume increases and the arguments offered become more wild and confused;[2] until finally, when war or tyranny comes, reason is driven out into the wilderness, and the open discussion of general moral problems, even when completely abstract, is paralysed by the dangers of lapsing into bad taste or treason.

In trying to deal with this flood of arguments—each of which claims to provide the best of reasons for acting in the way proposed—we are continually up against one central problem. How are we to distinguish those to which we should pay attention from those which we should ignore or reject?

This is a formidable problem, and some who have considered it have given it up as insoluble. They have concluded that all the judgements of value made by mankind are 'attempts to prop up their illusions with arguments',[3] that ''tis impossible they can be pronounced either true or false, and be either contrary or conformable to reason',[4] that our whole idea of value is 'a chimera'.[5] Of course, it is possible that the widespread interest in morality is evidence (of a sort) against the more extreme claims for its authority, but abdication is a drastic solution. Come to that, it is no solution at all, for we still need to know what to do, and we still have to choose between the conflicting courses and arguments with which we are presented.

That must be my excuse for reopening one of the oldest, hardest-worn questions in the world, for going over such familiar

---

[1] David Hume, *A Treatise of Human Nature*, ed. Selby-Bigge (1888), p. 455.

[2] I might instance the 'argument' being put about at the moment for the restoration of a ration of petrol for private motoring—that 'Basic Petrol is the Birthright of your Car'.

[3] Sigmund Freud, *Civilisation and its Discontents*, tr. J. Riviere (1930), p. 143.

[4] Hume, op. cit. p. 458.   [5] Loc. cit. p. 456.

ground in search of fresh clues. Which of all these arguments should we accept? Which of the reasons are good reasons? And how far can one rely on reason in coming to moral decisions? Is there always a place for reasons and further reasons or does 'giving reasons' sometimes become supererogatory? What, in short, is the place of reason in ethics? In this book I shall not be adding to the flood of ethical writing: instead I shall be trying to provide some kind of a dam with which to control it.

1.1 *How ought one to Approach the Problem?*

The very bulk of our subject-matter makes it a little difficult to know how to begin; but, fortunately, we can rule out quite a proportion of the arguments offered. A great many of the speeches, essays, sermons and articles which are directed at us consist purely of exhortations. These are comparatively straightforward, for they employ reason only in a secondary role. Their authors attempt to influence our actions chiefly by arousing our fear, our pity or our cupidity—and provided that we remember this we shall be on our guard.

The more detached, philosophical approaches are different: those who adopt them want to convince us less through our emotions than by cumulative argument, as a result of reflective thought and impartial reasoning. Their discussions at any rate appear more relevant than the pure exhortations, and we may hope to learn something from them.

However, one look at any of the traditional works will be enough to raise a doubt. Is it any good attacking our problem directly? Is the question of 'good reasons' really the central one? Or am I from the start begging the most important question— whether it is central? Will it not be said that, on the contrary, our question can only be answered as a corollary of some more fundamental 'ethical theorem'—that we cannot discover what are good reasons in ethics without first answering the question, 'What *is* goodness'? And is not any argument from 'good reasons' to 'good deeds' bound to be circular?

This last objection is quickly answered. To begin with, in talking about 'a good reason', I am not talking about ethics: we can equally well (and frequently do) talk of 'a valid argument' instead, and this has far less of an ethical sound—so that, even if there were any kind of circularity here, it would be a harmless one. We must not, of course, *assume* that X is a good reason, so as to prove that Y is a good deed—and then accept the very same argument as a proof that X is a good reason (Q.E.D.!)—for this is mere rationalisation; but it is quite in order to try to discover and justify further considerations Z, for deciding both whether we ought to do Y, and whether we should accept X as a reason for doing it.

The other objection (that our question is not really the central one) is more solid, and I shall not attempt to dispose of it at once. Our question is at any rate one which we cannot help encountering in every ethical situation. Whenever we come to a moral decision, we weigh the considerations involved—the relevant facts, that is, so far as we are acquainted with them—and then have to make up our minds. In doing so, we pass from the factual reasons (R) to an ethical conclusion (E). At this moment, we can always ask ourselves, 'Now, is this the right decision? In view of what I know (R), ought I to choose in this way (E)? Is R a good reason for E?' When considering ethics in general, therefore, we shall naturally be interested in the question, 'What is it that makes a particular set of facts, R, a good reason for a particular ethical conclusion, E? What is "a good reason" in ethics?'; and this will interest us to a greater degree than questions like, 'What is the analysis of "right"?', and 'Is pleasure better than knowledge, or knowledge than pleasure?'

The question of good reasons in ethics is therefore of capital practical importance; but this (it may be said) does not prove that theoretically it is the central one, or that there is no more fundamental question, whose answer embraces the answer to my question as a mere rider.

About this we need not express an opinion. The traditional method is so well established that nothing would justify passing it by without an examination. And if some people are dissatisfied, and want more of a justification at this stage, I can only ask for patience. It is no good calling for certainty of a type quite inappropriate in this context—the certainty of a mathematical proof—and it will do no harm to postpone until later the question of whether any deeper 'justification' is required.[1]

[1] This question will be discussed in §§ 11.9 and 11.10 below.

1.2 *The Traditional Method*

The traditional method has a very long and respectable history, having been popularised by Plato, who attributed it to Socrates. Its principal aim is not so much to discover what reasons and arguments should be accepted in support of ethical decisions, as to pin down—to characterise—ethical concepts by means of some kind of definition. 'What *is* goodness?', 'What *is* justice?'—these are the questions which it puts in the centre of the picture. And we had best consider these traditional questions, and the kind of answers which are given to them, for a start.

Even within this category of ethical argument there is so much variety and such an appearance of contradiction that it is not easy to discover what exactly is at issue. Some of the answers given (e.g. Spinoza's)[1] are extremely complex, and can hardly be understood unless one masters an elaborate metaphysical system; others (like G. E. Moore's)[2] are comparatively simple. It is possible, however, to cover the ground without too much unfairness if one begins by discussing the three chief, logically simple doctrines, from which the more complex theories are developed, and from the strengths and weaknesses of which they take their own strengths and weaknesses. According to these doctrines, to call anything 'good' or 'right' is

(i) to attribute to it a property of some kind or other (this may be called the 'objective' approach to the question);

(ii) to report on one's own feelings, or the feelings of some group with which one is associated (this may be called the 'subjective' approach); or

(iii) neither of these alternatives, ethical concepts being mere pseudo-concepts used for persuasion (the 'imperative' approach).

Discussing these doctrines in turn will be enough of a programme to start with. If we are to be satisfied with any of the traditional theories, it must be such as will help us to tell good reasoning from bad—we therefore have a test to apply in criticising them. And afterwards, if none of them helps us to find the answer to our central, practical question, we can always return and attack the problem head-on.

[1] I have in mind the type of argument presented in his *Ethics*.
[2] Cf. his *Principia Ethica*, *Ethics*, etc.

PART I
THE TRADITIONAL APPROACHES

2

THE OBJECTIVE APPROACH

L E T us begin by considering one of the oldest and most familiar doctrines of philosophical ethics, the doctrine that, in saying that anything is good or right, we are mentioning a *property* which it has, the property of goodness or rightness. This doctrine I shall call, for short, the 'objective' doctrine (for although the question, 'Is goodness objective?', may not be the most important one involved, it is one to which its supporters have traditionally paid great attention). In discussing it, we shall have to ask ourselves:

(i) What is the point of the doctrine?

(ii) Is it true?

(iii) How does it help us in answering our central question?

The first thing to notice about the doctrine is that it classes our concepts of value, 'good' and 'right', with those other concepts, which we call 'properties'. In order to understand it, therefore, we shall have to ask what kinds of concept are, most characteristically, 'properties'. I shall point out three types into which they may be divided, and in this chapter I shall pay special attention to two of these, that of 'unanalysable, directly-perceived' properties like redness, and that of 'analysable, directly-perceived' properties such as 259-sidedness. From a study of these, it will be possible to outline the things which make properties what they are for us.

After this, we shall have to ask whether the chief logical characteristics of properties are shared by values—for I take it to be the essence of the objective doctrine that they are. I shall show, by comparing the ways in which we talk about properties and values, that in at least one important respect values differ from *all* such properties; so that there is as much reason for saying that goodness and rightness are not properties at all as there is for saying that they are properties, of a special kind, 'non-natural' ones. Further, I shall call attention to certain facts which make it clear that, when we talk of goodness or rightness in their most typically ethical sense, we are not talking about any directly-perceived property of the object; to suppose that we are is to be misled by the similarity in the forms of words used of values and properties.

Finally, when we come to ask what help the doctrine is to us in solving our central problem—that of distinguishing valid ethical arguments from invalid ones—we shall find that, so far from being a help, it is a hindrance. Not only does it fail to lead to any answer to our question, but it actually distracts from that question the attention which it deserves and requires.

2.1   *Three Types of Property*

What is it that makes a concept a 'property'? What (that is to say) makes a word a word for a 'property'? Before we can answer these questions we must first ask, 'What words unquestionably *are* typical words for properties?'

Philosophers who treat goodness as a property often compare it to the qualities of sense (colours, etc.)—Moore goes in considerable detail into the similarities between goodness and yellowness[1]—and some even talk about our means of perceiving 'ethical properties' as 'the moral sense'. I shall therefore take colours as typical of one of the classes of things which we call 'properties'. Such properties are directly perceived by the senses, and differ in this from the third type to be mentioned below; they are also, unlike both the other two types, 'unanalysable'—that is to say, they cannot be verbally defined, either in terms of simpler qualities or in terms of any set of operations, without mentioning the property itself. I can tell a red tie from a green one at sight, and I can teach any normal person to do the same; but I cannot explain how I do it either by reference to other properties of the tie or in terms of any procedure, without using the words 'red' and 'green' or other words for the same concepts. I shall refer to redness and other similar properties as *simple qualities*.

Another familiar class of properties consists of those which are perceived directly in the same way as the obvious qualities of sense, but which one can safely attribute to an object only after going through a certain routine. That a particular regular polygon

---

[1] Cf. *Principia Ethica*, pp. 9-10; *Philosophical Studies*, pp. 272-5.

has a fixed number of sides I may be able to tell by looking at it, but I can only be certain that it is 259-sided (rather than 257-sided or 261-sided, say) after counting its sides. For the presence of properties of this sort we require *criteria*. These are detected by means of a more or less complex routine and the properties can be defined in terms of this routine—thus '259-sided' means 'having 259 sides', the operation of counting sides being familiar from other cases. Such properties are (that is to say) 'analysable', and they are distinguished by this from the simple qualities. I shall refer to them as *complex qualities*.

These two types include most of the properties with which we are concerned in our day-to-day life, but there is a third which must be mentioned: this consists of properties which are detected by means of routines, in the way that complex qualities are, but which are not perceived directly—in fact we might say not perceived at all. If, for example, I say that the sun, when shining through the fog, is really yellow, although it looks as red as a blood-orange, I am not referring to any directly-perceived property of the sun at all. My remark is to be understood in the context of a scientific theory; and the property which I attribute to the sun, of being 'really yellow', of radiating such-and-such types of electromagnetic wave, is defined in terms of that theory. Such properties I shall call *scientific qualities*.

Two cautions must be entered at this point. First, we need claim no deep epistemological significance for this classification. It may have some such value, but that does not concern us: all we require of it is that it shall simplify our analysis. Secondly, in saying that properties can be divided up in this way, and that such a classification exhausts the class of concepts we ordinarily refer to as properties, I do not mean that every property can be labelled once and for all as belonging to one of the types rather than another: I mean that whenever we talk about properties we talk about them in one or another of these ways—sometimes in one, sometimes in another.

Consider some examples:

(i) Under most circumstances, when we say that anything is red or blue, hard or soft, we treat these words as words for simple qualities. But when we say that a figure is square, we sometimes treat squareness as a simple quality, telling it by eye, and sometimes, when our purposes require greater precision, demand measurements with ruler and set-square before accepting it as square—i.e. we treat 'square' as a word for a complex quality, analysable into 'rectangular and equilateral', these again being complex qualities analysable in terms of measurements with a set-square and a ruler respectively.

(ii) Since I have not been trained to do so, I cannot say whether or no a carpet is turkey-red unless I am given a colour-card as a 'key'; I therefore treat 'turkey-red' as a complex quality. A carpet-dealer, however, may get so used to telling fine shades of colour by eye that he can treat 'turkey-red' as a simple quality.

(iii) We may say the sun is sodium-orange because we can see that it is (tell it by eye), *or* because we have a colour-card to compare it with, *or* because we believe a particular scientific theory: we may (that is) treat 'sodium-orange' as a simple quality, *or* as a complex quality, *or* as a scientific quality.

It is in one or another of these ways, however, that we treat all properties—and this is true of sense-qualities (red, green, hard, soft, loud, quiet, sweet, sour, rank and fragrant), personal characteristics (haughty and meek), shapes (square and thick), temporal distributions (rare and frequent), or what you like. In considering the objective doctrine, it will be sufficient to discuss the analogies between values and typical properties of each type.

Of course, there are cases in which our use of a concept makes it doubtful whether we should call it a property of the object or not. Judgements of taste—of what is sweet and what sour—are so erratic that we sometimes treat the concepts as though they were more like 'nice' than like 'red'; and by transference call the distinction between the pleasant and the unpleasant 'a matter of taste'. Such borderline examples draw attention to the way in which the two classes of concept shade into each other, but they do not obliterate the distinction between qualities like redness and 'subjective relations'—i.e. concepts like pleasantness. In consequence they need not worry us.

Philosophers who hold that goodness is a property of those things which are good must, therefore, be taken to mean one of three things, corresponding to the three types of property which we have distinguished. They may mean that goodness is directly-perceived and unanalysable, that it is directly-perceived and analysable, or that it is to be detected only through criteria—not being perceived directly at all. In this chapter I shall concentrate on the first pair of possibilities: viz. the suggestion that goodness is a directly-perceived property, to be recognised either immediately or by means of criteria. These are the possibilities with which philosophers, especially those who talk about 'the moral sense', have been most concerned. Most of the things to be said about complex qualities apply equally to scientific qualities, but I shall consider in more detail later[1] the idea that ethics is a science, and goodness a scientific quality, whose presence is to be recognised, not by direct perception, but only by indirect tests.

2.2 Simple Qualities

What, then, is involved in asserting that an object has a particular simple quality? I have said that I can tell a red tie from a green one at sight, and can teach any normal person to do the same, but how is this? How does one, in fact, teach people to use correctly concepts of this kind? Again, in what circumstances can disagreements about simple qualities arise? And what is one to say if they do? Are we justified in correcting other people's use of simple qualities in the way in which we should correct the arithmetic of a child who said, 'Seven eights are fifty-six; five and carry six; seven twos are fourteen and six makes twenty-two; so seven twenty-eights are two hundred and twenty-five'? Or can we pass over disagreements with a shrug of the shoulders, as we should the difference between one man who said, 'There's nothing like an afternoon's fishing for sport and interest', and another who said, 'Fishing's terribly boring'?

Imagine that I am trying to teach a foreigner (whose language I do not know and who has only a little English) to ice a cake, and suppose that I wish to explain the use of cochineal. 'Cochineal?', he may inquire, not understanding me. '*Red* liquid', I shall say, 'for making things *red*.' If he fails to understand 'red', what do I do?

The most natural thing, if I have some cochineal, will be to demonstrate to him, showing him how the icing-sugar takes up

[1] Especially in Chapter 9 below.

the colour of the liquid. And if that does not help him, I can try
to get the idea over to him by pointing out a red rose, a book, a
penny stamp or a pillar-box, and by contrasting these with 2½d.
stamps, the lawn, sugar and shoe-polish—afterwards showing him
the cochineal again. He should by then be able to understand
what I mean, and pick out red objects; if he remains at a loss, all
that I can do is to go through the same kind of process again and
again, more slowly and with more examples, in the hope that he
will get the idea. But if, whatever I do, he just fails to learn, I
shall begin to think, either that he is deliberately fooling me, or
that there is something wrong with him; and with reason, for the
normal means of communication will have broken down.

So much for teaching people simple qualities; but what if someone else comes along and says 'Cochineal is green'? Having
learnt the word 'red' in the ordinary way and used it successfully
in everyday life, I shall wonder what is up, and I shall try to
discover the cause of the contradiction. What I decide will depend
on what else I find out about him. If, for instance, this is the only
occasion on which I notice anything odd about his use of colour-
words, I may conclude that it was a slip of the tongue. But if I try
him out on pillar-boxes and penny stamps, and he calls those
green, and never calls anything green except those things I call
red, I shall conclude that he is talking a different language; and
that, in use, his word 'green' is identical with my word 'red'—
in fact that his 'green' *means* the same as my 'red'. In such a case,
I can learn to understand him by making appropriate substitutions
(translations).

Such an example—written out at length—may seem wildly
improbable, but in spoken language this kind of thing may happen
quite easily. If engaged in sorting things into colours, English
and Germans who understand only their own languages will get
on all right as long as they only have occasion to refer to green
(*grün*) things and brown (*braun*) things; but the English will be
as puzzled by the Germans' talk about vice, when referring to
white things, as I should be if anyone called cochineal green.

The type of disagreement manifested in these cases is one (and
only one) of those arising out of *linguistic* differences. Under
this heading may be included also those cases in which we should
say that there was no difference in language, but only a difference

of dialect, and those in which there is not even a difference of dialect, but only one of borderline usage.

This last category requires a little explanation. In everyday speech, the uses of words for properties shade into one another in ways which may lead to apparent contradictions. This fact is of great advantage to us; it would be intolerable if one might not name a colour without giving 'the absolutely-exact shade'—whatever that means—or talk of 'a fast car' without specifying its maximum speed in miles per hour on a level road with no wind. But there are always borderline examples which are puzzling. If two people are presented with the same object, whose colour is on the border between blue and green (i.e. such that we may not know whether to call it blue or green), one of them may be more inclined to say that it is blue, and the other that it is green. The fact that they are so inclined may reflect some difference between the sets of objects from which they learnt the words 'blue' and 'green': but, whether it does or not, we should expect the difference to be resolved (like so many of our disagreements) by specifying more exactly the limits being placed on the use of the words for the two properties. And if it were so resolved, we should not feel that there had been any more than a verbal difference between them.

It will, no doubt, be said that disagreements over simple qualities are not all of this kind; for what if the man is colour-blind? Colour-blindness, being exceptional and so ignored in our terminology, is a favourite source of philosophical puzzles, but it need not hold us up here. In such a case, no simple substitution or translation will be found to work: it will be found impossible to teach a colour-blind man to tell red from other colours, and indeed it is just this that leads us to call him colour-blind. There is in fact something odd in talking about a *disagreement* between a normal and a colour-blind person: the colour-blind man does not have *different* ideas about colours—he is just *without* some which most people have. In this respect his position relative to normal people is like that of normal people relative to those with absolute pitch. A man with absolute pitch can say straight off what is the position in the scale of any note which he hears: normal people do not *disagree* with him about this—they simply have no opinion.

Again, the man who says that cochineal is green may be fooling me deliberately, and he may go on doing so consistently, but this likewise leads to a situation in which we just do not know what to say—since communication breaks down—and does not lead to any relevant logical or philosophical problems. In a conceptual analysis, such as concerns us in this book, one need only examine the parts which concepts of different kinds (and words in so far as they stand for those concepts) play in our lives when language is being used literally, in the way in which we learn it—i.e. as the tool of reason (which Socrates called 'the universal medium of communication').[1] The use of language for deception is not a primary use—it is in fact dependent on its unexpectedness for its success—and we need do no more than mention it.

To sum up this discussion. Simple qualities are taught 'ostensively', i.e. by pointing out or instancing (which one might call 'verbally-pointing-out') objects having the quality: the learner is shown how to sort out red objects from green ones, or told, 'You know—like poppies and penny stamps'. If two people have a disagreement about a simple quality, when the object referred to is before them (if one says that it's blue, the other that it's green; one square, the other oblong; one rare, the other frequent); then, neglecting cases of deliberate deception or organic defect, we say, 'They can't mean the same by "so-and-so"'—and we are satisfied if we discover that they are of different nationalities, or come from different parts of the country, or if one says for example, 'Well, *I* should call three times a day frequent, anyway', and the other, 'Good heavens, *I* shouldn't'. Their disagreement, that is to say, has to be put down to a *linguistic* difference.

2.3   Complex Qualities

The case of complex qualities may at first sight appear considerably more elaborate, but all that is involved is one further step. If I have a difference of opinion with another man as to whether a certain regular polygon is 257-sided or 259-sided, I shall not say the disagreement arises from a linguistic difference: I shall say that one of us cannot count. In the event of a dis-

---

[1] See K. R. Popper, *The Open Society and its Enemies*, vol. I, p. 166; and cf. *Phaedo* 89 c: 'No greater evil can happen to anyone than to hate reasoning.'

agreement over a complex quality (or a scientific quality, for that matter), one's first reaction will be to ask whether the appropriate routine (counting, measurement or comparison) has been correctly applied by both parties.

This, of course, can easily be checked: I can, for instance, make a careful joint count of the sides of the polygon with my opponent, and agree with him, to begin with, that it has got 259 sides. And if after that he still calls it '257-sided', I shall have to conclude that his language or usage really is different from mine— say, that he calls a figure 'n-sided' if it has $n + 2$ sides. When talking to him after this I shall try making appropriate translations, using the rule, 'In my usage a figure is called n-sided if it has n sides; in his if it has $n + 2$'. I shall ask him whether a square is 'four-sided' or 'two-sided' and so on. Of course, I may not succeed in finding a general translation-rule of this kind—his usage may differ from mine only in its nomenclature for figures with 259 equal sides. But, whatever the result of that attempt, the disagreement which arises in such a case will be a linguistic one—a new type of linguistic one, characteristic of complex and scientific qualities. (Two more familiar instances—numerical ones again—of words which invite similar confusions are the French term *quinzaine* for 'a fortnight', and the Hebrew 'on the third day' for 'on the second day after'.)

Taking both types of directly-perceived property together, the possible sources of disagreement can be set out as follows:

(i) deception;

(ii) organic defect;

(iii) incorrect application of the routine (in the case of complex qualities);

(iv) linguistic differences

    (*a*) in language,

    (*b*) in dialect,

    (*c*) in borderline usage,

    (*d*) in verbal definition (for complex qualities).

This list is exhaustive. If I have a disagreement with any-one about a directly-perceived property, and appear to have good evidence that none of these is the source of the difference, I can only say, 'Well, one of them *must* be'. And the fact that this list is exhaustive, that it is only from these sources that

disagreement can arise over a concept, is part of what we mean
when we say that it is 'a property of the object'.

2.4   Is Goodness a Directly-Perceived Property?

This discussion of simple and complex qualities shows some of
the conditions which must be met if we are to say that ' X is good
(or right)' attributes to X a directly-perceived property of goodness (or rightness). We must now see if any of these conditions
are in fact met: this means asking about 'good' and 'right' the
same kinds of question as we have already asked about 'red' and
'259-sided'.

Suppose, then, that someone says to me, not 'Cochineal is red',
but a sentence which on the face of it is very similar, 'Meekness
is good'. If I do not understand it, how can he make me? Will he
point out to me instances of meekness, and hope to make me
understand 'good' in the way which would be effective if one
were teaching 'red'? Hardly! But this by itself is not a serious
objection: he may instead try instancing—'You know, like
loving your neighbour, and feeding the hungry, and honouring
your parents, and paying your debts. . .'. And if I then say, 'I'll
take your word for it that meekness is good if paying your debts
is, but how am I to know that paying your debts is?', he may
reply, 'Well, it just is—intrinsically'.[1]

It will be tempting to conclude from this that 'paying your
debts' is just part of his ostensive definition of 'good', just one
of the examples he uses to teach people the idea (and so in a way
it is); and it will be natural also to suppose that he will regard
'good' as sharing *all* the logical properties of the simple qualities.
But at this suggestion a supporter of the objective doctrine will
begin to get worried. 'It's not as arbitrary as that', he will
insist. 'Goodness is not a vague notion like the simple qualities—
we don't mark off the "good" from the "indifferent" and the
"bad" in the way we mark off the "blue" from the "yellow"
and the "green", or the "tall" from the "middling" and the
"short"'; and if we press him too hard at this point he will take
refuge in vague references to 'fundamental moral intuitions'.

Alternatively, and especially if I say that I see no resemblance
between meekness and debt-paying, he may adopt a different

[1] Cf. G. E. Moore, *Principia Ethica*, pp. 21 ff.

approach, saying, 'Well, meekness makes for smoother personal relations than assertiveness or truculence: that's why I say that it's better'. He may (that is) produce 'criteria of goodness' ('good-making characteristics'),[1] which are at first sight to be used in the way in which 'rectangularity' and 'equality of sides' are used in the case of 'squareness', or 'having 259 sides' in the case of '259-sidedness'. But again trouble arises if we ask about the standard routine for the application of the criteria. He will insist that the relation of 'good-making characteristics' to 'goodness' is different from the relation of the criteria for a complex quality to that quality. He will point out (quite justifiably) that the similarity between saying that a figure is 'rectangular and equilateral' and saying that it is 'square' is far more radical than the similarity between saying that a man beats his wife and saying that he is a 'wicked' man—however good a reason his wife-beating may be for condemning him. And he will conclude that there is no standard routine, that 'good' is unanalysable[2] and therefore a *simple* quality, and that the 'good-making characteristics' are only *signs* of goodness, not criteria after all.

From the first, therefore, there are difficulties about the view that goodness is a directly-perceived property. If we take it that a simple (unanalysable) quality is meant, the apparent arbitrariness of an ostensive definition is puzzling: if a complex (analysable) quality is understood, no definite routine for confirming its presence is forthcoming. But these are not the greatest difficulties which arise, and I shall do no more than point them out: we are in for more serious trouble when we consider the possible sources of disagreement over ethical questions.

2.5   *The Scope of Ethical Disagreements*

What if someone else comes along and says 'Meekness is bad'? What will the first man say then? Will he put the disagreement down to a linguistic difference?

No! The natural reaction will be for him to say, 'Well, he's wrong', or 'I may be mistaken, but I must say I like it myself', or

---

[1] Cf. C. D. Broad, *Proc. Aristotelian Soc.* vol. XXXIII (1933–4), on 'Is "Goodness" a Name for a Simple, Non-natural Quality?'; and also his contribution to the symposium, *The Philosophy of G. E. Moore*, pp. 43–67.

[2] Moore, op. cit. pp. 6–8.

'He may think it's bad but it's really good', or 'Of course, it depends upon the circumstances'. In exceptional cases he may say, 'He's pulling your leg—he doesn't really mean it', or 'Don't take any notice of him—he's notoriously insensitive over matters of ethics' (with implications of deliberate deception or natural defect). But the one thing I shall not expect him to say is, 'He doesn't understand plain English': and this, if goodness *were* a property, is just what he should say.

If I am confident that both men are candid and in full possession of their faculties, and that they employ the same language, dialect and usage (i.e. if all the sources of disagreement over simple qualities are removed), there will be no point in my asking whether they agree or disagree about the colour of a pillar-box: there is no room for disagreement. If, in addition, I know that they have counted together the sides of a given polygon, it will be as pointless to ask whether they agree about its 259-sidedness. But, though I know all this, it will still not be silly to wonder, for example, whether they will agree that meekness is good, or that such-and-such is the right decision. Even if there is neither deception nor defect on either side, even if both parties are fully informed about the case and both mean the same by 'good' and 'right', it still makes sense to inquire whether their moral judgements are in fact the same.

This difference between values and properties is crucial. A few comments may help to clarify the point:

(i) There is, of course, no reason why a disagreement over values should not be based on a linguistic difference. If, for example, someone takes his moral judgements from Authority, he may mistranslate *buono* as 'bad' and fall into an argument as a result. Or again, when talking about his own compositions, a musician may put on a display of uncommon self-depreciation, which leads to misunderstandings. But this kind of thing is trivial. We discover soon enough what is up—we notice that he only applies 'not too awful' in *exceptional* cases, and so on—and afterwards, by substituting 'all right' for 'terrible', 'good' for 'very poor' and 'excellent' for 'not too awful', we come to understand him.

(ii) Apart from all linguistic matters, it is possible, that, given all the relevant facts, people's moral judgements might always agree. Hume, in his ethical theory, had to assume that there would *in fact* be no ethical disagreements between fully-informed people.

The notion of morals [he wrote] implies some sentiment common to all mankind, which recommends the same object to general appro-bation, and makes every man, or most men, agree in the same opinion or decision concerning it.[1]

But this apologetic assumption only accentuates the difference between 'goodness' and the qualities that we have been dis-cussing. No one thinks it necessary to make any such assumption when accounting for the general agreement about ordinary simple qualities. No one suggests that the notion of redness implies any 'sentiment common to all mankind', which represents the same object to the vision of all in the same way, and so leads us to 'agree in the same opinion or decision concerning it'. And there need be no mystery about this, for it is a natural consequence of the function which our concept of redness serves.

This difference between values and properties, between con-tingent and necessary agreement, is fundamental. To contrast them, suppose that I say, 'If we know all the relevant facts, there will (apart from linguistic differences) be no disagreement as to what things are and are not X'. If X is a word for a property ('red', 'square' or '259-sided'), the form of my statement is quite likely to be misleading: it appears to be a factual prediction, but there is actually nothing to predict—once we know all the facts there *can* be no disagreement, and it is nonsense to suggest that there might. But suppose that X is an ethical word ('good' or 'right'); then my statement is a perfectly proper prediction, which may or may not be fulfilled. Ethical disagreements are not just a matter of using words differently. No set of translation-rules (like that from *weiss* to 'white' or that from *rouge* to 'red') would be com-prehensive enough to cover all possible ethical disagreements. And, furthermore, I do not believe that anyone would ever expect there to be: our ethical concepts are not of that kind.

2.6 *Is Goodness a 'Non-natural' Property?*

In one unquestionably important respect, therefore, values differ from all that we should normally call directly-perceived

[1] Hume, *An Enquiry concerning the Principles of Morals* (ed. Selby-Bigge), p. 272.

properties. This discovery puts us in a difficult position. Is the objective doctrine quite false? Is the value of an object purely and simply *not* a property of it? Or have we missed the point? Have we been taking the doctrine too literally, supposing that more is implied by it than its supporters intend?

If the latter be the case, if the doctrine does not mean what it says but is, even in part, *figurative*, we can abandon it straight away. If all it tells us is that goodness is 'as-it-were-a-property' and therefore 'what-you-might-call-objective', it might, for our purposes, just as well be false. What we want is a literally-true account of our ethical concepts, an account which will show us how to distinguish between good ethical reasoning and bad. Metaphor, for us, is worse than useless.

This may be too high an aim, but we are not alone in it: some supporters of the objective doctrine have the same ideal. Instead of admitting that the doctrine is metaphorical, and so a *cul-de-sac*, they insist on its literal truth. 'All that you have done', they tell us, 'is to show what we all know, that goodness is not just like other directly-perceived properties. Of course it isn't, but it's a directly-perceived property none the less, a special kind of property, a *non-natural* one.'[1]

What happens if we try to preserve the truth of the objective doctrine in this way? As a matter of logic, the suggestion seems at first sight pretty disreputable. A townsman on his first visit to the country might be excused for thinking of rams as small, woolly bulls. (After all, they both have horns.) But if he replied to an objecting zoologist, 'Ah! Don't mistake me—I know there are differences between bulls and rams. Of course there are: a ram is a very special kind of bull, a *non-tauroid* one', the zoologist might pardonably retort, 'Don't be silly—it's not a bull at all. This stuff about "non-tauroid bulls" is just verbiage conjured up *a posteriori*, in a hopeless attempt to hide the failure of your classification.'

Such a retort, however justified, would fail to convince; but the zoologist could go on to bring evidence in support of his classification—for example, the mutual infertility of rams and cows. In the same way, calling or refusing to call 'goodness' a 'non-natural property' gets us nowhere: some kind of *grounds*

[1] Moore, *Principia Ethica*, and *The Philosophy of G. E. Moore*, pp. 581–92.

must be advanced for the choice. Until we examine the case further, we have an equal reason for saying that goodness is a 'non-natural' property and for saying that it is not a property at all—either suggestion is just a way of overcoming the difficulties I have pointed out, namely, the distinctions between 'goodness' and 'rightness', on the one hand, and all that we should normally call directly-perceived properties, on the other.

2.7 *Goodness not a Directly-Perceived Property*

If we consider the contexts in which we normally use ethical concepts, we shall find that to treat them as properties ('non-natural' or otherwise) leads to paradoxical results.

Suppose that I am talking to a philosopher (who accepts the objective doctrine) about a mutual friend, a man noted for his high moral character, for his kindness, incorruptibility, thoughtfulness, sobriety, modesty, understanding, public spirit and wide interests; and who, when asked why he has done any particular act, always gives what we should consider good reasons, referring (for example) to the needs of others, the importance of fair dealing or the welfare of his family or community.

'Surely,' I may say, 'if ever a man knew what goodness was, he does!'

'I imagine that he does,' the philosopher will say.

'And yet,' I may reply, 'I have asked him whether, when making up his mind what to do, he is conscious of observing any "non-natural property", any "fittingness",[1] in the action he decides on, and he says that he isn't. He says that he does what he does because there's a good reason for doing it, and that he isn't interested in any additional, "non-natural properties" of his actions.'

To be consistent, the philosopher will have to answer, 'If that is the case, he may know *what things are good*, he may know *what it is to be good*, but he cannot know *what goodness is*'.

'But this is absurd,' I shall retort. 'Not know what goodness is? Is such a man to be classed with a kleptomaniac, a poor sneak-thief who doesn't know what goodness is? Is he to be put on the same level as a young delinquent, whose wretched home and

[1] C. D. Broad, *Five Types of Ethical Theory*, p. 219.

irregular upbringing have sent him into the world with no knowledge of what goodness is? How laughable!'

How far is it fair to laugh his argument off like this? Not
entirely. It is true that, in one sense, it would be ludicrous to
say that a golfer who won the Open Championship did not know
how to play first-class golf, even though he might not be able to
explain the secrets of his success. Yet the very fact that he could
not explain what was special about his strokes might lead us to
say that, in another sense, he did not 'know how it was done'—
that he just 'had the knack of doing it'. But if this is all that
lies behind our philosopher's objection, it has not the force he
requires. Our virtuous and reasonable friend will not necessarily
be able to give a *reflective account* of what is involved in reaching
a moral decision, any more than the Open Golf Champion will
necessarily be able to analyse his own technique—if he could,
there would be no call for me to be writing this book. But there
is nothing *wrong* with the way in which he reaches his own moral
decisions: providing he does the right things for the right
reasons, that is enough for us. A colour-blind man who over-
came his initial handicap by learning from others what things
were red and what green might indeed be said to be missing an
essential experience, because the two colours did not look any
different to him; and if goodness and rightness were 'properties'
our friend who is interested only in the reasons for his decisions
would have to be thought of in the same way—as missing the
one thing which really mattered. But this would be ridiculous.

Now this paradox shows that not even 'non-naturalism' can
preserve the literal truth of the objective doctrine, or justify us
in adopting the objective approach to our problem. For (leaving
aside the activities of moral philosophers) if I am told that someone does not know what goodness is, I shall expect him to break
his promises, to lie, steal or cheat, and in so doing I shall be
recognising what we do in fact mean by 'goodness' and by 'He
does not know what goodness is'. A philosopher who, out of
fidelity to a theory, is driven into saying that a thoroughly
virtuous and upright man does not know what goodness is, is
assuredly up the garden path. He may think that, in telling us
this, he is giving us factual information about the virtuous man,
but he is doing nothing of the sort. If he were doing that, his

remark would—philosophically—be trivial; as if he had said, 'One can be upright and virtuous and yet never have read the Bible'. The point of what he says is otherwise: he wants to deny something which is merely a piece of idiomatic usage—that 'to be virtuous and upright and to give good reasons for one's actions' is 'to know what goodness is'—and to demand instead that the phrase 'know-what-goodness-is' shall be reserved for 'intuitive insight' (or something) into the 'non-natural properties' of actions.[1]

Now this is to misrepresent our concept of 'goodness', and to burke the problem with which we began. As long as we take it literally, there is something seriously at fault with the objective approach, and it is not at all likely to elucidate for us the place of reason in ethics.

2.8   The Sources of the Objective Doctrine

At the same time, we can hardly be satisfied to leave the objective approach in this state. Those who have adopted it have evidently felt very strongly that 'goodness' was a property of some kind or other—in spite of the fact that, in the ordinary sense of the word, it is no such thing—and, being men of the highest intelligence, they would hardly have done so without some reason. Before leaving the subject, therefore, we are bound to inquire why anyone should have felt that goodness *must* be a property, and have trusted this feeling in the face of serious (and comparatively obvious) objections.

One explanation, which will occur to any student of psychology, is that this is an instance of the phenomenon of 'projection'; that is to say, that the philosopher, seeking some outside authority or standard to support and justify his own moral decisions and judgements, creates one himself, by treating the abstract noun 'goodness' as the name of a property possessed by the objects of his judgements. Now this may be valuable as a psychological account, but it does not reveal any logical reason for the plausibility of the objective doctrine. At the best, it only points to a predisposing factor, which makes certain philosophers particularly liable to fall for some kinds of deceptive argument

[1] For a discussion of this type of argument, see Norman Malcolm's contribution to *The Philosophy of G. E. Moore*, pp. 345-68.

rather than others. What we want to find is the faulty argument itself (the 'paralogism',[1] as Kant would have called it), which lends so much colour to the objective doctrine and explains the popularity of the objective approach.

We have already remarked upon one of the factors which may play a part—the superficial but far-reaching resemblance between the forms of words we use when talking of values and when talking of properties. The statement 'Meekness is good' is on the face of it a statement of the same form as 'Cochineal is red', and this similarity is apparent also in the comparative and superlative forms. 'Meekness is better than truculence' may be compared with 'Diamond is harder than carborundum', 'Meekness is the best of personal qualities' with 'Diamond is the hardest of materials'. 'This decision was immoral' may be paralleled by 'This hope was vain'; 'Would it be right?' by 'Would it be successful?'; 'Henry VII was the first of the Tudors' by 'Henry VII was the worst of the Tudors'.

These facts are suggestive, but they are not enough by themselves to explain the plausibility of the objective doctrine, as we shall see if we remember that the same forms are used with words for 'subjective relations'—'pleasant', 'amazing', 'incredible'—concepts from which the supporters of the objective doctrine are very much concerned to distinguish goodness and rightness. However, when an additional factor is borne in mind, a more adequate reconstruction of the argument can be given.

Consider under what circumstances disagreements amount to contradictions. Suppose that I ask two people, in turn, 'Which of the boys in this class is the tallest?', 'Which summer sport is the most enjoyable?' and 'Which of these courses of action is the right one?'—questions about a 'property', a 'subjective relation' and a 'value' respectively—and suppose that in each case they disagree, one saying, 'N', and the other, 'No, not N, but M'. In which cases do they contradict one another?

In the first case, the disagreement between them is certainly a contradiction, and it can be resolved by measuring the heights of the boys and seeing which is in fact the tallest. In the second, there is no contradiction, since the two people may very well

---

[1] Cf. the beginning of the second book of the 'Transcendental Dialectic, ch. 1; *Immanuel Kant's Critique of Pure Reason*, tr. Kemp Smith (1929), pp. 328–9.

enjoy different sports. In the ethical case, there is again a contradiction—or so the unsophisticated would say. (I realise that some philosophers, *after* thinking about this, have ended by saying that 'This is right' and 'This is not right' do not contradict one another. Still, the unsophisticated would regard that as paradoxical, and they have this very material fact on their side —that, if I ask which of two courses of action is the right one, there is usually no question of my doing both. And, as we shall see more clearly later,[1] the philosophical inclination to say that there is no contradiction in the ethical case is itself a reaction against the objective doctrine—a doctrine we have already rejected.)

It is these facts about contradiction—this similarity between properties and values and this dissimilarity between values and subjective relations—which the supporter of the objective doctrine wishes to emphasise. In addition, he has an idea that values must be classed either as properties or as subjective relations. The fatal conclusion follows at once.

But though it follows in the philosopher's mind, why does it not follow logically? Let us examine the argument more closely. Suppose that one man says 'O is X' and the other says 'O is not X'. If 'X' is a word for a property, say 'red', we may say that one man is attributing to the object the property of redness, and that the other is withholding it; or, that one is attributing the predicate 'red' to the object, and that the other is withholding it—in the case of simple qualities, these statements are equivalent and unexceptionable. We may also say that one is attributing to the object the very same predicate that the other is withholding from it; and we may go on to say that, since they are contradicting each other, there must be something in common to both and neutral between them, about which they are disagreeing. What is this neutral thing in common to them? Why, clearly, the property of redness!

Now let 'X' be 'right'; we may again say that, since there is a real contradiction, one must be attributing to the object the very same predicate that the other is withholding, and we may go on as before to conclude that there is something neutral in common to them, which one attributes to the object, but which

[1] Cf. §§ 3.7, 3.8, 4.5 below.

the other withholds. What is this neutral thing in common to them?. . . The model provided by 'red' is so compelling that the impulse to say 'The property of rightness' is almost irresistible.

However, as so often, the 'logical conclusion' is the most illogical thing in the world. 'Rightness' is not a property; and when I asked the two people which course of action was the right one I was not asking them about a property—what I wanted to know was whether there was any reason for choosing one course of action rather than another; and, provided that they are arguing about the reasons for my doing different things, we are perfectly justified in talking of a genuine contradiction between '*N* is right' and 'No, not *N*, but *M*'. The idea (which the philosopher takes for granted) that, if one man attributes the predicate '*X*' to anything and another withholds it, they cannot be contradicting one another unless '*X*' stands at least for a *property*, is a fallacy. All that two people need (and all that they have) to contradict one another about in the case of ethical predicates are the *reasons* for doing this rather than that or the other.

This reconstruction of the paralogism seems especially likely to be correct because the key premise, the fallacy upon which the whole argument depends, is in practice suppressed. As in other faulty philosophical arguments, the misleading model (here provided by 'red') determines not so much what steps are put in as what are left out—taken for granted, that is—and a faulty premise is, of course, more easily overlooked when it is suppressed than when it is explicitly stated.

Finally, this reconstruction explains why those philosophers who are attracted to the objective approach pay so little attention to what we regard as the central question—the place of reason in ethics. In adopting the objective approach (so as to 'preserve the possibility of contradiction' in ethics) they say, in effect: 'Reasons are not enough. Ethical predicates must correspond to ethical properties, and "knowing-what-goodness-is" means recognising the presence of such a property.' The objective doctrine is, therefore, not just unhelpful to us: it is a positive hindrance, diverting on to arguments about a purely imaginary 'property' the attention which should be paid to the question of ethical reasoning.

3

THE SUBJECTIVE APPROACH

Towards the end of the last chapter we remarked on a distinction which supporters of the objective doctrine have always wanted to emphasise, that between values and subjective relations, between 'good' and 'pleasant'. We must now turn and consider the 'subjective approach', which rejects this distinction, and puts forward the doctrine that, in saying that anything is good or right, we are reporting on the feelings which we (or the members of our social group) have towards it. We must ask about this doctrine the three questions which we asked about the objective doctrine—'What is its point?', 'Is it true?', and 'How does it help us?'

This means, to begin with, examining the logical characteristics of 'subjective relations', those concepts like 'pleasant' to which the subjective doctrine assimilates our ethical concepts; and then seeing whether they can properly be classed together.

In its simplest form, the subjective doctrine has an obvious defect: if it were true, there would be nothing to be said when two people asserted opposite views about the value of any object or action. Once again, however, ingenious emendations are offered in the hope of saving the doctrine: these I shall have to consider in detail. I shall show that any theory based on the subjective doctrine must have one fatal weakness; that the concept of 'attitudes' (or whatever concept the new theory relies on in place of 'feelings') cannot, as long as it retains a special reference to the speaker, do what is required of it—for no subjective theory can give any account of what is a good reason for an ethical judgement, or provide any standard for criticising ethical reasoning.

This weakness so far infects the subjective doctrine, that its supporters regard our central question as trivial, treat the difference between good ethical reasoning and bad as a matter of personal preference, and refuse to help us in our search at all.

3.1 *Subjective Relations*

In considering the subjective approach to ethics, remember first the similarity between the forms of words we use with values and with subjective relations, a resemblance as striking as that between the forms of words used with values and with properties. 'Meekness is good' is comparable with 'Meekness is gratifying', 'Meekness is better than truculence' with 'Sailing is more enjoyable than fishing', 'Meekness is the best of qualities in a man' with 'Shandy is the most refreshing of drinks when you're tired'. These examples indicate the important characteristic of subjective relations, that they are used to express the effects of things on people; etymologically, they spring from verbs which relate to feelings—'enjoy', 'gratify', 'refresh', 'please'. If we bear in mind the obvious fact that ethics has something to do with the effects of things on people, something to do with satisfaction, we shall begin to understand the charm of the idea that ethical concepts are concepts of the same kind, and that in some way or other 'good' just means 'satisfying'.

To bring out the logical characteristics of subjective relations, it is worth while setting them against a wider background and discussing, first, what we may call 'adjectival relations'—predicates involving a suppressed reference to the speaker or his hearer. 'Loyal', in one of its uses, is one example, 'patriotic' another, 'adjacent' a third. Like 'gratifying' and 'enjoyable', these are often used self-referentially.

The way in which the suppressed relation operates can be seen by contrasting adjectival relations with properties. Suppose, on the one hand, that two people are presented with an object and asked 'Is it red?' or 'Is it cubical?' They will both give answers which are obtained by the same method—direct inspection or measurement—and which refer to the very same property, the red colour or cubical shape; this property we describe as neutral between them. But if, on the other hand, they are asked 'What is there in the next room?', one man may look in the room next door to the one *he* is in, the other in the room next door to *his*; alternatively, either may go and look in the room next door to that in which the *questioner* is. If such a question includes the word 'next' or 'adjacent', it is ambiguous, and may be interpreted by the hearer either as about something adjacent to him, or as about something adjacent to the questioner.

Likewise with 'patriotic' or 'loyal': if an Englishman, a Frenchman and a German are in conversation, any question about whether a fourth man is loyal or patriotic is more or less ambiguous—it is open to interpretation by each of them either self-referentially, 'loyal' meaning 'to *my* social group' and 'patriotic' meaning 'to *my* country', or as meaning 'loyal to the *fourth* person's (or even the *questioner's*) social group', 'faithful to *his* country'.

When two people are asked a question containing an adjectival relation, which is left vague in this way, there may be something neutral between them or there may not. If they both interpret it as referring to the speaker, they have a common way of finding out the answer—going to look in the room next to his—but, if they interpret it differently, one as referring to the questioner and the other as referring to himself, or if they both understand it self-referentially, there is nothing neutral between them, nothing to be compared with the red colour or the cubical shape.

Subjective relations share some, but not all, of the characteristics of adjectival relations. Questions about adjectival relations, in general, may perfectly well be interpreted with reference to the questioner. When someone asks us, 'What is there in the next room?', for example, we can go and see what is in the room next to his. If two people are given glasses of shandy, however, and then asked 'Is it refreshing?' each will take a draught, swallow it and wait to see whether he himself is refreshed by it. There is nothing here neutral between them, to compare with the red colour and cubical shape, and it would be incorrect to interpret the question with reference to the questioner. He, too, may take a long draught, swallow it and sit back showing every sign of having relieved his thirst and tiredness, but it cannot be supposed that when he asks, 'Is it refreshing?', he means 'Does it refresh *me*?' If he did mean that, they would just say, 'Why ask us? You should know!', and, if all he wanted to know was whether he was showing signs of refreshment, he would ask, not 'Is it refreshing?', but 'Would you say that I was finding it refreshing?' The same is true of any subjective relation— 'pleasing', 'amazing', 'incredible', 'enjoyable'. You would not ask another person 'Is so-and-so X?', where X is any word of this type, and expect the question to be interpreted with reference to your own feelings.

There is an allied fact on which we have remarked before—that if one man says 'This is X' and another says 'This is not X', and X is a word for a subjective relation, there is no contradiction. If I ask two people whether a glass of shandy is refreshing and get opposed answers, 'It is refreshing' and 'It is not refreshing', there is nothing to wonder at, no contradiction, and all that I can say is that the shandy refreshed the one but not the other.

To summarise this brief discussion. If X is a word for a subjective relation, and two people are asked 'Is this X?', they will answer in logically *independent* ways: each will say whether X describes the effect of the object on *him*. They may without contradiction give opposing answers—for it may have opposite effects on the two of them—and they will not take the question as referring to the way in which the object affects the questioner.

3.2 Are Ethical Concepts Subjective Relations?

Now what if we are discussing whether something is good or right, and not simply whether it is pleasing or refreshing? Are the concepts we use in this case still subjective relations? How far (to ask the same question in different words) do the things we say retain the same logical characteristics?

If we take the subjective doctrine perfectly literally and straightforwardly, we very soon run into paradoxes, which should be enough to make us think again. To begin with, suppose that, when I ask, 'Is this course or that the right one to follow?', one man answers that this one is and another says, 'No, the other'. Then I shall regard their answers as contradictory, as incompatible. They cannot both be correct, for if they were I should be morally obliged to do the logically impossible—namely, to perform both of two mutually exclusive actions. Yet if the concept of rightness were a subjective relation—merely expressing their feelings about the courses of action—both their answers *might* be correct at once: it might easily be the case that they felt differently about the possible actions. According to the subjective doctrine, it seems, no two ethical statements can contradict one another and this—especially to a man in the position of having to choose—appears ridiculous.

Secondly (a related point), I often take other people's opinions about moral questions into account when making a moral decision myself, and they seem to me to be directly relevant. Yet this is something which it would not be at all right to do, if 'This is right' meant 'I approve of this', and all I wanted to know about were my own response to the possible courses of action.

However, the subjective doctrine has its strong points. It allows, in a way in which the objective doctrine fails to do, for the obvious connection between our notions of 'value' and 'satisfaction', and it appears to explain the fact which we took as fatal to the objective doctrine[1]—that there is no logical necessity for two fully-informed people to agree in their ethical judgements.

Indeed, the variation in ethical judgements and standards, both between individuals within a community and between members of different communities, is the main evidence produced in favour of subjective ethical theories.[2] And, in its way, this evidence is both relevant and interesting. But is it sufficient to justify the doctrine that, in saying 'This is good', I am just saying something about my own reactions to the object? It is worth while examining this inference more carefully.

3.3 *The Variations in Ethical Standards*

Consider, to begin with, what follows when you ask someone 'Were the lights red?' and he says 'Yes'. Unless you have any reason for believing that his report is unreliable—for example, because his memory or eyesight is bad, because he never thinks before speaking, or because he is likely to get a term in prison if the truth about his car-driving comes out in court—you are justified in taking it that the lights *were* red: this example just illustrates our conclusions about directly-perceived properties. But now suppose that you ask him 'Are cream-buns nice?' and he again says 'Yes'. You are not justified in inferring from this that cream-buns *are* nice, unless you have some reason for believing that his likes and dislikes are similar to yours: this

---

[1] See § 2.5 above.
[2] See E. Westermarck, *Ethical Relativity*, and J. S. Huxley, *Evolutionary Ethics*, for widely separated examples of this argument.

is just another way of putting our conclusions about subjective relations.

Both these questions, however, are of the same form—'Is so-and-so X?'—and one could order other people's answers to questions of this form according to the amount of weight one would be justified in giving them when deciding on one's own answer. Near one extreme would be the report of a man with good memory and eyesight on the shape or colour of a nearby, solid, stationary object: near the other extreme would be an eccentric gourmet's expression of delight on catching a whiff of birds'-nest soup. Now, can ethical judgements appear in such a series? And if so, where will they come?

The advocates of the objective doctrine take it for granted that they can be put in this series, and want to place them near the first extreme. To do this, however, is misleading, since it obscures the fact that, whereas normal, fully-informed people may agree about ethical matters, they cannot help agreeing about directly-perceived properties. The advocates of the subjective doctrine also put ethical judgements into this series without anxiety, but they want to place them near the other extreme. The question we must ask is whether (assuming that it is proper to put ethical judgements into this series at all) putting them at this extreme may not be as misleading in its own way as putting them at the other.

Now the tests which we apply in answering questions about subjective relations vary from person to person, and that they do vary is part of what we mean by calling a concept a 'subjective relation'. However 'normal' and 'fully informed' people may be, they cannot help using independent tests to decide whether things are 'pleasing' or 'incredible': the variation in tests and standards is a matter of logical necessity. In the case of 'good' and 'right', it may also happen that the standards differ from person to person, and this is the evidence so often called upon to justify a complete ethical relativity (or subjectivity). The standards appealed to in particular cases may in fact be self-referential—'Well, I just don't think it right' or 'Why mustn't you? Because I say not!' But they need not be. To put ethical judgements at the 'subjective' extreme is therefore misleading also; for, if 'good' and 'right' were words for subjective relations, the answers to 'Is this good?' or 'Is this right?' could only be 'Well, I feel such-and-such a way about it' or 'How can I tell you how you feel about it? You should know!'—and neither of these is what we accept as a complete reply to 'Is this good (or right)?'

We can perfectly well conceive of everybody's agreeing about ethical matters—agreeing, not only in the sense in which everybody liking cream-buns may be said to agree, in spite of having independent tests of 'niceness'; but also in the sense of having the same standards or criteria of goodness, of accepting the same reasons as good reasons for their ethical judgements—a thing which over subjective relations there is no question of doing.

This is an important difference. Philosophers who support the subjective doctrine confuse the contingent difference in standards of rightness and goodness (which there might not be) with the logically necessary difference (which could not be otherwise) in the standards of pleasantness, enjoyability and so on. In doing this, they are as seriously mistaken as those who equate the contingent agreement of normal, fully-informed people over values and the necessary agreement of the same people over directly-perceived properties. Many of us like to think that it may eventually be possible to get general agreement over ethical standards, so that the moral judgements of different individuals will not vary in the way they do at present; this hope may be futile but it is certainly not nonsensical. To hope for agreement over the tests and standards of pleasantness would indeed be nonsensical; but our concepts of value are different—they are not concepts of that kind at all.

In spite, therefore, of the subjective doctrine's two strong points, it appears to be seriously at fault. What are we to conclude? Is it to be dismissed as merely figurative? Is it really false? Or may it turn out to be true after all, if only we treat ethical concepts as subjective relations, not of the simple kind we have considered so far, but of a more complex variety?

3.4 *The Theory of Attitudes*

This last possibility leads us on to the more elaborate theories, put forward by supporters of the subjective doctrine to overcome its initial deficiencies.

In likening ethical concepts to subjective relations [one of them may say] you have been talking as though we treated ethics as a matter of *passive* reactions. In fact, of course, everybody recognises that persuasion plays as important a part in it as mere feelings.

Of course it is not enough to say that 'this is good' means simply 'I like this'—there's more to it than that—but one cannot get over the fact that in ethics (as with subjective relations) the tests which are applied when coming to a decision do vary from person to person. One man says meekness is good, another that it is bad, one says promise-breaking is always wrong, another allows that on occasion it may be right. It is proverbial that to the pure all things are pure—whereas they are obviously not! All that such a proverb can express is the fact that things interest the pure in a certain way, that the pure have a certain *attitude*[1] to them. And this can be generalised: ethical disagreement is disagreement in attitude, not disagreement in belief. This explains both how it is that we can regard people expressing opposed ethical judgements as disagreeing (which we could not do if they were only expressing their feelings), and the possibility that, when all the facts are known, disagreements can occur at all (a possibility not explained by the objective doctrine).

What exactly is this distinction between disagreements in 'attitude' and 'belief'?

Questions about the nature of light-transmission, the voyages of Lief Ericsson, and the date on which Jones was last in to tea, are all similar in that they may involve an opposition that is primarily of beliefs. In such cases, one man believes that p is the answer, and another that not-p, or some proposition incompatible with p, is the answer; and in the course of discussion each tries to give some manner of proof for his view, or revise it in the light of further information. These are cases of 'disagreement in belief'. But there are other cases, differing sharply from these, which may yet be called 'disagreements' with equal propriety. They involve an opposition, sometimes tentative and gentle, sometimes strong, which is not of beliefs, but rather of attitudes—that is to say, an opposition of purposes, aspirations, wants, preferences, desires, and so on. Such are the cases with which we deal in ethics.[2]

How, then, are we to regard a typical ethical judgement—'This is good' for example?

[1] I have chosen the most recent, and in some ways the most striking form of this argument, as given in C. L. Stevenson's *Ethics and Language*—a book from which I shall have occasion to quote frequently, and one to which I owe a good deal, in spite of my rejection of its central thesis.

[2] Stevenson, op. cit. pp. 2–3.

Well, it's a complex business. You see, our judgements always have two components of meaning—one referring to some matter of fact, which can be verified (the 'descriptive' component, we may call it), and another ('emotive') aiming at persuading our hearers to behave in some way or other—and what these two components are varies from case to case. As a working model, you might regard 'This is good' as meaning 'I approve of this: do so too'—for in saying that something is good one means, partly, that one approves of it and, partly, that one wants one's hearers to approve of it as well.[1]

But how can one close the gap if there is a disagreement? And what point would there be in closing it, if a disagreement represented only a divergence of attitude?

That's quite clear, for it's something that happens every day. We find ourselves in disagreement, compare notes to make sure that we both know all the facts and then more often than not we are ready to compromise. Take a simple example.[2] We're going out to dinner, and I say 'Martini's is the place to go' (because I like that restaurant best), while you say, 'No, the Crown and Anchor's better'. We talk it over, agree that the band at Martini's is too loud for talking comfortably, while the cooking at the Crown and Anchor has deteriorated, and end up by making the best of a bad job at one or the other or by going off to a third restaurant instead. As far as I can see, there is no reason why an effort to reach convergent attitudes should be any less of a modest, co-operative enterprise than is an effort to reach convergent beliefs.[3]

3.5   *The Fatal Weakness of the Subjective Approach*

How far does this kind of account take us? No doubt it may be interesting, illuminating and even valuable to examine in detail the things that we do when we are engaged in ethical discussions. There is no reason why, after a careful study of a large number of cases, we should not become able to give as accurate a psychological account as could be wanted of what happens in such discussions—and the same could be done for scientific arguments, mathematical arguments, theological arguments and arguments between bookmakers. But this by itself gets us no nearer the solution of our problem.[4]

---

[1] Cf. op. cit. p. 21.   [2] Cf. op. cit. pp. 3, 21.   [3] Cf. op. cit. p. 157.

[4] Cf. A. J. Ayer, *Language, Truth and Logic* (2nd ed. 1946), p. 69: 'Such empirical enquiries are an important element in sociology and in the scientific study of language; but they are quite distinct from the logical enquiries which constitute philosophy.'

What we want to know is in which of these discussions the arguments presented were *worthy* of acceptance, and the reasons given *good* reasons; in which of them persuasion was achieved at least in part by valid reasoning, and in which agreement was obtained by means of *mere* persuasion—fine rhetoric unsupported by valid arguments or good reasons. And it is over the criteria (or rather, the complete lack of criteria) given for the validity of ethical arguments that the most telling objections to this (and any) subjective theory arise.

Suppose that we put forward an ethical argument, consisting partly of logical (demonstrative) inferences, partly of scientific (inductive) inferences, and partly of that form of inference peculiar to ethical arguments, by which we pass from factual reasons to an ethical conclusion—what we might naturally call 'evaluative' inference.

'Clearly', the advocate of the subjective doctrine declares, 'this last inference will be neither demonstratively nor inductively valid, by hypothesis, so that the argument as a whole cannot be valid in these senses either. The only other interesting issue is of another sort. Granted that demonstrative and inductive validity are irrelevant to this step, is there not some other kind of validity, peculiar to arguments of this kind, that deserves equal emphasis?

'Certainly one might devise a broad definition of "validity" such that certain inferences from factual reasons (R) to ethical conclusions (E) could be called "valid": but to sanction it would be wholly impracticable and injudicious, as such a sense would be deprived of its normal connection with "true". For remember: the descriptive meaning of an ethical judgement simply reports on the speaker's attitudes; the emotive meaning has nothing to do with truth or falsity; and clearly, for the step we are considering, the reasons do not establish or call in question the truth of the ethical judgement's descriptive meaning. If A says "This is good" and B says "No, it's bad", and A then produces reasons R for his judgement, he is not calling into question the truth of B's judgement, for B has said only that he disapproves of the object; he is trying to redirect B's attitudes. In general, when E is supported or opposed by R, R neither proves nor disproves the truth of the descriptive meaning of E. So unless "valid" is to have a misleadingly extended sense, the question "Does R permit a valid inference to E?" is devoid of interest.'[1]

---

[1] This passage is a paraphrase of Stevenson's account, but it is substantially in his own words: cf. op. cit. pp. 152–6. Stevenson offers a number of alternative

This is the conclusion to which any supporter of the subjective doctrine must come—and it is fatal to every subjective theory. For common sense will immediately reply, 'Devoid of interest? If a man tells me that it is right for him to kick the niggers around, because everyone else does, is it of no interest whether his argument is valid or not?'—thus revealing the paradox involved. The philosopher will assert in reply that, if you do insist on talking about validity in this connection, all that you are doing is 'selecting those inferences to which you are psychologically disposed to give assent';[1] but this only makes matters worse, saddling the subjective doctrine with two paradoxes in place of one. For of course, though you are doing that, you are not simply doing that—you are insisting, in addition, that his argument really is an invalid argument, that his reason is a bad reason and one which no one should accept. And similarly, in saying that anything is good, you are of course saying that you approve of it (or at any rate would like to be able to approve of it), and that you want your hearer to approve of it also. But you are not simply doing that—you are saying that it is really *worthy* of approval; that there really is a valid argument (a good reason) for saying that it is good, and so for approving of it, and for recommending others to do so too. And any subjective theory, which makes the criteria of validity applicable to ethical judgements a matter of the 'feelings', 'attitudes', 'responses', 'psychological states' or 'dispositions' of the speaker or of his social group, must fail at this point. Although the inferences to which we are 'psychologically disposed to give assent' may *in fact* often coincide with the inferences to which we ought to give assent, they are distinct from them logically—and common sense recognises the distinction. And, as a matter of actual fact, the inferences to which we *do* give assent are bewilderingly different and even contradictory.

3.6 *The Deceptively Scientific Air of this Theory*

To observe just how paradoxical the consequences of the subjective doctrine are, and so underline the fatal fallacy, consider analyses of sentences including the word 'good', the 'descriptive meaning' of some of which is quite other than 'I approve of this': his account of 'validity' applies equally to all these analyses.

[1] Op. cit. p. 171.

the peculiar nature of the philosopher's assertions that 'the
question "Does R permit a valid inference to E?" is devoid of
interest' and that 'talking about "valid" or "invalid" evaluative
inferences is just selecting those inferences to which you are
psychologically disposed to give assent'.

These statements seem, logically, to be quite in order, and we
think we understand them. But we do so only because they remind us of other statements, which are superficially very similar.
Thus, the prosecuting counsel in a murder case may say, 'The
question where the accused was at ten past six is devoid of
interest: it is where he was at a *quarter* past six that we have to
establish'. Likewise, an anthropologist may assert on the basis
of his experiences in Africa: 'Adolescent Hottentots when sober
have an acute sense of moral obligation, but after a pint of beer
they lose all scruples and do only those things which they are
psychologically disposed to do.' And both counsel and anthropologist are interesting and informative, for they tell us something that is the case, by contrasting it with something that is not
the case.

The philosopher, however, is doing nothing of this kind. Although his assertions rely on their everyday and familiar air to
get past our guard, this air is deceptive. And indeed, if it were
not—if there were any question of the opposite of what he says
being the case—he could not draw the consequences from them
that he wishes to. He is not stating a matter of scientific fact.
He does not mean that, when forced to make moral decisions, we
all behave like drunk Hottentot adolescents—failing for some
reason to tell rhetoric from reason, or to distinguish between
those arguments which are really valid (and which we ought to
accept) and those which appeal to us, but are specious. He means,
rather, that to talk of 'valid' or 'invalid' ethical arguments is the
result of a misunderstanding, so that we ought not to call ethical
arguments 'valid' or 'invalid' at all.

This interpretation is confirmed when he says himself, 'One
might devise a broad definition of "valid" to cover this case, but
to sanction it would be injudicious',[1] and if this really is his conclusion he is seriously off-track. For he is not called upon to
devise or to sanction linguistic usages—especially when this

[1] Cf. Stevenson's discussion of 'validity', quoted above.

activity involves misrepresenting our existing concepts. It is more his business to analyse the sense of 'valid' (and the criteria of validity), which are already implicit in our ethical discussions, and whose existence cannot be explained away by this kind of psychological analysis.

If it comes to that, the change in our ideas which he recommends has little to be said for it. Whenever we are faced with a number of courses of action, we shall have to choose between different sets of reasons for acting in the different ways, and between different arguments in support of the different possible decisions: if this is to be done at all methodically, we shall need to distinguish between those which are worthy of acceptance ('valid', as we now call them) and those which are not worthy (or 'invalid').

The advantages of the existing usage are so great that even the philosopher has to go on talking of 'reasons' (and of 'well-proved reasons') for acting in this way or that.[1] In doing so, he excuses himself by explaining that, when he talks of 'well-proved reasons', he means 'relevant facts which have been proved to be the case', and not 'relevant facts which have been proved to support this ethical conclusion'. His very apology, however, shows that his fears are baseless and his demands self-contradictory. Of course, to establish an ethical conclusion one cannot appeal to the facts in just the way one does when establishing the facts themselves; for this would be to treat the ethical conclusion as a 'fact'. Few, however, apart from philosophers, would suppose that one could: and, if it is as a guard against this danger that he wishes to amend our usage, his fears can be ignored.

3.7   *The Common Source of the Objective and Subjective Doctrines*

Again we are left without answers to the central questions—'What types of reasoning are relevant to ethical conclusions?', 'What makes an evaluative inference valid or invalid?' If we compare the arguments given by the present philosopher with those given by the supporters of the objective doctrine, we may be able to discover why he shirks the questions in the way he does.

The supporter of the objective doctrine wishes to emphasise the resemblances between values and properties ('redness' and

[1] Cf. Stevenson, op. cit. pp. 29–30.

'goodness'); in particular, he takes it for granted that opposed ethical judgements cannot be regarded as incompatible unless there is at any rate a property of the object to which they both refer. And, since they seem to him to be incompatible, goodness, he concludes, must be a property.

The philosopher advocating the subjective doctrine is impressed not so much by the similarities as by the differences between properties and values; he is impressed still more by the resemblances, rather than by the differences, between values and subjective relations ('goodness' and 'pleasantness'). He therefore recoils from this argument. 'Goodness a property?' he protests, 'The whole argument's absurd! If two people assert opposed ethical judgements, there's no property, nothing neutral, nothing incompatible at issue between them at all!'

In consequence, when the two philosophers come to consider the question, 'What makes evaluative inferences valid, or particular facts good reasons for ethical conclusions?', neither of them can answer helpfully at all. The one has to declare, 'The presence of the non-natural property of "goodness", or "rightness" is required for drawing such a conclusion'; and the other replies, 'You really shouldn't talk about "good reasons" or "valid inferences" in this context, for such phrases have no use except to indicate those reasons and inferences you are psychologically disposed to accept.' As we have seen, neither of these answers will do.

But where does the second philosopher slip up? It was right, of course, for him to reject the first philosopher's conclusion—that goodness is a property: the error must therefore be in his reasoning. And, indeed, it turns out that, by rejecting the argument *as a whole*, and so declining to touch our central problem, he is deceived in just the same way as his opponent was before him. The supporters of both doctrines take it for granted that opposed ethical judgements can only be contradictory if they refer to a property of the object concerned; and that, unless they do refer to a property, such judgements must refer to some psychological state of the speaker—in which case they can never contradict one another at all.

This suppressed assumption is certainly plausible, but it is mistaken. In the ethical case, there need be no such property, nor such a 'psychological state'. All that is needed is a good reason for choosing one thing rather than the other. Given that, the incompatibility of 'This is good' and 'This is not good' is preserved. And surely that, in practice, is all we ever demand.

3.8 *The Deeper Sources of these Fallacies*

'But once again', it may be asked, 'What is the attraction of *this* particular suppressed premise, that it should (if you are right) have seemed self-evident to so many people?'

The intellectual ramifications of such a fallacy are practically endless, but it may be illuminating to see how it links up, at any rate one stage back, with more widespread, more general fallacies, and so to trace its attraction back to the deeper springs of unreason in our thoughts.

The philosophers' fallacies arise (as we have seen) from the idea that any ethical theory must classify values either as properties or as subjective relations. According to their inclination, they plump for the one alternative or the other, announcing as their slogan either 'Ethical predicates are *objective properties* of actions, situations and motives' or 'Ethical judgements express the *subjective responses* of the speaker'. In so doing, they introduce (and make much of) a question which we have not found it necessary to discuss explicitly—the question 'Is goodness subjective or objective?' This fact gives us the lead we want.

We often like to describe properties, such as redness, as 'objective', or as being 'in the object'. This description seems to us a particularly happy one, since we sometimes find actual physical or chemical processes, literally going on in the object, with which the presence of the property can be causally correlated. (When this happens, we may introduce a 'scientific quality' —'really red', say—which is defined in terms of theoretical concepts, and which, for scientific purposes, is regarded as more significant than the simple quality—'red'—from which we begin.) The sodium discharge lamps which cast their characteristic orange glow on to the streets of our towns do so (the physicists explain) because electrons in the atoms of the sodium vapour are continually making transitions from the energy-levels $^2P_{\frac{3}{2}}$ and $^2P_{\frac{1}{2}}$ to the level $^2S_{\frac{1}{2}}$, emitting, as they jump, light of a particular wave-length—(and, as a scientific quality, colour is defined in terms of wave-length).[1]

Subjective relations, on the other hand, we take as referring to something 'in' or 'in the mind of' the speaker, and this again seems to us a very happy way of expressing ourselves, for all subjective relations refer to a 'psychological response' on the part of the speaker—his pleasure, amazement or incredulity—and in some cases we actually find positive physical or chemical processes in the subject's body, with which the 'psychological response' can be causally correlated. The film is 'exciting', so his pulse and breathing quicken, his pupils dilate and adrenalin seeps into his blood-stream.

But what about values? Are they objective or subjective—'in the object', or 'in the subject'? Ingenuous application of the Law of Excluded Middle suggests that they must be one or the other, that if they are not 'outside' they must be 'inside'. Concepts not correlated with processes outside the speaker's body must (it seems) be correlated with processes inside the speaker's body: anything correlated with neither would (we feel) lack body, and so be in some way 'unreal' or 'non-existent'. 'Value', therefore (we conclude), must *really* be either a property of the object or a response of the speaker.

This conclusion is false: so the reasoning must be faulty, and it is not hard to see why. There is no reason in the world why all our words should act as names for definite and unique processes—physical *or* mental: only some of them, in fact, are of such a kind that it makes sense to talk of such processes. And we can easily see that the class of concepts for which it does make sense cannot include ethical concepts. For, if 'goodness' or 'rightness' were something which could be definitely correlated with such a process, that would make nonsense of the crucial fact we remarked on in the last chapter—that there may yet be ethical differences, even when all sources of factual disagreement have been ruled out.

Nevertheless, there remains a strong temptation (and one which is manifested in ways too complex and numerous to be explored here) to forget how figuratively we are talking when we describe the properties of an object as 'in the object' and

---

[1] See any standard text-books of atomic physics.

psychological responses as 'in the subject'; and so to *identify* the property 'in' the object with a process in the object, and the response 'in' the subject with a process in the subject. And once this mistake is made, it is no wonder if, in our endless search for an 'ethical' process, property or response, which does not and cannot exist, we overlook that which really matters—the reasoning behind our moral judgements.

4

THE IMPERATIVE APPROACH

THE last of the three traditional approaches for us to discuss is the 'imperative' approach. The starting-point of this approach is the doctrine that, in calling anything good or right, we are only evincing (displaying) our feelings towards it. In saying 'You ought not to steal', for example, we are (it is said) doing no more, from the logician's point of view, than if we cried 'Stealing!' in a peculiarly horrified tone.

This doctrine has a lot in common with the modified ('attitude') form of subjective theory discussed in the last chapter; much of what was said there in criticism applies again with equal force. I shall show that, in spite of the important resemblances between ethical statements, commands and exhortations, the imperative doctrine fails to lead to an adequate account of ethics, principally because it side-steps the question, 'What is a good reason for an ethical judgement?', rather as the theory of attitudes did. The philosopher who adopts the imperative approach has too narrow a view of the uses of reasoning—he assumes too readily that a mathematical or logical proof or a scientific verification can be the only kind of 'good reason' for any statement. As a result, he dismisses all evaluative inferences (arguments from facts to values or duties) as rationalisation or rhetoric, and regards our central problem, not merely as trivial, but as nonsense.

In this, his arguments run counter to common sense and common usage, and can be rejected. They do, however, raise our central problem again with the greatest force. Moreover, they make it clear that it is our question, rather than the question, 'What *is* goodness?', which is really the central one.

4.1 *The Rhetorical Force of Ethical Judgements*

It may seem odd to have ignored until now a doctrine according to which the very problem I am discussing is nonsense. I have done so (I hope and believe) justifiably.

In the first place, the imperative approach is the youngest and most artless of the three traditional approaches. The objective and subjective doctrines have, in one form or another, been bandied about and criticised for 2000 years and more; their weaknesses have been apparent for almost as long, and their advocates have been used to retire to their second lines of defence. Only ingenuous amateurs still call goodness a 'property', in the ordinary sense of the word, or regard ethical sentences as straightforward expressions of the feelings. For professionals, things have become more complicated—it is with the world of 'non-natural properties' rather than ordinary 'properties', of 'attitudes' rather than simple 'feelings', that they are concerned.

By contrast, the imperative doctrine is fresh and uncomplicated. It does not call ethical sentences 'non-natural commands', but wears its obvious paradox bravely and defiantly. To have disposed, at the start, of the imperative doctrine, and to have passed on later to consider the more hardy objective and subjective doctrines, would have been to shoot the sitting bird first. And, moreover, it would have been impossible, while rejecting the approach, to do justice to its force and importance.

This leads on to the second point. The imperative approach is the youngest of the approaches, by no mere chance, but because it is the result of a reaction against the two older ones. To appreciate its strength, it is necessary to have seen beforehand the weaknesses in the objective and subjective doctrines which it is intended to overcome. No doubt one might dismiss the doctrine out of hand, simply on grounds of factual falsehood— it is just not true that the phrase 'ethical reasoning' is self-contradictory, or that to talk of 'valid evaluative inferences' is nonsense. In the same way, one might dismiss Russell's conclusion that 'all one ever sees is a part of one's own brain'[1] on the grounds that we do as a matter of fact often see chairs and tables and motor-cars and trees, and rarely if ever see parts of our own brains. But to do this and this alone would be perversely common-sensical, for the imperative doctrine is only obliquely directed at preventing people from discussing our central problem, and we can learn a good deal by examining its more immediate aims.

---

[1] *The Analysis of Matter* (1927), p. 383.

The advocate of the imperative doctrine is determined, from the start, to avoid some of the mistakes in the subjective and objective doctrines. Ethical concepts, as he recognises, correspond neither to processes 'in' the object nor to processes 'in' or 'in the mind of' the speaker: there is no quality and no response which can plausibly be taken as that to which our value-sentences refer. Our philosopher, therefore, condemns the form of words 'So-and-so is *X*' ('Meekness is good', 'Promise-keeping is morally obligatory') as a misleading one—one which gives a false idea of the part that ethical sentences play in our lives. He insists that it is not possible to find a place for such sentences in that series of statements, of which a clear-sighted man's judgement of shape is near one extreme, and an eccentric's gourmandise near the other[1]—and not merely in fact impossible but wrong-headed, since (for him) the question 'Where on this series do ethical sentences come?' has no meaning. In contrast to those sentences of the form 'So-and-so is *X*' which give information of some kind, the whole force of ethical statements (according to him) is *rhetorical*. They are, he asserts, disguised imperatives or ejaculations; our least misleading ethical utterances being those like 'Good!', the cry of joy, and 'Naughty!', the command to desist.

'In saying "tolerance is a virtue"', he explains,[2] 'I should not be making a statement about my feelings or anything else. I should simply be *evincing* my favourable feelings towards tolerance; a very different thing from saying that I have them, or that there is something about tolerance, some quality which intolerance has not got. Again, if I said to someone, "You acted wrongly in stealing that money", I should not be *stating* any more than if I had simply said "You stole that money", cried "Stealing! Oh!" in a peculiar tone of horror, or written it with special exclamation marks.'

This doctrine often strikes newcomers as 'cynical' or 'pessimistic'; philosophers who advocate it seem to the unsympathetic to be 'fiddling and playing tricks while the world burns'.[3] Their reaction is significant, but to understand the doctrine we must

---

[1] See §3.3 above.

[2] Cf. Ayer, *Language, Truth and Logic* (2nd ed. 1946), pp. 107–9.

[3] Martin D'Arcy, 'Philosophy Now', in *Criterion* (1936).

discount this appearance, at any rate until we are in a position to account for it. As matters turn out, it is quite misleading. One soon discovers in practice that advocates of the doctrine are no less cheerful or 'idealistic' (in the everyday sense) than others, and that they will happily support the most rigorous of ethical judgements.

The point of the doctrine is logical, not empirical. Just as those who adopt the objective and subjective approaches assimilate ethical concepts to the logical categories of 'properties' and 'subjective relations' respectively, the supporters of the imperative doctrine assimilate all ethical sentences to the class of interjections—exclamations, ejaculations, commands and so on.

In order to see why they do this, let us consider typical members of the class. To start with, there are those spontaneous reactions, like blushing, smiling, laughing and weeping, which play an important part in our relations with our fellows, and which mean (indicate) so much to those we meet. Next, there are the manner and tone of voice in which we speak, which convey to a hearer nuances difficult to put into writing. With these we may class ejaculations like 'Blast!' and 'Hurrah!', which, without stating anything, release our feelings of annoyance or jubilation; and those stimuli, by means of which we move others to act—'Geeup!' and 'Whoa!'; 'Stop!' and 'Stand to attention!'[1] The whole force of each of these is rhetorical; the blush, the manner, the curse, the command, all evince feelings—and so (it is said) do ethical utterances.

Unquestionably, many of the facts to which our philosopher will draw attention in presenting his case are true and important. In practice, moral exhortation is often no more than straight persuasion or intimidation. Ethical remarks are, indeed, made with the intention that hearers should act or reflect on them. Certainly they evince our feelings: what we call 'wicked' horrifies us, the 'admirable' gratifies us. The schoolboy who, on hearing that he has won his cricket colours or a scholarship, exclaims 'That *is* good news!' might equally well cry out 'Good!' or 'Hurrah!' or 'I *am* pleased!' Likewise when, in your childhood, your father said to you, 'Naughty! Naughty! You mustn't take all the jam', he was not so much interested in conveying

---

[1] Cf. John Dewey, *Theory of Valuation*, pp. 6–13.

information to you—apart perhaps from information about your chances of the slipper—as he was in stopping you before you finished the pot. All these facts are true and important, and moral philosophers have in the past paid too little attention to them. But more is required in order to establish the literal truth of the imperative doctrine.

4.2 *The Impossibility of Disputing about Exclamations*

In addition to their rhetorical force, ejaculations and commands have important logical characteristics in common. First (though this must not be put too strongly), none of them can be said to 'give information', or to 'state' anything. Of course, if they 'mean a lot' to our friends, in one sense they do give information, but there is a clear sense in which they cannot be said to. If someone blushes, that is a sign that she is embarrassed, if he shouts it is a sign that he is angry, if he curses that is one too, and if he starts giving orders, you gather he wants things done. But it is 'gathering' in each case: you would not say that she had told you she was embarrassed, or that he had told you he was angry, or even that he had told you he wanted you to do anything (although he 'told you to do it'). Leaving aside the sense in which such signs do 'give you information', there is a common and important sense, which I am using here, in which his utterance does not give you information unless he tells you.

Again, there is no disputing about exclamations in the way in which we dispute about questions of fact, because no two exclamations can be said to be logically incompatible with one another. If Featherstone maximus blushes and says to Smith minor in a reproachful tone, 'Beast! You told him I was late for school. Do mind your own business in future', the only subject for dispute is the fact in question; namely, whether or not Smith did tell on Featherstone. The blush, the tone of reproach, the exclamation ('Beast!') and the imperative ('Do mind your own business') are to be distinguished from the fact in question; for, in spite of the considerable part that they play in the total situation, they *state* nothing whatever. To put this in another way: many things bear upon the statement of fact ('I heard you telling him', 'He told me you had', 'I knew that you must have from the way in which he carried on', etc.), in a way in which they cannot bear upon the other elements in the situation. One can quite properly ask about the 'verification' of a statement of fact; but there is no meaning to the 'truth' or 'falsity' of a blush or an exclamation.

4.3 *Are Ethical Sentences Ejaculations?*

Our philosopher maintains that what applies to interjections applies equally to ethical sentences. 'It is impossible to dispute about questions of value', he says.[1] 'When ethical statements appear to be subjects for dispute, or are opposed, the dispute—if it has any meaning at all—is reducible to differences regarding the facts of the case—such as whether anyone really did steal anything.' All we can do, he suggests, is to hope that, if we get an opponent to agree with us about the facts of the case, he will adopt the same 'moral attitude' towards them as we do. As for the question of good reasons and valid arguments in ethics, he declares bluntly that ethical judgements 'have no validity'.[2]

The position he takes up is similar to the 'theory of attitudes', which we considered in the last chapter, but with two main differences. Although both theories agree that the aim of ethical discourse is to achieve convergent 'moral attitudes', they differ in their accounts of these attitudes. The modified subjective theory identifies them as attitudes of approval and disapproval; the imperative theory leaves them unexplained, making no attempt to specify the peculiarities of the 'moral' attitudes and 'ethical' feelings evinced in the course of ethical discussions.[3]

Again, although they agree in ignoring the question of the validity of evaluative inferences, it is for different reasons. The advocate of the subjective theory does so because he regards the question as *trivial*, the supporter of the imperative doctrine does so because he regards it as *nonsense*. From their different points of view, however, both succeed in ironing out a distinction which is, in practice, central—the distinction between those ethical arguments we should accept and those we should ignore or reject.

In this lies the principal paradox of the imperative doctrine. We might dismiss it at once, having seen the ridiculous consequences to which, when taken literally, it leads; but this would

---

[1] Ayer, op. cit. pp. 110–11.   [2] Loc. cit.
[3] Cf. Dewey, loc. cit.

be a pedantic and disingenuous thing to do. It will be more interesting to examine, with the help of examples, the weaknesses of the approach, and see whether we can account for its origin and for its appearance of cynicism. If we can do this before abandoning it, we shall be better placed to appreciate its value.

4.4   *The Weaknesses of the Imperative Approach*

Consider, first, a genuine imperative. If the sergeant-major says to me, 'Stand to attention!', I do not stop to argue, but stand to attention at once. And if I ask him for 'a good reason for accepting what he says as true', he will put me on a charge, or send me to the Medical Officer for a psychological inspection. In such a case, no questions of truth, falsity or verification arise; and they do not arise, not just because of the threat of the 'glass-house', but because they have no meaning in this context.

Now consider a very similar ethical sentence. Suppose that the sergeant-major says to me instead, 'You ought to be standing at attention'. I shall stand to attention at once in just the same way—and this shows the justice of the imperative doctrine's claims about the rhetorical force of ethical judgements. And once again, if I ask him about 'a good reason for agreeing with what he says', he will act as before. Once again, that is to say, no questions of truth, falsity or verification will arise. But there is this important difference between the two cases: if these questions do not arise in this case it will be because of the threat of the 'glass-house', and not because it would be nonsense to ask them. If, for example, I had asked the sergeant-major, 'How am I to know that I ought?', he could with perfect logic have said, 'By consulting King's Regulations and Army Council Instructions, Section so-and-so'; and this would indeed have been to 'give a reason'.

Is this example a fair one? Or is the issue confused by questions of legal obligation, which can only be called 'ethical' as a courtesy matter? Questions of legal obligation, our philosopher may say, are of course open to dispute and verification—that is what the Law Courts are for—but questions of moral obligation are not.

This objection, however, does not get him very far: quite apart from legal considerations, questions of truth, falsity and rational justification (or verification, in a broad sense of the term) do continually arise in ethics. If you tell a child, 'You ought to take off your dirty shoes before going into the drawing room', and he asks 'Why?', then the answers, 'Because your Mama does not like you to dirty the carpet' and 'Because it makes unnecessary work', are 'reasons'—and pretty good ones, too—while the answer, 'Because it's the third Tuesday before Pentecost', seems a poor one. For that matter, we often talk of 'reasons' (some 'good', some 'bad') for commands, too. Thus, in an undisciplined army, with the threat of a court-martial absent, my response to the sergeant-major's 'Stand to attention!' might well be to ask, 'Why?'

In the case of commands, however, these reasons can never be 'reasons for agreeing to the truth of what has been said'. If, when the sergeant-major has bellowed his order, I go up to a private and say to him, 'D'you know; the R.S.M. wasn't telling the truth', he may stare at me or laugh, but he will certainly not understand. But if the sergeant-major has only said to him, 'You ought to be standing at attention', and I do the same, he will agree, ask for my reasons, or begin to argue with me. He will not regard my statement as strange or unintelligible, for he will be thoroughly familiar with such discussions. That being so, it is quite wrong to call it nonsense.

A major weakness of the imperative doctrine of ethics is, therefore, this: it treats the contingent proposition that questions of truth, falsity and verification often *do not* arise in ethical discourse, as if it were logically identical with the necessary proposition that, over exclamations and commands, such questions *cannot* arise. That is, it treats ethical statements, which approximate in some respects to commands and interjections, as if they were just commands and interjections. And this paradox is inevitable if one is to dismiss all evaluative inferences as beyond the scope of reasoning. If we are to overcome it, we must grant that ethical reasoning is possible, and so that some types of reasoning are 'good' and some 'bad'—some of the arguments leading to true conclusions 'valid' ones, and all which lead to false conclusions 'invalid'.

4.5   *The Sources of the Imperative Doctrine*

The nature of this weakness also helps to explain how the doctrine arises. Despite our ordinary usage, in which 'reasons' can be brought for anything from mathematical theorems to curses, the advocate of the imperative doctrine wishes to limit the meaning and scope of 'reasoning'. For him, 'truth', 'falsity' and 'proof' or 'verification' are features of logical, mathematical and factual statements only, and strict proof or factual verification the only kind of good reason which can be said to support any statement.

In view of the debt to Hume which the advocates of both the imperative doctrine and the theory of attitudes themselves acknowledge, it is interesting to remark that he, too, deliberately limited the scope of reasoning in the same way. Recall the famous outburst standing at the end of his *Enquiry Concerning Human Understanding*:[1]

> If we take in our hand any volume; of divinity or school metaphysics, for instance; let us ask, *Does it contain any abstract reasoning concerning quantity or number?* No. *Does it contain any experimental reasoning concerning matter of fact and existence?* No. Commit it then to the flames: for it can contain nothing but sophistry and illusion.

For him and them alike, logic, mathematics and experimental science alone are logically respectable: other attempts at reasoning are shams.

To do justice to Hume and his present-day followers: it is, of course, important not to apply to one mode of reasoning criteria of proof or truth appropriate only to another. Thus '$x^2 = 9$' is a bad reason for concluding '$x = 5$', 'I have thrown double-six three times running with unbiased dice' is a bad reason for concluding 'I shall throw double-six next time', 'I know of no-one over 7 ft. 6 in. in height' is a bad reason for concluding 'there is no-one over 7 ft. 6 in. in height' and 'Everybody kicks the niggers around' is a bad reason for concluding 'It is all right for me to kick the niggers around'; but each is a bad reason of a logically

---

[1] Ed. Selby-Bigge (2nd ed. 1902), p. 165. Ayer quotes this passage with approval (op. cit. p. 54); and Stevenson acknowledges a general debt to Hume in his *Ethics and Language*, VII, 273–6.

different kind, and it will not do to treat any two of them as logically indistinguishable.

One point which the imperative doctrine fairly emphasises is the difference between arguments from logical, mathematical or factual premises to conclusions of a *similar* logical type, and arguments from factual premises to conclusions of a *different* kind, conclusions about duties or values. It is this distinction which is the strongest point in any refutation of the 'naturalistic fallacy'[1] —that is, the idea that the value of any object can be identified with some ordinary property of it. Although factual reasons (R) may be good reasons for an ethical conclusion (E), to assert the conclusion is not just to assert the reasons, or indeed anything of the same logical type as R. It is to declare that one ought to approve of, or pursue, or do something-or-other. It is a wicked man who beats his wife; but to say that he is wicked is not just to say that he beats his wife—or, for that matter, to assert any other fact about him. It is to *condemn* him for it.

The bias in favour of logic, mathematics and science is not confined to the 'empiricists'. Logicians of all schools have traditionally concerned themselves, first, with deductive logic; next, with the logic of probability—a nice mixture of deduction and induction; and, lastly and more briefly, with inductive logic. The other uses of reasoning have commonly been ignored. In their books, the word 'reason' has been used primarily for the facts which support a factual conclusion, and then mainly when the support offered is conclusive.[2]

Even within philosophy, the use has naturally not been constant. In an inductive argument, data about the past and present are taken as 'reasons' for a conclusion about the future: in a syllogism, factual or logical premises are 'reasons' for a factual or logical conclusion: in a mathematical argument, the axioms and proof are the 'reasons' which establish the theorem. When these differences have been forgotten, there has been trouble: the history of philosophy is littered with the corpses of theories attempting to prove that there is no real difference between the canons of deduction and induction.[3] (And, likewise, the history

---

[1] Moore, *Principia Ethica*, pp. 9–10.
[2] See almost any text-book of logic for confirmation.
[3] Laplace's theory is of course the notorious example.

of philosophical ethics is largely a record of attempts to identify evaluation with some form of inductive or deductive inference.)

All the same, past practice does not justify present neglect. We are all familiar with the idea of 'giving reasons' in contexts other than logical, mathematical and factual. The most that can be said for the advocate of the imperative doctrine is that this wider use of 'reason' and 'valid' is an everyday and colloquial, rather than an esoteric and technical one. But this does not justify him in declaring that ethical judgements have *no* validity: all that it does is to help to explain the logical temptation to which he gives way.

Furthermore, past practice, conditioning present preoccupations, can hardly be the only reason for the plausibility of the imperative doctrine. It would be surprising if no deeper, 'para-logistic' source could be found—and I think it can.

Historically, as I pointed out, the imperative approach is a reaction against the objective and subjective approaches. Like so many reactions, it goes a little too far, and in doing so makes the same mistake as its opponents.

'When two people are in ethical disagreement', said the first philosopher, 'they contradict one another. If they are to do this, there must be something in the object they are discussing for them to contradict one another about. Therefore, goodness must be a property of the object.'

'Nonsense!' replied the second philosopher. 'Goodness is no property of the object. All they are doing is expressing divergent reactions to the object: the contradiction is only apparent. It is in their attitudes towards the object, not about any property of it, that they disagree.'

'A plague on both your houses!' retorts our third philosopher. 'You're both overlooking the rhetorical force of ethical judgements. People who have ethical disagreements are not talking about their own attitudes, and they are not talking about any property of the object either. The truth of the matter is that they are not "talking about" anything, for there isn't anything for them to "talk about"—all they are doing is answering each other back, and bringing pressure to bear on each other to behave differently.'

The objective doctrine relies for its plausibility on the premise (usually suppressed) that, if there is to be a contradiction between two people, there must at least be a property of some kind for them to contradict one another about: otherwise the judgement can only be personal, referring to the speaker's psychological state. This premise is tacitly assumed in the argument for the subjective doctrine, too. Now the advocate of the imperative doctrine is under the tyranny of the same idea—that, in order to be logically respectable, to be capable of being regarded as 'true' or 'false' or of being reasoned about, a sentence must be made up only of concepts *referring to* something, something either 'in the object' or 'in the subject'. The novelty of his paralogism is that he rejects both alternatives: he recognises that ethical sentences and ethical concepts 'refer to' nothing of the kind required[1] and concludes (paradoxically but firmly) that they can only be 'pseudo-statements' and 'pseudo-concepts'.[2]

We, however, have already seen the faultiness of the suppressed premise, and so of any argument depending on it. And, in seeing the nature of the fallacy involved, we have come to realise what it is that people in ethical disagreement really do have to contradict each other about—nothing physically or psychologically 'concrete' or 'substantial', but something which, for logical purposes, is quite as solid and important—namely, whether or not there is a good reason for reaching one ethical conclusion rather than another.

4.6 *The Apparent Cynicism of the Imperative Doctrine*

Can we, as a result of our discussion, understand why it is that people complain, when first presented with this doctrine, of its cynicism and pessimism? I think the reasons are directly connected with the central fallacy of the approach.

The fundamental doctrine of the imperative approach may be put in several forms: 'There is no good reason for passing from any set of facts to an ethical judgement', or 'There is never any good reason for saying that anything is good or right, or for ascribing to ourselves or others any duty or moral obligation to do anything', or 'All that happens, when anyone makes an ethical judgement, is that he bears the facts and the feelings of others in mind, and then exclaims in whatever sense he feels most like'. When

---

[1] See § 3.8 above. [2] Ayer, op. cit. p. 197.

anyone is first presented with such statements, he is likely to be misled by their form into thinking that they express ordinary matters-of-fact.

The statements, 'There is no good reason for passing from any set of facts to an ethical judgement' and 'There is never any good reason for saying that anything is good or right', are at first sight very like the statement, 'There is no good reason for supposing that he will come before five o'clock'. The assertion, 'All that happens, when anyone makes an ethical judgement, is that he exclaims in whatever sense he feels most like', immediately brings to mind statements of the form, 'All that happens, when anyone pokes a hippopotamus in the ribs, is that it turns over'.

If, in consequence, you suppose that the philosopher really is expressing an ordinary matter-of-fact—a natural assumption for a newcomer to the doctrine—what a terrible pessimist you must think him! 'Poor, deluded humans', he seems to be saying, 'spending their time looking for reasons for ethical judgements! If only they saw what a hopeless task they've taken on! Even looking for a needle in a haystack is a job with more prospect of success than that. And fancy their imagining that anyone making an ethical judgement ever does anything but exclaim! Why, I've watched thousands of them, and I've never *once* seen one who did.'

The point of his doctrine is (as we have seen) quite otherwise: his preoccupation is with logic, rather than with everyday matters-of-fact. If all he were saying were that in only a negligible proportion of cases do people *in fact* arrive at moral decisions on the basis of reason, he could not draw the conclusions he wants to. And this shows why the appearance of pessimism is deceptive.

The imperative doctrine arises out of a confusion between the logical proposition, 'There are (can be) no good reasons for ejaculations', and the matter-of-fact proposition, 'There are (may be) no good reasons for ethical judgements'. The philosopher formulates the differences between factual and ethical statements in the logical proposition, 'There are (can be) no good reasons for ethical judgements'. The newcomer mistakes this for the matter-of-fact proposition, 'There are (in fact) no good reasons for ethical judgements', and concludes that all his moral striving has been in vain. Hence the feeling of pessimism.

And it is not only the newcomer who is misled into behaving as if these were the kind of statements they seem to be: as often as not the philosopher begins to as well. Struck by the matter-of-fact appearance of his own remarks, and knowing that such statements are often enough true in spite of being paradoxical (see the 'Believe It or Not' feature in the Sunday paper), he starts to treat his theory as really true, and common sense as really mistaken in its firm belief that some reasons *are* good reasons for ethical judgemènts, and that sometimes people making ethical statements are *not* just exclaiming.

But the only 'matter of fact' with which the philosopher can be said to be concerned is whether or no the phrases 'ethical reasoning', 'an ethical dispute', 'a valid evaluative inference', 'a sound ethical judgement', 'a good reason for doing this rather than that', and the like, are all nonsense. He mistakenly believes that they are, and concludes that we ought not to call the facts, which we bring in support of our ethical judgements, 'reasons' for the ethical conclusions. He is afraid that, if we do, we shall confuse them (as philosophers sometimes have done) with the 'reasons' which, in deductive and inductive arguments, lead us to draw *factual* conclusions. 'You ought never to use the word "reasons" for the facts we feel justify us in drawing an ethical conclusion; or say that a man who calls anything good or right is making a "reasoned" statement—say, rather, that he is "exclaiming".'

The feeling of pessimism passes off, when we realise what it is that the philosopher is really asserting: that to ask for 'good reasons for ethical judgements' is like asking for 'the colour of heat', and not like asking for the moon. When, in addition, we realise that he wants us to *change* the use of our words 'reason' and 'validity', our natural conservatism will assert itself, and we shall lose the temptation to take his theory too seriously—that is, at its face value. For if, as he recommends, we stop calling the facts which support our ethical conclusions 'reasons', we shall have to find another name for them; and if we are to stop talking of the 'validity' of evaluative inferences, we shall have to invent another word for that too. The sensible thing to do is to bear in mind the facts to which he has drawn our attention, as an insurance against falling into philosophical errors, and afterwards to go on talking of 'reasons' and 'validity' in the way in which we always have done.

Our conservatism is justifiable. It is well over two thousand years since philosophers made the first recorded linguistic demands of this kind. About 430 B.C., Anaxagoras of Klazomene, under the impression that the everyday use of the concepts 'coming into being' and 'passing away' carried with it more in the way of metaphysical implications than it did, complained:

> The Hellenes follow a wrong usage in speaking of 'coming into being' and 'passing away'; for nothing comes into being or passes away, but there is mingling or separation of things that are. So they would be right to call 'coming into being' 'mixture' and 'passing away' 'separation'.[1]

As far as I know, nobody took any notice. Even the philosophers soon found something else to dispute about, so that the dangers of metaphysical confusion which Anaxagoras feared abated. Everyone went on using 'coming into being' and 'passing away' as before, and no harm (again as far as I know) resulted. Need we pay any more attention to the metaphysical scruples of our contemporaries than the Hellenes did to those of Anaxagoras?

4.7   Conclusion

Sometimes, when we make ethical judgements, we are not just ejaculating. When we say that so-and-so is good, or that I ought to do such-and-such, we do so sometimes for good reasons and sometimes for bad ones. The imperative approach does not help us in the slightest to distinguish the one from the other—in fact, by saying that to talk of reasons in this context is nonsense, it dismisses our question altogether. However, the doctrine is not only false but innocuous, for it draws its own fangs. If, as we must, we still refuse to treat ethical judgements as ejaculations, its advocate can produce no further reasons for his view. By his own account, all he can do is to evince his disapproval of our procedure, and urge us to give it up: it would be inconsistent of him to advance 'reasons' at this stage. And if, instead, he retorts, 'Very well; but nothing else will get you anywhere', that is a challenge worth accepting, a prediction worth falsifying.

---

[1] Anaxagoras, fr. 17, quoted by Burnet, *Early Greek Philosophy* (3rd ed. 1920), pp. 260–1.

5

INTERLUDE: A CHANGE OF METHOD

5.1 *Vale...*

This has been an unpromising beginning. We started by asking the question, 'How are we to tell good ethical arguments from bad ones?', and turned for an answer, first, to the moral philosophers—since they, of all people, should have been able to answer it. But their theories gave no help. Some bade us talk of 'goodness' as an 'objective property', and spent their time in arguments about this 'property' (invented by themselves), so that they never even reached our question. Others tried to explain ethics away, by giving a psychological account of valuation, or by describing it as 'mere ejaculation', denying that we had any right to ask our question at all.

This was bad enough. But not only were their theories unhelpful; on closer inspection they turned out to be false. Each of the three lines of approach starts with the false assumption that something which is sometimes true of our ethical judgements is essential to them:

(i) the advocates of the objective doctrine talk as though two normal, factually-informed people could not help agreeing about values (in the way in which they agree about properties);[1]

(ii) the advocates of the subjective doctrine talk as though people could not help having different standards of value (in the way in which they have independent tests of, say, pleasantness);[2]

(iii) the advocates of the imperative doctrine talk as though the purely hortatory nature of some ethical arguments were something which applied to all ethical arguments, and could no more be helped than the hortatory nature of exhortations.[3]

Each approach, if taken literally, misrepresents our ethical concepts in a way which cannot be ignored. And in each case, being in a false position to start with, the theorist spends the

---

[1] § 2.5 above.   [2] § 3.3 above.   [3] § 4.4 above.

greater part of his time trying to redeem his initial failure by *ad hoc* modifications—one explaining that he is concerned with 'non-natural' properties; another insisting that he is discussing 'attitudes', not just feelings; a third talking of the 'interplay' of our feelings. But this is like trying to overcome a mistake in natural history by saying, 'Of course a ram is no *ordinary* bull', instead of admitting that it is not a bull at all and starting afresh. All they can do is to elaborate their terminology, in the double hope of hiding their initial mistakes, and of getting their theories to fit our ideas of goodness and rightness in spite of these mistakes. And, in so doing, they make their arguments vague beyond redemption.

The spinning of such theories is a singular kind of activity. One apologist for philosophical ethics, feeling uncomfortable at the complexities of his argument, has suggested that ethical theories are related to right action in the way that the mathematical theory of the flight of the golf-ball is related to the game of golf; that its interest is thus almost wholly theoretical; and that 'to try to understand in outline what one solves *ambulando* in detail is quite good fun for those people who like that sort of thing'.[1]

From our examination, however, it looks as if he were pitching his claim too high—as if the ethical theorist were discussing neither a scientific question nor a logical problem, but were playing a private game. And it is important to realise this: to see that, logically, an 'ethical theory' is less like physics or mathematics than it is like talking entirely in rhetorical questions, or walking on one's hands, or making up acrostics, or playing at 'lines and squares'—or, at the best (to adapt the simile offered), like 'proving' that the trajectory of a golf-ball is 'circular' by constructing it entirely out of circles.

This, of course, is far from what the theorists announce themselves as doing. They like us to think that by adopting their method we shall find the answers to those questions about ethics which we most want to answer; and sometimes we are taken in—for a time. But we never get anywhere to speak of. We always end up as we have now—back where we started.

---

[1] C. D. Broad, *Five Types of Ethical Theory*, p. 285.

5.2 ...*et Salve*

For all that, the first round has not been quite in vain. We may be back at our original question, but this discussion of the traditional method of attacking it has reminded us incidentally of several important facts about ethics:

(i) Unless there can be a 'good reason' for an ethical judgement (as the objective approach reminds us), there is nothing to account for its incompatibility with opposed ethical judgements.[1]

(ii) Our feelings, especially feelings of approval and obligation, are (as the subjective approach emphasises) closely bound up with our moral judgements.[2]

(iii) The rhetorical force of ethical judgements is one of their most important features (as the imperative approach shows).[3]

Although we must give up the traditional, oblique approach of asking, first, 'What *is* goodness?' and 'What *is* rightness?', and attack our central problem from scratch, we have discovered already three important things to bear in mind: the incompatibility of opposed ethical judgements, their close relation to our feelings, and their rhetorical, imperative force.

But in one respect more than all others this discussion has been of value to us. It has underlined the importance of our central problem, emphasised its magnitude, and shown beyond reasonable doubt that it is upon it directly that we must concentrate our attention.

The *practical* importance of our problem we saw from the start. And herein lay our salvation, for it meant that, in considering the traditional approaches to the problem, we had a safe test by which to tell whether any theory even neared the truth. This test the oblique approaches all failed.

In failing it, however, they showed up the magnitude of our task. We have insisted, and insisted *ad nauseam*, that there is a distinction between good and bad reasoning in ethics; but how little positive have we said about it! When the advocates of the objective doctrine misrepresented the distinction, all we could say was that being upright and virtuous, knowing what goodness is, was not like being able to count, or knowing red from green.

---

[1] § 2.8 above.   [2] § 3.1 above.   [3] § 4.1 above.

When the other philosophers tried to skate over it, all we could do was to reiterate that the distinction existed, that its existence was recognised by common sense, and that, at any rate in some cases, it was not just a matter of what kinds of reasoning the speaker preferred. In refusing to lose our heads and abandon common sense, and in undertaking to answer the central question without the unhelpful assistance of the traditional doctrines, we have accepted no mean challenge.

We shall have to go right back to the beginning, to the first form in which we asked our question: 'What kinds of argument, of reasoning, is it proper for us to accept in support of moral decisions?' We shall have to examine the question itself—abandoning most of our intellectual machinery and presuppositions, and attempting to discover, from our knowledge of the practical situations in which this and similar questions become important, what kind of answer it calls for. And, finally, we shall have to see if we can work out an alternative way of answering it, more fruitful than the traditional method.

PART II
LOGIC AND LIFE

6

REASONING AND ITS USES

LET me quote, in place of an introduction, what Tolstoy says in *War and Peace* about Platón Karatáev, the old peasant: in this single paragraph is contained the germ of all that we shall discover.

Sometimes Pierre, struck by the meaning of his words, would ask him to repeat them, but Platón could never recall what he had said a moment before, just as he never could repeat to Pierre the words of his favourite song: 'native' and 'birch-tree' and 'my heart is sick' occurred in it, but when spoken and not sung no meaning could be got out of it. He did not, and could not understand the meaning of words apart from their context. Every word and action of his was a manifestation of an activity unknown to him, which was his life....His words and actions flowed from him as evenly, inevitably, and spontaneously, as fragrance exhales from a flower. He could not understand the value or significance of any word or deed taken separately.[1]

6.1 *Widening the Problem: What is 'Reasoning'?*

'What kinds of argument, what kinds of reasoning is it proper for us to accept in support of moral decisions?' In all our attempts to answer this question up to the present, we have begun by asking, 'What is goodness?' or 'What is rightness?' This approach, for reasons which we have examined, has got us nowhere. Let us now try approaching the question from the other end—asking instead, 'What is "reasoning"?' If we can come to understand reasoning in general, we may be better prepared to solve the special problems of ethical reasoning.

What is 'reasoning'? Let us take a look at a number of typical cases of reasoning. The circumstances in which we talk of 'reasoning', and of 'reasons' being offered in support of conclusions, are so many and so diverse that it is hard to see what is common to them, and the choice is embarrassing. I shall therefore begin by giving four examples chosen from very different

---

[1] Tolstoy, *War and Peace*, bk. XII, ch. 13; tr. Maude, World's Classics Edition.

types of reasoning, but each characteristic of its kind. I shall present them in the form of dialogues:

(i) *An arithmetical example*

A. 'You should have at least four shillings left.'

B. 'Should I? I thought I'd spent more than that.'

A. 'No. You began with fifteen shillings. Then we took a bus-ride, which cost us a shilling; then we had tea—that was three shillings; you bought a five-shilling book, and finally spent one-and-ninepence at the grocer's. One, and three, and five, and one-and-a-bit makes ten-and-a-bit: eleven from fifteen leaves four....'

B. 'Oh yes, so I should. Well, I seem to have dropped half-a-crown somewhere.'

(ii) *An example from science*

A. 'Why, of course the fuse would blow if you tried to use that bulb.'

B. 'I don't see why. After all, it was a 5-amp. fuse.'

A. 'Yes; but the bulb was only a 50-volt one.'

B. 'I know, but it was marked 100 watts; and a 100-watt bulb should only take half-an-amp. off 200-volt mains.'

A. 'Ah, but the marking only applies if you're using it with 50-volt mains. If you put a 50-volt bulb across the 200-volt mains, the filament immediately overheats and melts, and the surge of current passing through it is quite enough to blow a 5-amp. fuse.'

B. 'Yes, I suppose it would be. But let's get on and find a torch; then we'll be able to see where we are.'

(iii) *An example from ethics*

A. 'Jones is fundamentally a good man.'

B. 'Why do you say that?'

A. 'His harsh manner is only a pose. Underneath, he has the kindest of hearts.'

B. 'That would be interesting, if true. But does he ever manifest this kind heart of his in actions?'

A. 'He does. His old servant told me that Jones never uttered an unkind word to her, and recently provided her with a luxurious pension. And there are many such instances. I was actually present when (etc.)....'

B. 'Well, I confess I do not know him intimately. Perhaps he is a good man.'[1]

(iv) *An everyday example*

A. 'Come and have a drink!'

B. 'We can't go yet. What's the hurry, anyway?'

A. 'Don't you know? It's my birthday.'

B. 'Many happy returns, old man; but what difference does that make?'

A. 'The boss said I could pack up early and go and celebrate. I'm sure he wouldn't grudge me your company.'

B. 'Fine. In that case, give me a moment to put my things away and I'll be with you.'

The most obvious thing that these examples have in common is the form of their dialectic. In each case, one of the speakers, *A*, starts off by saying one thing (a_0). In each, the other speaker, *B*, wavers, is sceptical or positively disagrees (saying b_0). *A* goes on to make a different remark (a_1). *B* is, perhaps, still unconvinced, and does not yet agree (b_1). The conversation continues, *A* presenting a series of fresh considerations ($a_2, a_3, \ldots a_n$) and *B* still wavering or disagreeing ($b_2, b_3, \ldots b_{n-1}$); until, at the end, *B* agrees (b_n) not only to *A*'s last remark (a_n) but also to his first one (a_0) and, in many cases, to all the intermediate ones ($a_1, a_2, a_3, \ldots$) as well.

Even if the two speakers were using a language so strange that we could do little more than recognise whether two remarks were the same or different, we might very well surmise, if their conversation had this dialectical form, that *A* was 'giving reasons' to *B*, and that the utterances a_1 to a_n were the 'reasons' for his original utterance a_0.

If this is what all the cases of 'reasoning' have in common, can we perhaps *define* 'reasoning' as argument having this dialectical form, and 'reasons' as those utterances occupying the places a_1 to a_n in a 'reasoned argument' (so defined)?

[1] Cf. Stevenson, *Ethics and Language*, p. 29.

6.2 *'Gerundive' Concepts*

The answer is that we cannot: the dialectical pattern is too wide. Although the most typical dialogues in which 'reasons' are offered for a conclusion do fit it, so do dialogues of other kinds, ones which are emphatically not instances of 'reasoning'.

If we are to conclude that $a_1, \ldots a_n$ are 'reasons' for a_0, it is not enough that B should end up by saying what A wants him to. He might very well do the same in response to threats, or taunts, or jeers:

> *A.* 'You call me that again!'
> *B.* 'Shan't.'
> *A.* 'Go on! I don't believe you dare.'
> *B.* 'Shan't.'
> *A.* 'Oh, won't you? Cowardy-cowardy-custard!...'
> *B.* 'All right; I shall then—You're a beastly bully!'

Again, for $a_1, \ldots a_n$ to be 'reasons' for a_0, it is not enough that B ends up by agreeing sincerely and genuinely to what A wants. There are all sorts of situations in which a conversation of the right form may lead to this result, and $a_1, \ldots a_n$ may still not be things we should call 'reasons':

> *A.* 'Come and have a drink!'
> *B.* 'I can't: it's not time to go yet.'
> *A.* 'Oh, come along! Don't bother about that.'
> *B.* 'O.K. I don't mind if I do.'

If it comes to that, it is not enough that B should end up by saying, accepting and *believing* what A wants him to. His judgement over the question at issue may be faulty. He may be misled into accepting a mathematical conclusion by taking a special case as proving a general theorem. Or, if a_0 is a scientific hypothesis, he may be too readily impressed by experimental evidence which is in fact inadequate or irrelevant. If the argument is an ethical one, he may take 'everybody does it' as a reason for adopting a pernicious habit. And there is a multitude of specious excuses for having a drink, by which he may be led astray at any time of day or night.

As long as we confine our attention to what A says, or B agrees, or C believes, we shall fail to find the answer we want. And this shows the weakness of our approach: it is not the form of the dialectical pattern, whether alone or in conjunction with the attitude of the speaker and hearer, that makes the utterances $a_1, \dots a_n$ 'reasons'.

When we talk about the 'truth' of a proposition, or the 'validity' of an argument, we are interested in something which applies to the proposition or argument regardless of who believes it. To conclude that a proposition is true, it is not enough to know that this man or that finds it 'credible': the proposition itself must be *worthy of* credence. Likewise, in order to decide that an argument is valid, we cannot rely on the fact that such-a-one regards it as 'plausible': the argument itself must be *worthy of* acceptance, as making its conclusion *worthy of* belief. And the same kind of considerations apply to all logical concepts—'correct', 'sound', 'relevant' and so on.

Questions of logic, that is to say, are concerned, not with 'subjective relations'—with what is 'credible' (to-A), 'plausible' (to-B), etc.—but with concepts of a *different* kind.

In this, they resemble questions of ethics (and, for that matter, of aesthetics). I have analysed at length the 'subjective' approach to ethics, which attempts to account for ethical concepts in terms of the attitudes of the speaker and hearer alone, and shown that it is fallacious. If we are to conclude that some past deed was 'good' or that some proposed course of action is 'right', it is not enough for us to know that we ourselves are psychologically disposed to approve of the deed, or that the proposed course seems right to the agent: we must have reasons for thinking that the act was *worthy of* approval, or that the course of action is *worthy of* selection. (And, in the same way, for a picture to be 'beautiful', it is not enough for it to attract *me*: it must be *worthy of* admiration.)

Questions of ethics and aesthetics, as well as of logic, are evidently concerned, not with 'subjective relations'—with what is 'attractive' (to-A), or with what 'seems right' (to-B)—but with concepts of a *different* kind.

These concepts—logical, ethical and aesthetic alike—we can class together as 'gerundives', thereby opposing them to such logical categories as 'properties' and 'subjective relations'. The name 'gerundives' is appropriate because they can all be analysed as 'worthy of something-or-other'; in this resembling the grammatical class of 'gerundives', which appears in one's Latin primer—consisting of such words as *amandus*, which means 'worthy of love' (or 'meet-to-be-loved'), and *laudandus*, which means 'worthy of praise'.

In the light of this distinction (between 'subjective relations' and 'gerundives', between the 'credible' and the 'true') we can make more explicit the problem before us—the problem we expressed vaguely at the beginning of this chapter in the question, 'What is "reasoning"?' What we have to discover is why some of the arguments which fit our dialectical pattern deserve the title of 'reasoning' and some do not. We must therefore ask: 'Of what kind do the utterances a_1 to a_n have to be in order to make the conclusion, a_0, worthy of acceptance, in a way in which others do not?'

Put in this way, the present problem clearly resembles our central problem. It differs from it, in fact, only in being more general—in applying to arguments of any kind, and not simply to those from factual reasons to ethical conclusions.

6.3 *Philosophical Theories of Truth*

One might have supposed, from a quick look at this question, that the answer depended entirely upon the kind of conclusion to be justified, and upon the circumstances of the case. One might have supposed, that is, that the kinds of thing which make a scientific conclusion worthy of belief were so different from those which make (say) a mathematical, ethical, psycho-analytic or aesthetic conclusion true, that nothing valuable could be said which would hold for them all. And one might have doubted, in consequence, whether there was any hope of finding an explicit answer to the question, since any verbal formula comprehensive enough to cover all modes of reasoning must be so vague as to be useless.

Once again, however, the philosophers claim to know better. For most of them, our fears and doubts are unreal; and they are ready to produce, in answer to our question, a comprehensive verbal formula of the kind which seems to be required. To tell the truth, they produce between them a large number of such formulae, many of them at first sight appearing to be incompatible with one another. In considering the question we are, in fact, in the position of having too many answers to choose between rather than too few.

Some of the philosophers declare that, to make the conclusion worthy of belief, the arguments must show 'that it corresponds to a fact'.[1] Others declare, instead, that they must show 'that it coheres with our other beliefs'. A third school—'that it is of benefit to those who use it'. A fourth—'that the members of the proletariat believe it'. And these are only a few of the answers given.

These 'philosophical theories of truth' are comparable with the 'philosophical theories of ethics' discussed in our earlier chapters. They may be divided into two classes, according as they regard the 'truth' of the conclusion as a property of the conclusion itself—these we may naturally call 'objective' doctrines—or as concerned with the attitude, interest or welfare of the speaker, or some limited group of people to which he belongs —that is, 'subjective' doctrines.[2] (In some ways, the thing which surprises me most is that I have never come across an 'imperative doctrine of truth'; especially considering that it would be easy and entertaining to develop one—and quite a plausible one, too. Could one not argue, with considerable force, that to say that a conclusion is 'true' is not to attribute a 'property' to the conclusion, or to express one's 'attitude' towards it, but is just to evince one's belief in it, and to bring pressure to bear on one's hearers in the hope that they will assent to it and believe it as well?)

The question we must ask ourselves, at this point, is whether such philosophical theories of truth—and, for that matter, the corresponding theories of aesthetics, the 'objective', 'subjective' and 'imperative doctrines of beauty'—can hope to succeed in distilling the essences of 'truth' and 'beauty' into comprehensive verbal formulae.

If we hark back to our earlier discussion of the theories of 'goodness', and recall the reasons why the philosophical theories of ethics failed to do, for 'goodness', what these theories want

---

[1] See John Wisdom, *Problems of Mind and Matter*, ch. XI.

[2] The distracting effect of spatial metaphors can be shown as well in the 'theory of truth' as in philosophical ethics (cf. §§ 3.8 and 4.5) and metaphysics (cf. § 8.9). Recall the old tag, *Judicium est 'locus' veritatis.*

to do for 'truth' and 'beauty'; and if we remember also how it was that we came to class 'beautiful', 'true' and 'good' in one category as 'gerundives'; then our answer to this question must be 'No!' The arguments which led us to reject all three types of 'ethical theory' could be applied equally well to the 'theories' of truth and beauty. And they would demonstrate, as rigorously as they did for the theories of philosophical ethics, that such philosophical doctrines of truth and beauty cannot succeed.

In consequence, we may conclude:

(i) That the questions, 'What is truth?' and 'What is beauty?', if answered directly, are no more fruitful than the corresponding questions, 'What is goodness?' and 'What is rightness?'

(ii) That all the short answers given to these questions are, if taken literally, false; and that, if taken figuratively, they can at the best only focus attention on some special feature of the concept, all-important, perhaps, over a limited range of instances, but not of universal application.

(iii) That the central practical questions, 'What kinds of thing make a conclusion worthy of belief?' and 'What kinds of thing make a work of art worthy of admiration?', are to be answered, not by verbal pantechnicons with room for every case, but by a discussion of the ways in which, when faced with some particular variety of sentences, or works of art, we should set about making our selection.

It would be tedious to repeat in detail for 'true' and 'beautiful' the arguments we have already given for 'good'. We can be content with illustrating the force of our conclusions as they apply to a typical 'theory of truth'. I shall choose, for this purpose, a theory which is at once the most fashionable, and in some ways the most plausible—the 'correspondence' theory of truth.

6.4 The 'Correspondence' Theory of Truth

According to the 'correspondence' theory of truth, to say that a proposition is 'true' is to say that it 'corresponds to a fact'. (This is to locate the 'truth' of the proposition 'in' the proposition itself, rather than 'in' the speaker or hearer, so the theory may be classed as an 'objective' one.) Supporters of this theory argue that the utterances a_1 to a_n can only make the conclusion, a_0, 'true' if they show that it 'corresponds to a fact'.

Now, to do justice to the theory, and to its advocates, it does seem to give a life-like picture of what we require of certain types of utterance when passing them as 'true' or 'false'. There are some sentences which we can describe, with almost literal vividness, as 'corresponding to', or even as 'giving a picture of', those features of the world which they describe. Sentences of this kind (we may say) have a 'structure': that is, the sentence can be split up into a number of elements; each of these elements 'refers to' something in the world; and the mutual relations of these elements, in the sentence, are like (if the sentence expresses a 'true' proposition) or unlike (if it expresses a 'false' one) the mutual relations, in the world, of the things to which the elements 'refer'.

Consider, for example, the sentence 'The cat is on the mat', which appears in a child's first reader. This sentence can be split up into three elements thus:

'1 (The cat) 2 (is on) 3 (the mat)'

or, more symbolically, thus:

The situation which this sentence describes may be drawn thus:

and this state-of-affairs, fact, or what-you-will can be represented, in its turn, thus:

When one allows for the conventions governing the writing of the English language[1]—that it shall consist of horizontal rows of

---

[1] One can imagine a language in which these conventions were less rigid—in which, for example, spatial relations were expressed pictorially, so that one wrote

'Cat
mat'

instead of   'The cat is on the mat'.

One can even imagine a people among whom photographs or drawings took the symbols, and so on—it will be clear that we can regard the 'structure' of the sentence 'The cat is on the mat' as reflected in the 'structure' of the situation which it describes, but as different from that of any of the situations falsifying the statement.

We can do the same kind of thing with other simple descriptive sentences. Suppose, for example, that I say 'Jones left the house after Smith'. Then, if my statement is true, the temporal order of the words 'Jones' and 'Smith' is directly related to the order in which the two people referred to passed through a certain doorway. And, if it is false, this correspondence between the elements of my sentence and of the situation described is absent. Again, we might display the things which make the sentence true diagrammatically, thus:

Sentence: (Jones) (left) (the house) (after) (Smith)

Elements: 1   2   3   4   5

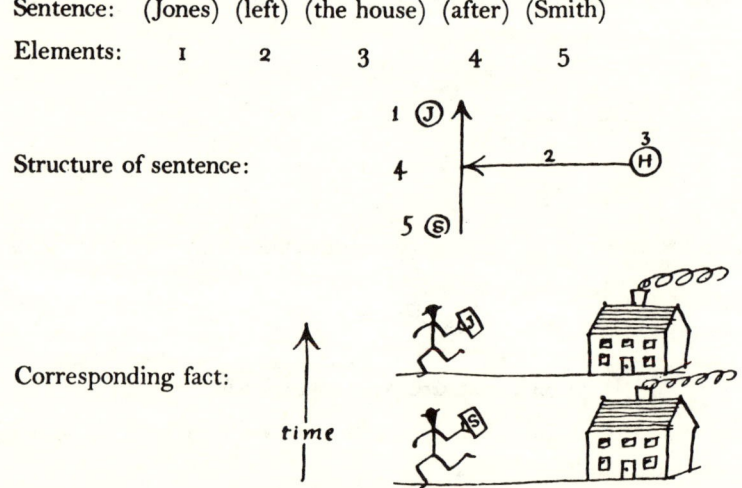

Structure of sentence:

Corresponding fact:

And again the 'truth' or 'falsity' of the sentence depends on there being a 'correspondence' between two 'structures'—the 'structure' of the elements of the sentence and the 'structure' of the things in the world to which the elements 'refer'.

(Incidentally, this second example underlines an important point which is obscured in the case of the first. In looking for the 'correspondence' between the two 'structures' in any particular

place of descriptive sentences—so that the drawing I have included in the text was used as a 'hieroglyph' or 'pictogram', taking the place of the sentence. But on this point, see §6.5 *ad fin.*

case, we require a rule of interpretation specifying the exact nature of the 'correspondence'. We have, for example, to learn that, when the spoken sentence 'Jones left the house before Smith' is true, the events referred to have the same temporal order as the words 'Jones' and 'Smith', whereas in the case of 'Jones left the house after Smith' the temporal order of the events is reversed.)

The 'correspondence' theory of truth does, therefore, give a vivid and illuminating account of one feature of the truth of a certain range of sentences, a range which could be made much wider than I have done by examining in more detail the ways in which words are made to 'refer to' things. In this, the theory resembles the philosophical theories of ethics: but, in order to bring out the full force of the analogy between 'truth' and 'goodness', I must also show that it resembles them in another respect —that, if the 'correspondence' theory is assumed to be of universal application, its consequences are paradoxical and even nonsensical.

6.5 *Correspondence and 'Description'*

It is natural enough, if one is looking for a single, exhaustive answer to the question, 'What is truth?', to choose as that answer 'correspondence with fact'. The vividness of this phrase, in the cases to which it most exactly applies, commends it above other possible answers; and it is not surprising to find that those who have set out to 'exhaust the universe of logic' (for example, Wittgenstein, in his *Tractatus Logico-Philosophicus*) have taken it as their starting-point.

The failure of such attempts is, however, guaranteed before they begin. It is implicitly assumed in any statement of the 'correspondence' theory of truth that all our significant utterances are intended as *descriptions*. I could not have explained the theory without giving a 'descriptive sentence' as an example, and without talking about the features of the world to which it 'corresponds' as those which it 'describes'. Indeed, the fact of the matter is that, if one starts off from the 'correspondence' theory of truth, the only logical category one can 'exhaust' is that of 'descriptive sentences': all other types of utterance slip through the net.

When Wittgenstein wrote, in the *Tractatus*: 'The specification of all true elementary propositions describes the world completely. The world is completely described by the specification of all elementary propositions plus the specification, which of them are true and which false'[1] (where an 'elementary proposition' is one which 'describes' and 'asserts the existence of' an 'atomic fact'), his explicit use of 'describes' and 'described' should have made this limitation doubly clear. And yet, at the same time, he seems to have supposed that his remarks were relevant to logic as a whole, for he went on to remark that many of our utterances cannot be regarded as expressions, either of elementary propositions, or of combinations of them, and concluded that such utterances are not logically respectable. 'There are', for instance, according to the *Tractatus*, 'no ethical propositions.'[2]

All that one can prove about ethical utterances by these means, however, is that they are not descriptive: and this is not news. The first step in applying the 'correspondence' test for truth is to split the sentence concerned into elements, each of which 'refers to' something in the world:[3] until one has done this, all talk about 'comparing structures' or 'looking for a correspondence' is useless. But, when we are interested in ethical sentences, the instruction to 'split' the sentence into 'elements' of this kind can mean nothing to us; for ethical concepts, as we saw when we discussed the objective and subjective doctrines of 'goodness',[4] cannot be said to 'refer to' anything at all, either in the speaker or in the world about him. In consequence, the 'correspondence' theory, so vivid and life-like as applied to one range of utterances, becomes nonsensical and obstructive when applied to another, equally 'respectable', but inappropriate range. And if the criterion of truth that it emphasises does not make sense when applied to at least one range of utterances, what can be the use of exalting it into a universally applicable theory of truth?

---

[1] Wittgenstein, *Tractatus Logico-Philosophicus*, 4.26, p. 91.
[2] Op. cit. 6.42, p. 183. I do not want to suggest that Wittgenstein still holds the views quoted here: I am quite certain that he would be prepared to criticise them at least as severely as I have. Still these quotations have a great *historical* importance.
[3] As we did in § 6.4 with the sentence: (The cat) (is on) (the mat).
[4] See § 3.8 above.

Is there any way of explaining why the 'correspondence' criterion of truth should apply only to descriptions? I believe there is. For consider what we do when we make up a description. Suppose, for example, that 'Slimy Joe' has been given ten years' hard for forgery, and that he arrives at the jail. One of the first things now to be done is that 'full particulars' will be taken of him: that is to say, he will be stood in the light and a warder will make a note of the colour of his hair—'fair'—and his complexion —'ruddy'—his height, chest circumference and other dimensions will be measured—'6 ft. ½ in., 35 in. expanding to 39 in.', etc.— and any special features will be noted down—'scar over left eye'.

If, now, 'Slimy Joe' ever comes to escape, or goes back to his old occupation after his release, a 'Wanted' notice will be prepared for distribution to all police stations. The purpose of this notice will be to bring about his *recognition*, and so his apprehension. It will, therefore, give a full 'description' of him, based on the prison records—'6 ft. ½ in. in height, fair hair, ruddy complexion, with a scar over the left eye', etc. In so far as this is a good description, it will help its readers to recognise him: if, however, by some mistake, someone else's particulars get sent out instead—'About 5 ft. 4 in. in height, sandy hair, pasty complexion'—recipients can justifiably complain that no one could be expected to recognise 'Slimy Joe' from *that* description. In so far as the circulated notice helps people to recognise the wanted man, it is a good description: in so far as it fails to assist this recognition, it fails *as a description*.

This gives us our clue. In composing a description, we have to produce an utterance *corresponding recognisably to* whatever it describes: in verifying a description, we have to confirm that it does *correspond to* the thing described. The reason why the 'correspondence' criterion of truth applies so aptly to descriptive sentences is, therefore, because with its help we can discover whether they have *served their purpose*—and, if the rules that it gives for verifying descriptive sentences look like the rules for giving a description 'in reverse', is that at all surprising?[1]

---

[1] Some will complain that I am here being too kind to the 'correspondence' theory: that I am appearing to concede its main claims. Nothing that I say about its *figurative* value as applied to a limited range of sentences should, however, be taken as affecting in any way my earlier remarks about its *literal* falsity: 'structure', 'reference', 'correspondence', these terms are all used here figuratively.

The example of the 'correspondence' theory of truth confirms our suspicion that the answer to the question, 'What makes utterances "reasons" for a conclusion?', depends, and must depend, upon the circumstances, and upon the type of conclusion involved. No single answer, no verbal formula comprehensive and general enough to cover all cases, can be hoped for.

Still, although we do not share the philosophers' hope for a universal answer to the question, 'What is "reasoning"?', we have no cause to be discouraged by this example in our search for particular answers, applicable to limited ranges of utterances. Indeed, the example is heartening, since it shows how natural and intelligible the logical criteria appropriate to a particular kind of conclusion can appear, when one bears in mind the circumstances in which utterances of that kind find their primary use.

Let us return, in conclusion, to the example with which this discussion of the 'correspondence theory' began: there are two things we must now notice. First, though some descriptive sentences *are* in some ways like pictures, this resemblance is not essential. Indeed, there is no reason in the world why a pictogram of a cat on a mat should necessarily serve as a 'description' or as a 'report' of a state of affairs at all. A picture, when used for linguistic purposes, is just as much a conventional symbol as a sentence written in a more normal fashion. Suppose, for instance, that a man comes up to me and hands me a photograph of a cat on a mat, saying, 'This is to be treated as a sentence'. Must I necessarily know what to do with it? How am I to tell whether he is trying to give me a report, say, rather than asking if the cat is on the mat, exclaiming at the beauty of cats, or issuing the injunction, 'No cats are to be allowed on mats'? After all, the metal discs bearing the head-on silhouette of a car, erected at the ends of some streets on the Continent, mean 'Cars are not allowed down this street', not 'There is a car coming down this street'—and even when one knows that they are intended as an injunction of some kind, one has to learn that it is this one, and not, 'Cars *are* to go down this street'.

Secondly, notice why it is that all those words like 'structure' and 'correspondence' which we have been using in this discussion are *figurative*. The reason is, that there are not two independent methods of identifying the two 'structures'—in the sentence, and in the world—*before* comparing them. Nevertheless, knowing as we do on what occasions we can properly and correctly say 'The cat is on the mat', we can *afterwards* point to the cat and the mat and the words 'cat' and 'mat', or the equivalent pictograms, and give a limited sense to the notions of 'structure' and 'correspondence'.

6.6 *Playing with Words*

In the case of descriptive sentences, the problem why one particular criterion of truth is appropriate was solved when we examined the purposes for which descriptions are used. The same intimate connection, between the logic of a mode of reasoning and the activities in which the reasoning plays its primary part, can be strikingly illustrated with the help of an especially simple (though artificial) example—that of an activity in which the reasoning operates as near as may be *functionlessly*.

In my childhood, we used to play a game with the following rule: starting from the letter A, and working through the alphabet, one had to make up sentences of the form:

> I love my love with an A, because she is artful;
> I hate her with an A, because she is arch;
> I take her to the 'Anchor'
> And feed her on artichokes;
> She comes from Aberdeen,
> And her name is Agnes Anstruther.

The primitive mode of reasoning involved in this game is the example required.

According to the rule of the game, only some of the possible reasons one might give for 'loving-with-an-A', or 'hating-with-an-A' are to be accepted. That your love is 'bashful' or 'comic' is a bad reason to give, either for 'loving-her-with-an-A' or for 'hating-her-with-an-A'; that she is 'awkward' or 'ambidextrous' is a good reason for either. Good reasons and bad reasons, correct and incorrect inferences, sound and unsound arguments, all are decided in this case by the rule of the game.

The exact nature of the rules we employ is comparatively arbitrary. The game would be none the worse, if one changed

them so that different 'reasons' were 'good' and 'bad' respectively, and so that the form of sentence required became:

> I love my love with an A because she is bashful;
> I hate her with an A because she is comic;
> I take her to the 'Dog and Duck'
> And feed her on earwigs;
> She comes from Fotheringay,
> And her name is Gertrude Gibson.

Despite the fact that the logical properties of the concepts 'loving-
with-an-A' and 'hating-with-an-A', and the reasons relevant
to each, are now distinct, the game could go on just as well as
before.

The two most striking things about this example—the arbitrariness of the logical criteria, and the fact that it is only a game
—are clearly connected. It is just because, being a game, this use
of speech is comparatively *pointless*, that the logical criteria can
be what you please. Rules there must be, rules for telling acceptable rigmaroles from unacceptable ones and good reasons
from bad, if there is to be a game at all; but it makes no difference
in the long run what these rules are, and the choice is therefore
arbitrary.

You may, of course, object that in such a game one is just
playing with words; and that, in consequence, one can hardly call
it a *use* of reasoning, or a *use* of speech, at all. And it must be
confessed that it is at the best only a borderline instance of
'reasoning'. But this only reinforces my point in citing it. All
our more typical modes of reasoning are far from pointless, and
the rules for distinguishing 'good' reasoning from 'bad' are
correspondingly far from arbitrary.

6.7   *The Versatility of Reason*

In the case of word-games, as of descriptions, the nature of the
logical criteria we are to apply is best understood from a study of
the activity—and especially the point of the activity—of which
the type of speech forms a part. But the example of a word-game
has an additional value: that of showing what extremes of variety
our uses of speech (and 'reasoning') include and, by implication,
what a travesty of our practice it is to argue as though all our
utterances were intended as descriptions.

If it is not completely nonsensical to talk of 'good and bad reasons' and of 'valid and invalid inferences', even over a mere word-game, how much less can it be so over the arguments we use in more important fields—in mathematics, in science, in ethics, in aesthetics, in expressing our reactions to things, in explaining our motives, in giving commands, and in our thousand-and-one other ways of using speech! And since, when we employ many of these modes of reasoning, it would be far-fetched to say that we were 'describing' anything, it is not to be expected that the logical criteria appropriate to these modes will be those relevant to descriptions. Rather, we must expect that every mode of reasoning, every type of sentence, and (if one is particular) every single sentence will have its own logical criteria, to be discovered by examining its individual, peculiar uses.

Hence arise the dangers of dogmatic attempts to define 'reasoning' uniquely. Some philosophers (like Hume) limit the scope of 'reasoning' to mathematics and science. Some stigmatise as 'pseudo-concepts' all concepts which do not 'refer to' specific objects or physical processes. Some are obsessed with particular, limited facets of 'truth'. And some dismiss all utterances other than those expressing factual propositions, on the ground that one cannot establish them in the way in which one establishes a factual hypothesis (as if one would want to!).

They would do none of these things if they recognised the full variety of purposes for which speech is used. Speech is no single-purpose tool. It is, in fact, more like a Boy Scout's knife (an implement with two kinds of blade, a screw-driver, a corkscrew, a tin-and-bottle opener, a file, an awl, and even a thing for taking stones out of horses' hooves); and, further, it is one which we continually shape and modify, adding new devices (modes of reasoning, and types of concept) to perform new functions, and grinding old ones afresh, in the light of experience, so that they shall serve their old, familiar, well-tried purposes better.[1]

6.8   *A New Approach to Our Problem*

We have examined two simple types of utterance—'descriptive sentences', for which the 'correspondence' theory specifies

---

[1] Wittgenstein makes use of the image of a tool-box in this context, likening different types of concept to different types of tool.

the criteria of truth and falsity, and the rigmaroles used in 'word-games', for which the logical criteria are what you choose to make them. The way in which each utterance is used, we discovered, was to be understood fully only as part of a larger activity: as soon as this frame was borne in mind, the logical properties of the mode of reasoning were seen to be related directly to the function it performs, and this again to the purpose of the activity of which it is a part. The logic of the utterances, on one side, and the point of the activity with which they are bound up, on the other, are as intimate and inseparable as the two faces of a coin.

Whether the same kind of relation holds for more complex modes of reasoning, and more complex types of sentence, remains to be seen. Our success so far at any rate encourages us to hope that, although the search for a general, universal answer to the question, 'What is "reasoning"?', was a mistaken one, we may still find answers applicable to individual modes of reasoning; and in particular that, by looking in the right way at the circumstances and activities in which our ethical utterances play their part, we may come to see how the logical criteria applicable to them are generated. Our central question, therefore, now takes the form:

Can we discover, from our knowledge of the kinds of human situation and activity in which ethical sentences find their primary use, the kinds of thing that are relevant as arguments for one course of action or another?

Can we, in other words, give an account of our ethical mode of reasoning which will bring out its characteristic function—that is, its contribution to the activities in which it is used?

Before we attempt to give such an account, let us try out our method on a mode of reasoning which is at once as complex as the ethical mode and less contentious. There is more agreement (because there is less general concern) over the purpose of science, and over the logic of scientific explanations, than there is over ethics and ethical standards; and yet the arguments which are presented in science are at least as complicated as any which are relevant to a moral decision. In both, there is the same duality, of individual judgements and general principles. In both, one encounters a contrast between the 'appearance' and the 'reality' —the scientist distinguishing between the 'apparent' colour of the sun at evening and its 'real' colour (quite apart from atmospheric refraction and so on); the moralist distinguishing those things which are 'really' good, and those actions which are 'really' right, from those things which we simply like and those actions which we simply feel like doing. Let us spend a little time, therefore, investigating the relation between the reasoning involved in a typical scientific argument, and the features of the situation to which it applies; and see what bearing this has on the special function of scientific argument, and of science itself. After we have done this, we can return and consider,

(i) whether ethics is a science—that is, whether the results of this investigation are immediately applicable to ethics;

(ii) if not, how the function of ethics differs from that of science; and

(iii) what kinds of argument are, in consequence, relevant to moral decisions.

7

EXPERIENCE AND EXPLANATION

'...How build, unbuild, contrive
To save appearances....'

MILTON, *Paradise Lost*, VIII, 81

7.1 *The Desire for an Explanation*

Suppose that we are going for a walk with some friends, and that I am carrying a walking-stick with me. If I pass the stick round, everyone will agree with me that it is straight; it will both look straight and feel straight to all of us. However, if we come to a stream and I plunge it half-way in, there will not be the same certainty. If we run our hands down the stick, we shall not feel, at the surface of the water, any change in the direction in which the stick is pointing—it will still feel straight to us all. But, if we are standing around, and each gives his own account of how it looks to him, we shall differ in what we say. Some will say, 'It's bent to the left'; others, 'It's bent to the right'; and one or two, 'It's just foreshortened'.

On encountering this phenomenon, you may react in any of a number of different ways. Your reaction may be one of wonder: you may simply gaze at the stick, ask me to pull it out and put it in again several times, so that you can take in what happens, and say, 'Isn't that marvellous?' Your reaction may be one of admiration: you may be struck by the way in which the contours of the bank enhance the bending of the stick, ask me to keep it there, and say, 'Isn't that a picture?' You may feel indifferent, wonder why anyone should be interested in the phenomenon, and turn away, saying, 'Well, what of it?' Or you may be surprised, not having expected this to happen, and say, 'Isn't that strange?' What you go on to do and say, what questions you ask, what consequences you draw, what investigations you undertake; all depend on the nature of your reaction—wonder, admiration, surprise or whatever it may be. For the moment, let us concentrate on the last of these—surprise.

Suppose that, in your reaction, what dominates is surprise at the unexpectedness of the phenomenon. The thing which disconcerts you about the situation is the way in which the evidence of our senses, originally unequivocal and unanimous, has become ambiguous and conflicting. There are obvious conflicts of three kinds:

(i) between the reports of the same observer about the same property at different times—first he said, 'It's straight'; now he says, 'It's bent';

(ii) between the reports of different observers about the same property at the same time—some say, 'It's bent to the left'; others say, 'It's bent to the right'; others again, 'It's just foreshortened';

(iii) between the evidence of different senses about the same property at the same time—looking at it, you would say it was bent but, to feel it, you would say it was straight.

In consequence of these conflicts, you ask, 'What is *really* the case? Is it really bent, or not? If so, to the left or to the right? And, if not, why does it look as though it were?' And, in asking these questions, you begin to demand an *explanation* of the phenomenon.

7.2 *Explanation and Expectation*

If what impresses you about the phenomenon is its unexpectedness, I can do a number of things to help you, and to satisfy your demand for an 'explanation'. To begin with, I can show you that this is something that always happens in such circumstances; that it is not a peculiarity of this particular stick or this particular stream, but that any straight piece of wood, metal or other solid, plunged into any smooth, level stretch of water, in stream or pond, in tank or wash-basin, looks the same. I can point out that the amount through which it appears to bend in such circumstances depends solely on the angle at which it is inserted and the direction from which one looks at it, and I can give you an equation connecting the angle through which it appears to bend with the angle of insertion and the direction of viewing; given this formula (Snell's Law), you will be able to decide beforehand how it will look when inserted at a new angle, or viewed from a fresh direction. Then I can show you that the same kind of thing happens when the stick is embedded in substances other than water—in petrol, alcohol, glass or ice—but that the amount of bending differs from substance to substance; and I can give you a table of constants, with the help of which you can extend Snell's Law to cover these substances too (thus introducing the concept of 'refractive index'—that property of a substance, constant over a wide range of conditions, upon which the degree of bending depends). Again, I can relate this phenomenon to others with which you are familiar. By talking about the way in which the 'refractive index' varies with the density, and so with the temperature of the substance, I can connect up the bending of the stick and the shimmering of objects seen through the air over a fire. By referring to the way in which, in some materials, the 'refractive index' depends upon the colour of the light passed, I can connect this phenomenon with the colouring which appears round the edges of objects viewed through a cheap magnifying-glass—but there is no need to go on.

All these things will help to make the phenomenon seem less surprising. All of them will help to satisfy your demand for an 'explanation'. All of them do so by giving an explanation of the same kind, an explanation taken from *physics*, the appropriate science.[1] And each explanation is designed to show that, from our experience of optical phenomena, the bending of the stick was 'to be expected'.

If such an 'explanation' does satisfy you, that is no accident. The situation we have been considering is typical of those in which a 'scientific explanation' is called for, and to deal with which science was developed. And it shows us what, if anything, we must take as the special function of scientific explanation: namely, to bring our past experience to bear upon our present and future expectations, in such a way as to 'save appearances'[2] and turn the unexpected, as far as possible, into the expected.

---

[1] I believe the facts which I have quoted to be more or less correct. Nevertheless, it does not matter particularly whether they are or no: all that is necessary is that my 'explanation' should sound plausible, and be correct in form. If it is also correct in substance, that will simply help to avoid irrelevant objections.

[2] Cf. Milton, *Paradise Lost*, bk. VIII; and recall the old Greek phrase, σῴζειν τὰ φαινόμενα, discussed by Burnet, *Early Greek Philosophy*, p. 28.

7.3 The Scientific Limitations of Everyday Concepts

But why do we need a special mode of reasoning in order to do this? To understand the reason why, we must examine the way in which scientific theories and scientific concepts develop out of everyday life, language and experience.

The demand for an explanation arose, in the example given, out of discrepancies between different judgements about the 'straightness' of the walking-stick; that is, about something which, in everyday life, we treat as 'a single property'. It arose, that is, because the criteria of identity—of what is and what is not the 'same' property—which we take for granted in everyday life and crystallise in our everyday speech, turned out to be inadequate in the new situation. Let us analyse the nature of this crisis more closely.

When, in our ordinary life and affairs, we talk about the properties of objects, we are accustomed to using a variety of tests for the presence of any particular property. In sorting out 'straight' objects from 'bent' ones, for example, we treat straightness and bentness in different ways on different occasions:

(i) As 'simple qualities'
    (a) to be told by eye;
    (b) to be told by touch.

(ii) As 'complex qualities'
    (a) to be told by sighting along the object, and taking the path of a light-ray as the standard;
    (b) to be told by measurement, by comparing the length of the object with the distance between its ends, and taking the shortest distance as the standard;
    (c) to be told by putting the object up against a template, and taking the edge of the template as the standard.

And, as a matter of fact, there is a large range of circumstances over which these tests give indistinguishable results.

A surveyor, when using his theodolite, and a carpenter, lifting his work to his eye to check his planing, take it for granted that a ray of light is straight—that is to say, they take the path of a ray as their standard. The same men, when working out a trigonometrical problem or setting out a job, take the shortest distance between two points as their standard instead. Neither of them runs into any trouble as a result of using two logically independent criteria. If I look down a road, and see it stretching out directly before me to the very place I want to reach, I can be confident that by following it I shall be taking the shortest route to my destination. If, from a pile of brushwood, we pick out those branches that look straightest, we shall, as a matter of fact, make the same selection as we should if we picked out those which feel straightest, or compared their lengths with the distances between their ends, or sighted along them.

The success and utility of our concept of 'straightness' depends upon facts such as these. If either we or our environment were sufficiently different, it would be impossible for us to employ our present, everyday distinction between the 'bent' and the 'straight', impossible for us even to learn it. And things might very well have been so.

You could not, of course, teach anyone this distinction if all the instances you gave him were of the 'stick-in-water' variety: you have to start him on unambiguous ones—on sticks in air, broken and unbroken, lines drawn with and without rulers, Roman roads and English lanes, and such-like things. Yet, if the optical properties of the atmosphere were only fuller of discontinuities (like that between air and water) or of fluctuations (like those in the air over a fire) all the available instances would be of the ambiguous kind. And, given no favourable instances, we should have no chance of learning, and so no use for the distinction.

Again, if everyone were colour-blind—that is, if no one were able to learn our present distinction between the 'green' and the 'red'—we should have no use for the two everyday concepts 'green' and 'red': we should have only one. And, if our vision were such that we could no more tell the 'straight' from the 'bent' by eye than a colour-blind man can the 'green' from the 'red'—if we were all, by present standards, 'shape-blind'—then the existing distinction between the 'straight' and the 'bent', which we now regard as obvious and natural, would be useless, recondite and artificial.

The eventual breakdown of our everyday concepts, and the consequent demand for an 'explanation', are, therefore, pretty well inevitable. As long as we use multiple criteria for 'properties', sometimes telling them in one way, sometimes telling them in another (and there is every reason why, for ordinary purposes, we should go on doing so), we are likely, sooner or later, to encounter a situation in which they lead to conflicting judgements. Our ordinary ideas about the 'properties' of the world can only lead us to predict and anticipate the developments going on around us under a limited range of conditions. Something unexpected always happens, and we are liable to be disconcerted when it does. If we want to be able to predict these occurrences, and not to be surprised by them, we have to give up the everyday account. Instead, we must try to find a more reliable one— a 'scientific' one.

7.4 *The Development of Scientific Theories and Concepts.* (I)

As a start, we tighten up our criteria of 'straightness', 'redness', 'rectangularity'—treating all properties as 'complex qualities', and demanding more accurate measurements, more specific descriptions. When this fails, we discard the everyday concepts, and replace them by a new set of concepts, defined by reference to the theory adopted.

These new concepts are of two kinds, those which are refinements of everyday concepts ('scientific qualities', I have called them) and those which have no counterparts in everyday speech —for example, physical and chemical constants like 'refractive index'. In either case, the danger of conflicts of the kind I have described is deliberately made as small as possible: the criteria for any 'property' are, as compared with those for everyday concepts, uniquely defined and highly specific. For the scientist, except in special circumstances which we shall come to later,[1] 'straightness' is completely unambiguous. The look, the feel, the ray of light, the template, all are of secondary importance. For him, a line is only 'straight' if it is the shortest line joining its end-points.

This unique choice of criterion, this particular definition of the scientific quality 'really straight', has a further, incidental advantage, of the greatest historical importance. It allows us to carry over bodily into science all the resources and paraphernalia of Euclidean and Cartesian geometry—the whole method of representing 'position' by three numerical co-ordinates, and

[1] §§ 8.5 and 8.6 below.

other physical properties as mathematical functions of these numerical co-ordinates. By adopting this unique definition of 'straightness', we can (so to speak) 'gear in' the results of mathematical research to the body of physical theory.

In our chosen example, it is the discrepancies between different criteria of 'straightness' and 'bentness' which lead to the demand for an explanation: physics explains away the apparent bentness of the stick as an optical effect. But the fact that it explains it away does not mean that the discordant observation, the look of bentness, is regarded as less important, at this stage, than the concordant ones. When we are searching for relatively constant and consistent factors in the situation, and formulating a new hypothesis to take account of them, it is the apparently conflicting reports which occupy us: we do not ask any more questions about the concordant reports until the discordant ones have been accounted for. If, adopting the classical physicist's definition of 'straightness', we say that the stick in the stream is 'really straight', then its *feel* does not worry us: if it still feels straight, so much the better—so much the less to explain! On the other hand, the look of the stick does puzzle us. It does not satisfy us to say, 'Now and then my eyes mislead me'—we must know when and how and why: so it is to the theory of optics that we turn for an explanation.

The theory of optics starts off from data about artificially simplified situations; for instance, the results of experiments in which extra-narrow rays of light are passed in precisely known directions through accurately ground prisms or lenses of unusually homogeneous glass. On the basis of data of this kind, formulae (such as Snell's Law, to which I have referred) are suggested relating the amounts by which the light-rays are deflected when they strike different prisms and lenses in different directions. Now, since the purpose of these formulae is to provide a more reliable indication of what was and is to be expected than any that can be given in terms of our everyday notions, the first test they must pass is that of accounting for all trustworthy past observations in the relevant field of study. And, when I say 'account for', I mean that they must show that these observations were to be expected: in other words, the theory must relate all the past phenomena to the conditions of the experiments concerned in the way which was actually found. Further, although the physicists who developed the theory of optics may have started by experimenting with prisms and lenses, the results of their work must be applicable also to the familiar kind of phenomenon we have taken as our example.

A theory which accounts in this way for all the observations made so far takes us half-way to our provisional goal. But as our account becomes more accurate, it looks less at the present and past, and more to the future. Our next step is to make trial predictions from the theory, using the methods of deductive logic—and of mathematics, where these are available—as a guide. Our theory will perhaps lead us to predict that, when I put the same stick into my bath, it will look bent again, and that while it stays in the air, it will continue (other things being equal) to look straight. As long as we find the relevant predictions confirmed by experience, we retain the theory. If, however, we are led to predict that the stick will only look bent in running water, and this expectation is falsified, so much the worse for the theory: we modify it, or abandon it in favour of a new one.

7.5 *The Development of Scientific Theories and Concepts.* (II)

Now we are hard to satisfy, and we do not want there to be any unpleasant surprises; so we keep on predicting and checking, first within the original field of experience, later changing the initial conditions one by one so as to pass beyond it. Eventually, we start making predictions in a field covered by another theory. At this stage, one of a number of things may happen.

(I) Our theory may, with no more than trifling changes, lead to the same predictions as the established theory, and the mathematical parts of the two theories may turn out to be formally similar. In this happy circumstance, the two theories can at once be unified and their concepts compared—'Light and radio waves are fundamentally of the same nature', we may explain; 'they are simply two manifestations of the same fundamental mechanism'.

(II) There may be a conflict: our theory may break down in the new field, and so prove inferior to the established theory: or it may do better than the established theory. In either case, we try to change the concepts and calculus of the deficient theory so as to make them fit: we dislike unexplained limitations on our theories as much as any other unexplained phenomena.

(III) We may, however, be unable to do either of these things. Each theory may explain well enough the phenomena in its' original field and their fields of study may be clearly connected, but neither may be able to touch the phenomena in the other's field; and this deadlock may continue for some time. An example is the deadlock between the 'electro-magnetic' (wave) theory of light and the 'photon' (particle) theory during the first quarter of this century. The wave-theory explained the propagation of light, the particle-theory the interaction of light with matter, and both with elegance and success; but neither of them seemed to apply in any way to the subject-matter of the other. In such a case, the solution lies in the development of a comprehensive set of concepts and a mathematical calculus embracing those of the two seemingly irreconcilable theories as special cases. This was done, for the wave-particle conflict, by the development of 'quantum mechanics' in the years beginning 1925.

(IV) Lastly, the two theories may lead to the same predictions, and yet their concepts and mathematical methods be totally dissimilar. An example of this, though for historical reasons not a completely pure one, can be found in the contrast between 'classical' and 'relativistic' physics. At the turn of the century, physicists were faced with certain experimental results—apparent anomalies in the behaviour of light—which would clearly be explained only after severe changes in physical theory. Einstein pointed out two ways of solving the problem. First, in his *Special Theory of Relativity*, he went half-way towards explaining the recalcitrant phenomena, without abandoning the framework of classical physics; and there is no logical reason why his work should not have been completed along these lines. Before this was done, however, he pointed out himself that the results could be more elegantly accounted for otherwise; and, in his *General Theory of Relativity*, he introduced an entirely different kind of mathematical framework, employing 'non-Euclidean' instead of 'Euclidean' geometry, and involving (as we shall see)[1] a different scientific criterion of 'straightness'. In the fields to which it is best applied, this 'relativistic' physics

[1] §§ 8.5 and 8.6 below.

has great advantages. The fresh mathematical methods introduced with it, such as the 'tensor calculus', make it possible for Sir Arthur Eddington to quote an equation, and then remark, 'There are about 280 billion terms on the right, and we proceed to rearrange those which do not vanish'[1]—an undertaking from which one might excusably shrink if one had at one's command only the less wholesale and sophisticated mathematics of classical physical theory. At the same time, over the greater part of physics, these more elementary methods can be made to produce the correct predictions without resort to marathon algebraic feats; and, since they *are* more elementary, they are generally preferred. The decision whether to develop a particular branch of physical theory along 'Euclidean' or 'non-Euclidean' lines is made, in practice, on an estimate of the relative difficulty of the mathematics involved in either case.

In deciding what scientific theory to adopt, therefore, we apply not one but a number of tests. The initial, and most important test is that of *predictive reliability*: the theory must show us that all the observations we have made in the relevant field of study were such as might have been expected, and it must give us the power to predict correctly future observations in the same field. The next test is that of *coherence*: if there are two theories which cover the same field of study with equal predictive reliability, we choose the one which fits in best with the theories established in adjacent fields of study—preferably in such a way that we can unify the mathematical and conceptual equipment of the two theories, and go deductively from the one to the other by different routes without inconsistency. Finally, if we have to choose between two theories which are both reliable, but which belong to different bodies of theory—e.g. one 'Euclidean' and one 'non-Euclidean'—we apply the test of *convenience*: the theory which produces the results with less effort on our part is the one we prefer.

7.6 The Scope of Scientific Explanation

This will do as an abbreviated account of the way in which scientific theories and concepts develop, and of the things which,

---

[1] A. S. Eddington, *The Mathematical Theory of Relativity*, p. 108: comment following equation 48.41.

at different stages in this development, lead us to accept and reject them. In the light of this survey, we can see in what kinds of situation the different questions which naturally arise in science can be answered and so, by elimination, the limits to the scope of science.

(I) Recall the situation from which we started. If, in your surprise at the appearance of the stick, you ask me, 'Why does this happen?', 'What is the explanation of this phenomenon?', or 'How do you explain this?', I shall know what you want; and I shall give you an answer demonstrating that the phenomenon might, from our experience in similar situations, have been expected. Your inquiry about the stick is intelligible because physics deals with just such phenomena; and the question, 'What is the explanation of this?', has the same force as, 'How would a physicist have come to predict this?' And I shall continue to understand you, so long as your inquiry is about phenomena which, from our experience, it is some good hoping to predict— phenomena, that is, with which we have some method of dealing, about which we have some kind of theory.

On the other hand, if you ask for a 'scientific explanation' of something which, in our experience, there is just no reason to expect, I shall be at a loss to know how to answer you. If, for example, you are impressed by the fact that the three Jones children all learnt to stand (or all died) on their respective birthdays, you may feel that you want an 'explanation' of the fact. But this is not the kind of event which we could have hoped to predict (and we mark this by calling it a 'coincidence'). Nothing which we did could 'show that it might have been expected', and I cannot therefore employ the familiar techniques of science to satisfy you. In consequence, if you do insist on asking me 'how I explain it', all I can do is to shrug my shoulders and reply that I do not attempt to. And, if you protest that I must have *some* explanation (still meaning a 'scientific' one), that is your mistake; for there are some situations in which the demand for a scientific explanation is out of place.

(II) Another class of questions naturally arising in science consists of those like, 'Is this explanation correct?' and 'Which of these explanations is correct?' If you ask me, 'Is this explanation correct?', I shall take your question as an inquiry as to whether this explanation would lead us to predict correctly all the recorded observations in the relevant field, or about the phenomena it leads us to expect, and the ways in which we can test it experimentally. Likewise, I shall know how to deal with the question, 'Which of these explanations is correct?', when it is equivalent to

(i) 'Which of them leads to the more reliable predictions?', or

(ii) 'Given that they are both satisfactory experimentally, which of them fits better with the established theories in adjoining branches of science?', or

(iii) 'Given that they are predictively equivalent, and both form parts of coherent bodies of science, which adopts the more laborious approach?'

But, once I have given you all the evidence about prediction, coherence and convenience, and you have agreed to it, I shall no longer understand what you are after, if you still ask, 'Is this explanation *true*?' or 'But which of these explanations is the *true* one?' As scientific questions, these no longer arise. Science is an activity of such a kind that there is no room for them.

(III) A third request, natural for a scientist, is for a 'unified theory', a comprehensive explanation covering more than one branch of science. If two branches of science are adjacent, and the established theories employ logically comparable concepts, it is proper to wonder about the relation between them, and to look for a theory covering both fields and embracing both established theories. You may very naturally and intelligibly inquire about the relation between (say) the physical and geometrical theories of optics—theories which, at any rate partly, lead to predictions about the same phenomena—and it is a physicist's business to provide the answer.

On the other hand, if two theories have been developed to explain phenomena in widely separated fields, or if they employ concepts whose logical characteristics are greatly different from one another—for example, the kinetic theory of matter and the psychology of musical composition—there is no question of their predictions being relevant to one another since, experimentally, they have no common ground. In such a case, it is only asking for trouble to try and 'unify' the theories.

Take a familiar example. Despite all the successes of classical physics in its own field (the explanation of the properties of gases, and so on), it is right to insist, with J. W. N. Sullivan, that

> the extension of the theory to the whole of phenomena was little more than an idle speculation. To suppose, e.g. that the Ninth Symphony was produced by the random collisions of little hard particles was never more, from the experimental point of view, than a pleasing fancy.[1]

And indeed, from the logical point of view, it was hardly even comprehensible. I can understand what it is to explain the apparent bending of the stick by reference to the shimmering of a heat-haze, but what would it be to 'explain' the genesis of the Choral Symphony by reference to the expansion and contraction of hydrogen? Nothing which I said about the properties of gases could ever quite remove your amazement at Beethoven's genius, or prove to you that the composition of the Choral Symphony 'might have been expected'.

(IV) A fourth class of questions, which we encounter when connecting up theories in adjoining fields of study, consists of conceptual questions, such as 'What is the nature of light?' If you ask me about the nature of light, I can talk to you about the close relationship between the physics of light and of electro-magnetism. I can point out the important similarities between optical and electro-magnetic phenomena, and I can demonstrate the formal equivalence of the mathematical theories (to confine myself for the moment to pre-quantum physics). And, as long as there is a place for an answer of this sort, these conceptual questions are intelligible. But once all this has been done the question, 'What is light?', has no further scientific answer. You may still feel worried, and want to go on asking, 'Is light *really* no more than very-very-high-frequency radio waves?' But, since all that science can do to satisfy you has been done, surprise is no longer appropriate: scientifically, at any rate, your question no longer has any sense.

7.7   The 'Justification' of Science

An examination of the situations in which one first looks for a 'scientific explanation', and of the function of the explanation

[1] J. W. N. Sullivan, *The Bases of Modern Science* (Penguin Edition), p. 206.

in these situations, can give one, therefore, an understanding of the *logic* of science. In talking of 'logic' I am here including both

(i) the tests to be applied to a 'scientific explanation' before one decides whether to accept it as 'correct', reject it as 'incorrect', or suspend judgement upon it, and

(ii) the limits to be placed on the scope of science, from which one is to decide when something that looks like a 'scientific' assertion or question has become either nonsensical or non-scientific.

Furthermore, such an examination shows us how self-contained an activity science is; how buttressed, cross-beamed and supported by one another its members are; and how solidly the whole structure rests upon its foundations of human life and purposes. Indeed, so natural and inevitable does the logic of science come to appear that one cannot help being a little taken aback, when a philosopher comes along and asks us how we justify, not just a particular one, but *all* scientific explanations.[1] For, apart from a more detailed and accurate account than I have had room to give of the way in which science develops—an account which could only be of use to us in justifying *this* explanation, as opposed to *that* one, and not 'explanations in general'—what kind of answer can be needed?

It is clear from the start that there is no room *within* science for the philosopher's inquiry. As a scientist, I can understand the questions, 'Is *this* explanation correct?' and '*Which* of these explanations is correct?': each presents me with a genuine choice, and requires from me a genuine decision. But if, instead, I am asked, 'Can *any* scientific explanation be correct?', what is wanted is completely mysterious: there are now no genuine alternatives, and so no choice or decision to be made. All that I can do is to explain the criteria which we do have for deciding whether or not to accept a scientific explanation, and point out how natural it is (bearing in mind the origins of science) that these should be our criteria.

[1] I am thinking in particular of the 'problem' of induction, as raised, for example, by Bertrand Russell in *The Problems of Philosophy* (1912), pp. 93 ff. It is interesting to reflect on Russell's desire for a 'justification' of science, in view of his parallel conviction that reason has no place in ethics: cf. footnote to § 11.10 below. One consideration which helps us to understand both of these views is this: it is possible, with the help of a 'Principle of Limited Variety' or such-like, to produce a demonstrative argument, which presents quite a vivid caricature of simple science, but there is no chance of doing the same for evaluation.

And it is not only within science that the philosopher's question is an odd one. For suppose that he explains what kind of 'justification' it is that he is asking for: then, either the results of such a 'justification' will be consistent with the conditions which we at present require a scientific argument to meet, or they will run counter to these conditions. Consider first the former case: what can his 'justification' do? It can only pay exaggerated attention to one feature of the situation at the expense of the others (in the same kind of way as the 'correspondence' and 'coherence' theories of truth), or else (like the 'pragmatic' theory) underline the fact that the process as a whole is one that pays.[1] (Needless to say, neither of these things is what the philosopher sees himself as doing.)

On the other hand, what are we to say if his results run counter to our present criteria? Shall we be asked to conclude that a scientist who has a reliable, coherent and convenient theory is nevertheless at fault in adopting it? There is something highly ridiculous and paradoxical in such a demand. Yet let us try to suppose that we do adopt the philosopher's new criteria in place of our present ones. Even if all that he does is to abolish some of our present tests as superfluous, we shall be in Queer Street.

Suppose, for instance, that he makes predictive reliability the only test that matters. Then, when faced with questions about why the Jones family all died on their birthdays, we can no longer excuse ourselves from taking any interest on the grounds— perfectly good grounds before we changed our criteria—that we are scientists, and that nothing in the results of science could have led us to predict that this would happen to them. We must now go in for fortune-telling and clairvoyance as well for, although they may be no more successful than science in this field, they can certainly be no less. And once we set up as clairvoyants there will be the same difficulty about calling us 'scientists' as there is about calling God a 'mathematician'[2] or a calculating-

[1] Cf. J. L. Austin on 'Other Minds', *Aristotelian Soc. Supp. Vol.* xx (1946), summed up by the author thus: 'Believing others, as it occurs in communicating, is one of the things we do, like giving promises or making inductions or playing games. If we press for an ultimate "justification" we shall only succeed in reducing it to something other than it is, or in proving that it pays.'

[2] Cf. Ayer, *Language, Truth and Logic* (2nd ed.), pp. 85–6.

boy an 'arithmetician':[1] going through all the proper steps (whether inductive or deductive) is something essential to genuine 'science' or 'mathematics'—jumping to the conclusion, even correctly, will not do.

The question, what makes a reason a 'good' reason in science, and what makes an argument or explanation a 'valid' one, can only be answered in terms of the reasons, arguments and explanations we *do* accept—namely, those which are predictively reliable, coherent and convenient. If we give up these criteria for others, we change the nature of our activity and, whatever we are now doing, it is no longer 'science'. The logical criteria applicable to scientific explanations are, in this respect, quite as intimately connected with the nature of the activity which we *call* 'science' as the logic and the activity of 'describing things' and the logic and the activity of 'loving-with-an-A'.

One possibility remains. Perhaps the philosopher is calling upon us to *give up* science. But, if this is the case, where are we to draw the line? In giving up science, are we to give up the activity in which natural science finds its use, for which science is our most highly developed tool? Are we, that is, to stop basing our expectations upon past experience?

These are not real questions, since we could not do so, even if we tried. The habit of basing our expectations upon experience of the past is so ingrained in us that it could only be suspended by a sustained effort of will—which itself could only be achieved by reference to experience of our own behaviour in the past. And, even if, by some miracle or misfortune, we were to lose the habit involuntarily, we should not do so for long, since the results would be quick, violent and fatal.

---

[1] Let me quote a paragraph from *The Times* for 17 December 1947:

'The *Cape Argus* reports a remarkable series of tests carried out by the professor of applied mathematics at Stellenbosch University on a broker's clerk who is reputed to have remarkable powers of mental calculation.

'In the presence of mathematical witnesses, and with careful safeguards, the young man was asked to answer the following questions: What is 58 times 73 times 67? What is 734 squared? What is 89 cubed? Multiply 961 by 579. Find the cube root of 84,567. He gave all the answers correctly in 39 seconds....

'Efforts are being made to enable the young man, who is one of a family of eight, to go to the university. *When at school his marks for mathematics were never high, because, although his answers were always right, his method of solving problems was always either unexplained or unorthodox.*' (My italics.)

8

REASONING AND REALITY

8.1 *'Modes of Reasoning'*

The outlook is now more promising. When discussing the nature of 'reasoning', we discovered that the best way to understand the logic of descriptions and rigmaroles was to consider the situations and activities in connection with which these forms of speech appear, and the purposes which they serve. In consequence, I suggested that, if the same kind of relation held between the logic of more complex kinds of reasoning and the purposes they served, we might hope to discover the rules for selecting 'true' moral judgements from 'false', and 'valid' arguments from 'fallacious', from our knowledge of the situations in which ethical utterances are used. Our next worry was how to set about such complex activities as those associated with ethics, and we took 'science' and the activities of scientists as a 'pilot' problem.

This 'pilot' investigation has been a success to this extent:

(i) it has shown that the same kind of relation does exist between the logic of scientific explanations and the function of science, as we found before between the logic of descriptions and rigmaroles and their uses; and

(ii) it has helped us, not only to discover logical criteria applicable to scientific explanations, but also to see that these are *the* logical criteria applicable to them—since to abandon these criteria would be to stop doing 'science'.

Further, as a result of this success, I can excuse and repair an omission. Although I have appealed at intervals to our recognition that there is a difference between 'describing things', 'expressing one's feelings about things', 'giving scientific explanations' and so on, and although I have used the phrase 'modes of reasoning' to refer to these different uses of speech, I have left the nature of the classification vague. (We certainly would say that giving a scientific explanation of a phenomenon was not the same as—say—describing it, but how do they differ?)

Our 'pilot' investigation shows that we must differentiate 'modes of reasoning' by reference to the larger activities of which they are a part, and to the ends which these promote.

A classification of 'modes of reasoning' along these lines has one particular advantage: it can be interpreted perfectly literally. In consequence, it is capable of giving us a greater depth of understanding and a clearer grasp of the logic of each mode than the metaphorical definitions to which we are more accustomed.

Suppose that one asks, 'What is science?' As soon as one puts the question, a flood of possible answers presents itself: 'Science is organised common sense', 'Science is systematic and formulated knowledge', 'Science is the set of beliefs men form to explain the wonderful universe around them'. However, if we turn these over in the mind, we begin to feel an uneasy suspicion that they do not do for us all we want, that none of them is quite the kind of definition we want, in fact that they are more like 'epigrams' than 'definitions'. For, whatever we are told— whether 'science' is defined as 'organised common sense', as 'systematic and formulated knowledge', as 'the explanation of the universe' or as 'the discovery of the pattern in events'—we are left asking, 'And how are we to know when we have organised common sense in the right way?', 'What is a "correct" formulation and what an "incorrect" one?', 'What makes an explanation "valid"?', 'How does one tell "the pattern in events" when one has found it?' And in each case the answer begins in the same way: 'The correct organisation (formulation, explanation, pattern) is one which leads us to expect what actually happens.'

I do not wish to suggest that there is anything *wrong* with such 'definitions': if what you want is an epigrammatic rather than a literal 'definition', something which gives warmth rather than light, and which must be judged as 'happy' or 'unhappy' rather than as 'true' or 'false', then they will do you very well. All that matters is that you should not be misled into taking them over-literally.

The point of my account is not so much to *compete with* or *contradict* the more figurative definitions as to *elucidate* them. I am not denying that scientists 'investigate the nature of reality' (or whatever figure you like to couch your definition in). I am arguing that it is the business of scientists so to correlate our experiences in different fields that we know what to expect in the future. And I am saying that if you like to call this 'investigating the nature of reality' you are welcome to; only, if you do, then this (for the purposes of your argument) is what 'investigating the nature of reality' *is*, and nothing you say about it will contradict or confirm any ideas you have derived from other kinds of situation in which we talk of 'reality'.

Since the notion of 'reality' is one that keeps cropping up in philosophy, and one that we shall not be able to avoid using ourselves, let us see what bearing the functional analysis of science given in the last chapter has upon it.

8.2   *The Concept of 'Reality'*

What does our notion of 'reality' amount to, anyway? To begin with, notice that we first learn to talk and think, not about 'reality', but about what is 'really this' and 'really that': 'reality' only comes in later.

Now the notion of 'what is really so-and-so' is one which we encounter in many types of context. The scientist explains that, in spite of looking bent, the stick is still 'really' straight; the moralist argues that, in spite of its temporary benefits, the practice of giving money to beggars is 'really' an undesirable one, and so on. Further, it is a notion about which there is not always agreement, or even consistency. An artist may take us into a wood and say, 'Look upwards, and compare the colour of the sky seen through the branches with its colour over the fields: you'll find that it's a deeper blue in the first case than in the second'; and, when the physicist replies, 'Of course, it isn't really a deeper blue: that's only an illusion', the artist may retort, 'Isn't *really* a deeper blue? What do you mean? Why, if you'll only use your eyes, you'll *see* that it is!'

The artist's retort may take us by surprise for, as his clinching piece of evidence, he picks on the way it *looks* in the two cases— the very thing the physicist has to regard as irrelevant! But need it worry us? Is there any material difference between them? Are the distinctions which the artist, on the one hand, and the scientist, on the other, draw between what is 'really' and what is 'not really' a deeper blue, drawn on the same grounds? And is 'reality' any more than a label which we invent, when we come to catalogue those things which are 'really something-or-other'? We have seen that there are some situations in which the request for a 'scientific explanation' is out of place; and that, in some circumstances, an argument about which of two scientific theories is correct becomes otiose. May not therefore the demand for a unique and unambiguous answer as to what is 'really' so-and-so also lose all meaning, sometimes?

In order to answer these questions, let us see how the notion of 'reality' arises in the development of science and art, and on what grounds the artistic and scientific distinctions between what is and what is not really a deeper blue are drawn.

8.3 'Reality' and Explanation

Consider, first, how the scientist's distinction between 'appearance' and 'reality' is related to his method of giving explanations.

Ordinarily, we are puzzled by the way in which our experiences change, and try to 'make some sense of them'. So, when we encounter unexpected phenomena, like the apparent bending of a stick in water, we ask both for an 'explanation' of the phenomenon, and for what may be called an 'interpretation' of the explanation. That is, we ask not only, 'Why does this happen? Why does it look bent?', but also, 'What is really the case? Is it really bent or straight?' And, at first sight, the question, 'What is really the case?', seems to be deeper than any request for an explanation—for how can we know which observations we can accept as 'veridical', and which we have to 'explain away', until we have discovered which represent 'reality' and which are 'illusory' or 'mere appearance'?

But this suggestion of priority and depth is misleading. For suppose, for the moment, that we stop sifting, comparing and 'explaining' our experiences; and that we relax our attention. Instead, suppose that, in tranquillity and contentment, we sit back and drift, letting the 'wonderful kaleidoscope of Nature' turn and change before us, neither bothering to anticipate the experiences of the next moment, nor concerned to advance or avoid any of the developments going on around us, seeking no ends. Then all that happens will be one to us, nothing will be 'expected' or 'unexpected', and we shall talk neither about 'reality' nor about 'mere appearance'.

These ideas only enter in when we begin to explain the flux of experience, to describe it in terms of things having more or less constant characteristics; when we seek to replace the 'contradictory' reports of our senses by 'self-consistent' descriptions, and to talk to others in a common language; and when we try to predict and control the developments going on around us. Only then do we demand (for instance) that the stick shall be regarded, neither as changing abruptly from straight to bent when put into the stream, nor as being both bent and straight, to different senses or observers, at the same time. And only when we make this demand do we draw any distinction between the 'reality' and the 'appearance'; between what is really the case, corresponding to those experiences we explain, and what is only apparently the case, corresponding to those experiences we explain away.

Again, if you say to me, 'Of course, that stick is not really bent', but cannot produce any explanation or evidence tending to discredit the appearance of bentness, I shall regard you as a fraud. You can always say, 'It *can't* really be bent', meaning 'This is a very surprising phenomenon, which goes against all my previous ideas about sticks: I wonder how it is to be explained'—even then, you will be invoking all your previous ideas and experience as evidence, and very good evidence they may be. But if, instead, you reject my request, saying, 'Why ask me for an *explanation*? I can tell *directly* that it isn't bent in reality', you cannot expect me to accept this—the scientific distinction between 'reality' and 'appearance' is one which we learn and understand only in conjunction with an explanation.

The connection between them is so intimate that, in the absence of some kind of an explanation of a phenomenon, it does not make any difference in which way we describe it—as 'real' or as 'apparent'. If I catch a glimpse of something unlike anything I have come across before, my description of it can be in terms of 'fact' or 'appearance', with indifference. It does not matter, that is, whether I say, 'It was red and elliptical and it buzzed like a bee', or 'It looked red and elliptical and it sounded to me like a bee'. It is, in fact, only when we have a number of reports to compare, and wish to give a 'reasoned explanation' of an experience, that the scientific distinction between 'appearance' and 'reality' has any significance at all.

8.4 *The Limits of 'Physical Reality'*. (I)

Since questions about 'physical reality' and 'mere appearance' only acquire any substance when we begin to grope after an explanation—however rudimentary—of our experiences, we can enquire, from our earlier analysis of 'explanation', what this 'substance' is, and how the scope of such 'interpretations' is limited; that is to say, under what circumstances questions about 'physical reality' cease to have any point.

To begin with: questions of the form 'Is O really X?'—'Is this stick really bent?', and so on—can only be asked about properties having counterparts in science. Many of our familiar, everyday properties have no such counterparts: they are never used as 'scientific qualities', but only as 'simple' or 'complex qualities', for the measurements which are found to be important in science include none corresponding to them.

The colour 'brown' is such a property. As an everyday concept, 'brown' is on the same footing as 'blue', 'green', 'red' and 'black'. However, the principles on which physicists base their classification of 'colour'—in terms of the wave-length of electromagnetic radiation—are so different from those on which the everyday classification is based that the colours 'brown', 'white' and 'black' are treated as secondary (for purposes of physics) to the colours, 'red', 'yellow', 'orange', 'green', 'blue', 'indigo' and 'violet'—colours whose names are applied to different parts of the visible spectrum. In consequence, questions about whether anything is 'really brown' will be of interest only in simple cases, where a fully-fledged physical explanation is not called for—where, for instance, the point at issue is only, 'Is this object being illuminated through brown glass, or is this its natural colour?' They will not arise in the interpretation of fully-fledged scientific explanations: one can ask whether an object is 'really red', meaning 'Does its emission spectrum have its principal maximum in the "red" region of the spectrum?', but there is no 'brown' part of the spectrum so, over 'brown', the corresponding question cannot arise. A biophysicist may understand what I want if I ask him whether the leaves falling from the trees at autumn are really dead, but if I ask him also, 'And are they really brown, on your theory?', he cannot begin to answer me.

8.5   *The Limits of 'Physical Reality'.* (II)

Consider, therefore, only those properties which do have counterparts in science; which can, that is, be treated as 'scientific' as well as 'simple' or 'complex qualities'. As 'scientific qualities', they are defined by reference to the established theory. Questions about them are therefore limited in the same kind of way as questions about the theory itself. They can only arise when there is a genuine doubt about what to expect, or a conflict between the predictions of two theories. Otherwise, the possible answers—'It *is* really X' and 'It is *not* really X'—will not represent genuine alternatives.

This condition has two important consequences:

First, I cannot question the standards adopted in the established theory. For instance, I can say to a physicist, 'This stick looks and feels straight, but is it really?', or 'Here is the template I have been using as a standard; tell me whether it is really straight', or 'Under the conditions of this experiment, can I expect light to be propagated in straight lines?'; and in each case he will have some means of answering me. But, if I say to him, 'This line is the shortest one between its end-points; is it really straight?', I cannot expect him to answer me, for this is to query the standard and definition of 'straightness' upon which the whole of classical physics is built up. With my very question, I take away from him the means of answering me. (Likewise, if I am talking to an astro-physicist about phenomena in some field which is usually covered by a 'non-Euclidean' type of theory, I can question the 'straightness' of anything except a light-ray. The question, 'Is this ray of light really straight?', can mean nothing to him, for his application of non-Euclidean geometry depends on the use of this standard.)

Secondly, if two theories account equally well for the phenomenon in which we are interested, and each of them uses a different criterion of 'straightness' (or whatever it is), there is again no place for the question, 'Is this, or is this not, really straight?' Once again, that is, the alternatives offered are not materially different, and no scientific purpose is served by demanding an unambiguous answer to the question.

This can be illustrated. When, in answer to the question, 'Is this stick really straight, despite its appearance of bentness?', we reply that it is, we rely on the fact that our theories of optics and elasticity employ the same criterion of 'straightness'. But suppose that they did not; and suppose that we had a fully verified theory of the elastic properties of solids, which was mathematically simpler than our present optical theory, and which led us to say that the stick really did bend when put into water. Under such circumstances, we should soon get used to saying, 'It's odd: although a stick really bends when you put it into water, and although you can see it bend, it still continues to feel straight!' And suppose that no experiment ever could decide between this theory of elasticity and our theory of re-fraction, since the scientific concepts of the two theories were logically independent. If this were to happen, the question, 'Is the stick really straight?', would begin to look a little odd. The way of answering it would be so much less obvious than it is now: and what you chose to answer would begin to be a matter of taste—'Call it which you like!'

Of course, I do not suggest that it *is* a matter of taste whether we say that the stick in water is really bent or straight: that would be the case only if the example were completely unequivocal. There are, in fact, good reasons for saying that it is really straight—for preferring our existing optical theory to an imaginary theory of elasticity. In consequence, someone may object: 'Maybe, if what you have described *were* to happen, we should do as you predict; but the very fact that it does not, and that our optical theory is successful, shows that, physically, the world isn't like that. In reality, the stick *is* straight.' He may, that is to say, insist that no mere change in theory could account for the differ-ence between something's being 'straight' and its being 'not straight'—that the difference must be a 'physical' difference. A more striking example is needed to bring out what our 'good reasons' are, what evidence we actually do accept for the 'reality' of anything's straightness and, above all, the extent to which taste *is* involved.

8.6   *The Limits of 'Physical Reality'*. (III)

We can get what we want from theoretical astronomy. In talking about phenomena in outer space, an astronomer finds it convenient to use a 'non-Euclidean' type of theory, taking light-rays as the standard of straightness. As long as he does so, there can be no question of his calling them anything but 'straight'. But on other occasions, the same astronomer will happily talk of light-rays being 'deflected'—for instance, by the gravitational attraction of the sun. In describing the state of affairs around the sun, he finds it more convenient to use a 'Euclidean' system of geometry, in which 'a straight line' is defined as 'the shortest distance between two points': in such a system, of course, there is nothing self-contradictory in the idea of a light-ray being deflected. In talking to the astronomer, we may feel like asking whether the light-ray is really straight or not. But, since the two theories which he uses on different occasions give opposite answers, it is no good asking him this question in isolation: it no longer has any meaning.

This example illustrates very well the point I want to make. As long as we have to choose between the look and the feel on the one hand, and a scientific criterion of 'straightness' on the other, the answer to the question, 'Is it really straight?' is unambiguous: we have a good reason for preferring the scientific criterion—the reason being just that it is a scientific criterion, i.e. one chosen for its predictive reliability. But, when there is an equally balanced conflict between two scientific criteria, any theory of Absolute Reality, which requires that there shall always be an unambiguous answer to the question, is in a hopeless position; there may be no reason at all for treating one criterion rather than the other as 'ultimate'.

The distinction between the 'reality' and the 'appearance', between the look of bentness and the real straightness, is not a material distinction, like that between a straight stick and a stick which I have broken across my knee. It is, rather, 'in the explanation', like the geometrical axes to which a surveyor refers his measurements. The reason for saying that anything is 'really straight' or 'really bent' is just the corresponding explanation. If the corresponding explanation is a good one, there is a good reason for saying, 'This is really straight'. And, when there are two equally good explanations, there may be nothing to choose between saying 'This is really straight' and 'This is really bent'.

But this leaves us uncomfortable: we feel that the light-ray cannot really be both straight and not straight. And, in a way, we are right. But we must be clear just what it is that makes us right. If we mean that it cannot be correct to say, at the same time, 'This ray is really straight', and 'This ray is not really straight', we are dead right, for, as long as we are giving our explanation in terms of any particular theory, these two statements will be contradictory and incompatible. But, if we mean that it cannot be correct to call the same ray 'really straight' when using one theory and 'not really straight' when using another, we are simply mistaken.

It is not altogether surprising that we should make this mistake. We are so used to asking questions of the form 'Is O really X?' in everyday cases (in which there is no ambiguity) that we cannot immediately recognise those situations in which they do not arise. It is easy enough to see that it is no good questioning the straightness of a light-ray when that ray of light is the astronomer's standard—when every ray of light just is straight, because in his terminology 'straight' means 'like a ray of light'. However, when two explanations can be given of the same state of affairs, one in terms of a Euclidean and the other in terms of a non-Euclidean geometry, the inappropriateness of the question is less obvious. We feel a strong desire to say, 'Surely this light-ray *must* be either straight or not!', and to demand a definite answer to the question. We have the idea that, if only the light-ray could talk, it would be able to tell us how it felt, and that what it would say would have a peculiar authority—for surely it must know! But, of course, even that would not help us: whatever it felt, it would have the same difficulty as us in expressing itself. The ambiguity of 'straight' in such a context—the equally balanced choice between the Euclidean and non-Euclidean senses—would leave it in no better position to say whether it was 'really straight' or not than we are.

At this stage, apart from pointing out the convenience of having alternative theories, each with its own standard of 'straightness', no answer can be given. And this is not because no one has found out the answer (as with questions like 'What causes cancer?'), but because the question is not a real question at all. If anyone insists on asking such a 'question', all that we can say is that scientific theories can be interpreted in terms of everyday concepts in many different ways, and that in some contexts there may be no reason why one definition of 'straight' or 'red' rather than another should be taken as giving us the only 'real' straightness or redness.

8.7   *The Contrast between Scientific and Everyday Judgements*

Even within a science, therefore, there need be no real contradiction between the judgements, 'This is really straight' and 'This is not really straight'; and when the judgements which appear to conflict with one another are taken from different kinds of context and different modes of reasoning, there is simply no question of their being incompatible.

Suppose that a scientist and a layman are admiring the sunset:

'The sun is yellow', declares the one (using his indirect, 'scientific' criteria of colour).

'No, it's red', replies the other (using the familiar, 'ostensive' definition).

'Ah, it may *look* red to us', explains the first, 'But it's really yellow!'

His qualification shows that, in calling the sun 'yellow' originally, it was the scientific quality 'really yellow' that he had in mind. This is confirmed if he is forced to put his cards on the table. When he does so, he talks about 'refractive index', 'wavelength' and other such concepts, and it turns out that the force of his remark was: 'There is no change in the radiation leaving the sun itself, when it passes out of our sight below the horizon: the appearance of redness is produced near at hand, in the atmosphere—at *our* end, not in the *sun*.'

When the scientist declares that the sun is 'really' yellow, not red, he is not denying that anyone (least of all he himself) is seeing a red patch in the western sky; nor does the fact that he explains away the apparent colour of the sun affect that colour in any way. Physics or no physics, the sunset remains as red as ever—the suggestion that it might not, rightly sounds ludicrous.

As a scientist, he is in no place to question an account of experience given in everyday language, on the grounds that it fails to do what it sets out to do—everyday speech describes the objects of our experience in a way which serves our usual purposes perfectly well. He can only question it because he has special, out-of-the-way purposes and, for these purposes, everyday language is inadequate. The table at which I write is solid, and so is the chair on which I sit, and I should be justified in using either as an instance of a 'solid' object, when teaching anyone the idea. Upon my knowledge of their solidity I base my confidence that, if I bump into either in the dark, I shall bruise myself, and that, if I put the tea-tray down on the table, it will not fall through.

The scientist, however, discards the everyday notion of solidity, because it may lead him to suppose, mistakenly, that nothing, not even a beam of α-rays, will go through my table or chair. And this is a perfectly proper thing for him to do—as a physicist. But it is wrong or, at the best, whimsical of him to say, 'That table is not solid at all; α-rays go through it, so it must be full of holes'—if he imagines that the results of his experiments *discredit* the everyday concept of 'solidity'.[1]

8.8 *The Independence of Different Modes of Reasoning*

As between scientific and everyday judgements, so also between scientific judgements and judgements of other kinds, there are no contradictions. The opposition between the artist (who says that the sky seen through trees really is a deeper blue) and the scientist (who says, 'It isn't really a deeper blue') does not reflect a material difference, like that between a pillar-box painted red, for surface-mail, and a pillar-box painted blue, for air-mail; it represents only a divergence between the modes of reasoning which they are using—the choice of mode being determined by their activities and interests.

The scientific distinction between 'appearance' and 'reality' 'only arises when we try to predict and control the developments going on around us. For the physicist, therefore, the 'real colour' of an object is that which a predictively reliable theory

---

[1] Recall the famous battle between Stebbing and Eddington, in *Philosophy and the Physicists*, *The Nature of the Physical World*, etc.

would lead one to attribute to it; and what worries him about the artist's statement is that, if we supposed that the (scientifically) 'real colour' of an object might change simply because we happened to be looking at it through the trees, we should never know *what* to expect. The artist's business is different. He is not so much concerned to predict our future experiences as to record our present ones. It matters less to him whether the appearance of an object is expected or unexpected than it does whether it forms an interesting pattern or not.

This explains how the artist and the scientist come to differ in the tests which they regard as relevant. For scientific purposes, how the sky looks through trees is comparatively unimportant: for artistic purposes, what could be more relevant or important?

In general, then, when two people say, respectively, 'O is really X' and 'O is not really X', their remarks will not contradict one another unless both are of the same logical type. Each remark has the force of 'One should treat O (for these purposes) as X', or 'One should pay attention (for these purposes) to the similarities between O and objects of the class X'. What 'these purposes' are can only be discovered from the context, and varies with the mode of reasoning employed. 'Treating O as X' may, in consequence, be any of a number of things, as different from one another as 'expecting similar phenomena' and 'applying similar paint'.

'Reality', in any particular mode of reasoning, must be understood as 'what (for the purposes of this kind of argument) is relevant', and 'mere appearance' as 'what (for these purposes) is irrelevant'. And, since these purposes differ from case to case, that which is, say, 'aesthetic reality' may yet be, for physics, 'mere appearance'.

In consequence, there is simply no room for the question, 'The sky *can't* be both a deeper blue and not a deeper blue; so which is it?' In the situation described, there is no way of choosing, and no genuine opposition between the 'alternatives'. The form of words 'Which is it *really*?' ceases to express a genuine question at all: the most it can call for is a decision—'Which am I to treat as relevant, for these purposes; the scientific or the artistic criteria?' To suppose that it still expresses a question, to continue looking for the one and only really real meaning of 'reality', is to enter upon a wild-goose chase of the most meta-phorical kind—not just a literal wild-goose chase (for a wild goose is a very solid object in spite of being so elusive), but the endless pursuit of an imaginary bird.

8.9 *More Unnecessary Work for Philosophy*

This brings us back to the point from which we started the chapter: the difference between an account of 'modes of reasoning' in terms of the activities with which they belong and the purposes these serve—an account of the sort I tried to give for science—and the more figurative definitions, in terms of 'the pattern of events' or 'the nature of reality', which we more commonly encounter. It underlines for us, first, the value of an account which can be interpreted literally and, by contrast with this, the things which make phrases like 'in reality' so misleading (as deeply and thoroughly misleading, if the figurative use of 'in' is misunderstood, as the phrases 'in the object', 'in the mind' and 'in the subject').

Let me give an example of this. It is understandable that a philosopher should write (as Prof. J. S. Haldane does, in his Gifford Lectures, *The Sciences and Philosophy*):[1]

> For the purposes of communicating needs from person to person, language embodying abstract ideas is indispensable. The words them-selves represent only abstract aspects of what they refer to, but for practical purposes these abstract aspects are often sufficient. Words referring to extension and number are, to take one example, of a different class from words referring to beauty; and out of the different internally consistent systems of words applying to different abstract aspects of experience the different sciences or branches of knowledge have arisen.

(We have seen ourselves the importance of examining the ways in which the different branches of knowledge arise, and of reserving to each mode of reasoning the appropriate logical criteria.) However, when he goes on to call it 'a natural enough further step to imagine that the different systems of abstract ideas correspond to separate realities', we cannot help pausing to ask what on earth it is that we are invited to 'imagine'.

[1] The passages I cite are taken from pp. 312 and 313.

It is true that, when visualising the results of science, we find it useful to have a mental picture of 'reality', as a kind of vast box, the nature of whose 'contents' it is the calling of the scientist to 'identify'; and, in its place, this picture may be helpful enough. But what are we to do if we are presented with several 'separate realities'? To demand that we visualise them all in the way in which we do 'physical reality' is to ask us to imagine 'several separate boxes all occupying exactly the same space'—that is, 'several separate, un-separate boxes'—and this demand is a self-contradictory one, before which the mind can only boggle.

There is a further difficulty. Once we get into the way of thinking that 'in reality' means any more than 'really', the phrase may come, for us, to *mean* 'in this box': and, since we never talk of 'more than one object' occupying a given volume, we may get the idea that nothing can 'occupy' 'more than one reality', and in consequence become worried at the apparent opposition between the scientist and the artist over the colour of the sky. We may want to insist that, *in reality*, the sky must either be a deeper blue between the branches or not, and hanker after a decision between the unopposed 'alternatives'.

Perhaps this explains the way in which Prof. Haldane continues. Seeing that 'the assumed separate realities are inconsistent with one another', and being (very properly) concerned at 'the clash between different sciences, and between science and religion', he invokes philosophy as the impartial judge which must 'mediate between the different sciences', whenever they seem to conflict. 'It goes without saying', he explains, 'that no science ever represents reality itself, since it deals only with abstractions from reality': 'reality itself' he reserves for philosophy to deal with. Metaphor, once again, gives birth to metaphysics.

But need the problems ever have arisen? Is not the difficulty which we feel in the face of Haldane's 'separate realities' the same as that we feel when presented with Freud's famous description of the Mind[1]—as a city in which all the buildings ever erected on one site continue to stand, along with those erected in the same place in later times? And is not the reason for our

[1] Freud, *Civilisation and its Discontents*, p. 18.

perplexity the same in both cases—that a spatial metaphor (the figurative 'in'), valuable enough in its own place, has been taken too literally, and its use extended in a way which leads to self-contradictions? Surely the soundest instinct is not Haldane's, nor even Freud's (for he does at least recognise the source of our difficulty), but Platón Karatáev's:[1] to understand the meaning of words only in their contexts, and to trust logic only so long as it keeps in touch with life.

[1] Recall the quotation at the head of Chapter 6, above.

PART III
THE NATURE OF ETHICS

9

INTRODUCTION: IS ETHICS
A SCIENCE?

AFTER examining the nature of reasoning in two simple cases, we decided to apply the method which was successful in these cases to a more elaborate mode of reasoning—namely, that of science. This experiment has occupied us during the last two chapters, and has given us a guide with the help of which we can approach once more our central problem: the place of reason in ethics. As a reintroduction to this problem, it is worth inquiring whether the results of our examination of science can be applied to ethics directly. Or is there some fundamental obstacle, something about the function of ethical reasoning, which makes the logical criteria of science irrelevant? If we discover any such obstacle, we shall have to deal with the problem from scratch; but, having recognised the nature of the obstacle we shall be better equipped to avoid it.

Is ethics a science? How far (to put the question in our own way) is the function of ethics like that of science? 'Well, for a start', someone may say, 'both ethics and science aim at the discovery of Reality—separate Realities, different aspects of Ultimate Reality, maybe, but Reality nevertheless.'

The value of this remark is not that it *answers* our question for, if one is to be strictly literal, it is no 'answer'; it is that it suggests a means of finding out the answer, of reformulating the question in a more illuminating way. What lies behind the remark, and what it reminds us of is this: first, the fact that what we call 'fully-developed moral judgements' are concerned, not with the things we *like* or the actions we *feel* to be right (since we may be misled as to their value), but with what is *really* good or right; and, secondly, the parallel between this ethical preoccupation with the *real* value of objects and actions, and the scientific preoccupation with, for instance, the *real* colour of the sun (discounting the effect on its apparent colour of atmospheric refraction, and so on).

As a literal definition, 'the discovery of reality' tells us no more about ethics than it does about science. Just as in the one case it leaves us asking the question, 'And how are scientists to distinguish between "physical reality" and "mere appearance"?', so now we are left with another unanswered question, 'And is the distinction between the "really good" and what we just like a distinction of the same kind as that between the "really yellow" and what just looks yellow, or that between the walking-stick which "just looks bent" and the one which "really is bent"?' We shall have to consider this parallel in some detail: let us begin by remarking on the points of similarity between the distinctions.

9.1   *Physical and Moral 'Reality'*

Recall the scientific distinction first. When you encounter the phenomenon of the stick-in-water, you may do any of a number of things. You may, at one extreme, simply report on what you see and evince your surprise: at the other extreme, you may know how to relate this phenomenon to other phenomena, with which we are all familiar, relying on the 'explanation' so developed to demonstrate that the appearance of bentness might have been expected, and so to justify your lack of surprise.

In the first case, you may evince your feelings in an inarticulate exclamation of surprise—'Oh!' Or you may be more explicit, and cry, 'Bent!' You may express what you see in the form of a personal report—'I see a bent stick', or 'I see what looks like a bent stick'. Or, finally, you may declare, impersonally, 'The stick is bent', or 'The stick looks bent'.

Any of these six remarks can act as a direct report of your experience—they differ only in the balance between rhetorical force and articulateness. As long as there is no thought of doing anything but record the experience—no interpretation, no relation to other experiences, no explanation—questions of truth and falsity, of evidence and reasoning, do not arise. Indeed, they *cannot*. It may always be, of course, that you are dissimulating, or making a verbal mistake—the kind of thing which you can correct later, by saying, 'What I saw was turkey-red, not carnation'. But, apart from deceit and verbal errors, these reports are not open to question. (In consequence, it is a matter of taste whether you classify them as 'empirical propositions which can be verified conclusively', or as 'mere ejaculations': they are neither typical propositions, nor typical ejaculations, but borderline instances.[1])

In the second case, you may declare, 'The stick is not really bent; its appearance is an optical illusion'. This judgement is intended as the fruit of all our experience in such situations: it is therefore far from 'incorrigible'. It is, indeed, open to question on any of three grounds:

(i) that the past experiences upon which your judgement is based are not as you believe;

(ii) that, though the data are as you believe, they do not refer to situations sufficiently similar to justify your conclusion; or

(iii) that, though the data are as you believe and are relevant, they do not lead to the conclusion you assert, but to a different one.

The fully-fledged scientific judgement, 'This stick is really straight', is therefore in sharp contrast to the more-or-less exclamatory expression of surprise at what you see, feel, smell or taste. And, to be 'true', it must follow correctly from a theory which accounts for all normal people's sense-experiences in similar situations—'accounting for them' here having the force of 'showing that they were to be expected'.

The fully-fledged moral judgement can similarly be contrasted to an immediate, unconsidered report or exclamation. A pleasant surprise, for example, may lead us to exclaim in any of five equivalent ways: 'Hurrah!', 'Good!', 'I am pleased', 'That seems good news' and 'That is good news'. The differences between these five remarks again depend on the balance reached between rhetorical force and articulateness. The first is more forceful than articulate, vigorously evincing our feelings; the last more articulate than forceful, expressing a quieter

---

[1] These two, seemingly opposed points of view appear in successive editions of Ayer's *Language, Truth and Logic.* In the first edition (1936), Ayer plumps for 'mere ejaculations' (1st ed. p. 127; 2nd ed. p. 91): in the second edition (1946), he changes his position, following his own treatment of the problem in *The Foundations of Empirical Knowledge.* In doing so, however, he admits (2nd ed. Introduction, pp. 10–11) that his arguments on this point only 'suggest motives' for agreeing or refusing to 'apply the term "proposition" to statements that "directly record an experience"; and this is a terminological point which is not of very great importance'.

satisfaction. Logically, however, they are equivalent: all act as direct reports of our feelings, and all lead an observer to the same conclusion—that, provided we are not dissembling or making a verbal mistake, the news pleases us. Further, like the direct reports of our sense-experiences, they are 'incorrigible': no questions of truth and falsity, evidence and reasoning, can arise over them and, in spite of the propositional form of the last three, one could argue with considerable justice in favour of calling them all 'exclamations'.

As long as we are only concerned with spontaneous remarks of this kind, there is no room for the distinction between what is 'good' and what 'pleases' us; and in this respect, too, there is a parallel between feelings and sense-experiences. Unless the evidence of our senses is 'conflicting', giving us grounds for regarding the appearance as 'illusory', the statements, 'This is bent' and 'This looks bent', convey the same.[1] So too, when we have to make a moral decision in a situation without precedent for us, or in such a hurry that we cannot fully consider the case, our feelings are our only guide as to what is 'good' or 'right'. Under such circumstances, there is no effective difference between 'I approve of your conduct' and 'You have done well', or between 'I feel obliged to help him' and 'I ought to help him'. 'I approve of your conduct' then conveys as much as 'I think you have done well' or as 'You have done well': all three are equally 'incorrigible'. And the same is true of the triad, 'I feel obliged to help him', 'I think I ought to help him' and 'I ought to help him'. (This is not to say that 'good' *means* the same as 'what I approve of', or that 'right' *means* just 'what I feel obliged to do': of course they do not. At its lowest, however, 'what *seems* good to me' means the same as 'what pleases me', and 'what I feel obliged to do' the same as 'what *seems* to me the right thing to do'.)

By contrast, the fully-fledged moral judgement, like the fully-fledged scientific judgement, is far from 'incorrigible'. It also is (in some sense) the fruit of all our experience in such situations, and can be disputed accordingly. It, too, will have (in some sense) to 'account for' all our relevant experiences, enabling us to sort out those cases in which the things that seemed to us good

---

[1] See § 8.3 above.

(or right) were really good (or right) from those in which our feelings were a bad guide, what seemed good being really bad, and what seemed wrong being right. In ethics, as in science, incorrigible but conflicting reports of personal experience (sensible or emotional) are replaced by judgements aiming at universality and impartiality—about the 'real value', the 'real colour', the 'real shape' of an object, rather than the shape, colour or value one would ascribe to it on the basis of immediate experience alone.

9.2 'Disposition' and the Function of Ethics

The scientific distinction between 'appearance' and 'reality' reflects the function of science—'to correlate our experiences in such a way that we know what to expect'. Can we now, from our analogy between science and ethics, define the function of ethics similarly? If so, it will be 'to correlate our actions and responses in such a way that...', but here we must leave a blank, for we have reached a point where the parallel between ethics and science breaks down.

Moral judgements are certainly not intended to help us *predict* our actions and responses. In the limited range of cases in which this can be done, it is the job of *psychology* to do it; and the judgements that emerge—'This will amaze him', and 'Loud bangs frighten civilians more than soldiers', for example—are certainly not *moral* ones. Our analogy will take us no further, and we must leave unspecified for the moment the precise senses in which moral judgements are the 'fruit of our experience', and 'account for' our actions and responses.

However, the very factor which is responsible for the breakdown of the parallel between science and ethics—the variability of our 'dispositions'—can help us to see the next step. Let us, therefore, examine the ways in which 'dispositions' affect the problem.

The fact that one talks of the colour which something '*appears* to have', but of the value which it '*seems* to have', is itself symptomatic. Though, in many situations, we use 'seem' and 'appear', 'seemingly' and 'apparently', interchangeably, there are still some uses which reflect (with varying force) the difference between the two concepts. If I see from a distance a man shaking his fist at a small girl, I may say, 'He *seems* to be cross with her': but if I go closer to him and he gesticulates to me and talks rapid Czech or Urdu (or some other language I do not understand) in an indignant voice, I shall more likely say, 'He *appears* to be cross with her'. (Of course, if he tells me how he feels in a language that I know, I shall be able to say, 'He *is* angry with her'—but we can leave that case aside.)

What I am after is this: as long as my evidence is slight, I shall be justified in speaking only for myself—if I say straight off, 'He appears to be cross with her', someone may reply, '*I* shouldn't have said he was: I should have said it was a game of some kind', and I shall have to fall back on to, 'Well, he seems to *me* to be'. But when my evidence is stronger, so strong in fact that I feel that anyone in my position would get the same impression as I do, I can safely say, 'He appears to be cross', eliminating the explicit or implicit reference to myself that there is in 'He seems (to me) to be angry'.

As its etymology suggests, that which is *apparently* the case is the same for all normal people in the same position. When the setting sun turns red, it appears red to all who care to look—so much so that we could even say, 'It really appears red'; the 'apparent' is primarily the 'manifest', the 'palpable', and only secondarily the 'seeming'.[1] That which is *seemingly* the case, on the other hand, carries with it a strong air of deception, unreality or fraud; the 'seeming' is primarily the 'ostensible', the 'apparent only', the 'apparent but perhaps not real', and only secondarily the 'apparent and perhaps real'.[2] About that which only *seems* to have any characteristic, we are prepared for differences of opinion which would surprise us if they occurred over something which *appeared* to have it.

But this is a point which we have encountered before. When discussing the 'objective doctrine', we noticed that there was a wide range of situations over which there might very well be differences about the 'value' of something, although disagreements over its 'properties' were unthinkable.[3] What we can now do is to remark on the connection between this logical distinction and the concept of 'disposition'. Differences over the properties

---

[1] *Pocket Oxford Dictionary*; entry against 'apparent'.
[2] Op. cit. entry against 'seeming'.   [3] See § 2.5 above.

of an object cannot (like differences over its value) be put down to differences in 'attitude' or 'disposition': if one were asked, 'How is it that *you* say this is red, and *he* says it's green?', to say, 'We just *feel* differently about it', would be no answer.

The importance of the element of 'disposition' can, however, be shown more strikingly. When a scientist distinguishes between 'real' colour and 'apparent' colour, his raw material is confined to observations which are the same for all normal observers in the same situation—the evidence of those with jaundice, or of the colour-blind (for example), is ignored in physical optics. In consequence, no scientific theory can modify the experiences it explains. The sun still looks red at sunset, although we know that it is not really red; physics may explain why a stick looks bent, when it is really straight, but it cannot stop the stick looking bent. And even to say, 'No explanation *can* modify the corresponding experiences', may be misleading, for it is the logical conditions we impose on 'scientific observations' rather than any feature of the 'physical world' that accounts for the impossibility—no experience which could be altered by a change in one's beliefs alone would be acceptable to us as a 'scientific observation'.

The relation between a 'moral experience' and the corresponding ethical judgement is different. The schoolboy, who discovers that he has been given his colours as a result of favouritism and not merit, no longer gets the same satisfaction out of them; the man, who discovers that his feelings of obligation to clean his teeth five times a day have a psychopathic origin, no longer feels the urge so strongly; the soldier, who discovers that his superior officer is using him to feather his own nest, no longer feels it his invariable duty to obey him. An ethical argument—in answer to the question, 'Is this *really* good (right, obligatory)?'—may, that is to say, change the corresponding experiences (our feelings of satisfaction or of obligation). It may reinforce them, so that we say, 'As a result of what you report, this seems even more wicked than it did'; or remove them, so that we declare, 'On thinking it over, his behaviour seems to me less immoral than it did'.

To contrast science and ethics in this respect: we none of us wonder at the fact that people's dispositions and attitudes change, when they are presented with ethical arguments (and why should we?); but we should feel a little disconcerted and misunderstood, if anyone were to say to us, 'I'm glad you explained to me about the scattering of solar radiation, for since you did I haven't been taken in once—the sunset never looks red to me now'.

This is all as it should be, for it reflects the difference between the jobs which scientific and moral judgements perform. If I accept a scientific law as true, my disposition need only alter in one respect: I now expect what I did not expect before—in my scientific work, my feelings about these future events are irrelevant. And if I try to persuade someone else of the truth of a law, it is his expectations rather than his emotions that concern me. Suppose that at sunset I say, 'Of course, the sun has not really changed colour, but at the moment the upper layers of the atmosphere are scattering its radiation in such a way that it looks red to us at ground-level'. I shall know that my hearer has understood me if, for instance, he replies, 'You mean that, if I were now in mid-Atlantic, it would still look as it did', or 'So to-morrow midday it'll look yellow again', or 'I suppose that if one lived in a balloon at a height of 80 miles one would never have red sunsets'. Scientifically, indeed, some expectations of this sort must be relevant to my judgement, if it is to be of any use at all.

On the other hand—and here appears the crucial difference between science and ethics—if I say, 'Meekness is a virtue', I may be concerned with no expectation whatsoever; rather, I am encouraging my hearers to feel and behave differently. Likewise, when I accept an ethical maxim, I begin to approve and disapprove, praise and condemn, look forward to, hope for, seek, avoid and fear different things; and all this, maybe, without any change in my situation. And more: the habit of reflecting on moral questions, and of changing the objects of our approval and disapproval accordingly, is the essence of 'conscientiousness', a personal characteristic which is generally considered a morally good one—in fact, the very best. (Kant even declares that none other deserves to be called 'good': 'In order that an action should be morally good, it is not enough that it *conform* to the moral law, but it must also be done *for the sake of the law*.')[1]

---

[1] Kant, *Fundamental Principles of the Metaphysics of Ethics*, tr. Abbott (10th ed. 1926), p. 5.

9.3   *Conclusion*

This difference in function between scientific and moral judgements—the one concerned to alter expectations, the other to alter feelings and behaviour—helps to explain the mistaken identification (popular among 'empiricist' philosophers, writers about psycho-analysis and others) of 'science' with 'reason', and of 'ethics' with 'rhetoric' or 'rationalisation'. One's hopes and fears, likes and dislikes are (it may be) more easily swayed by rhetoric than one's expectations. At the same time, the rhetorical element in ethics can be paralleled in the actual practice of science (and of mathematics, too, for that matter). If, as supporters of the 'imperative doctrine' suggest, we regard 'Good!' and 'Don't steal!' as the most characteristic ethical sentences, then we shall have to choose as 'typical scientific judgements' their analogues —for 'Good!' and 'Hurrah!' (the expressions of joy), the expressions of surprise, 'Blimey!' and 'Bent!'; and in place of the injunction, 'Don't steal!', the corresponding injunctions, 'Don't be surprised!' and 'Look out for an eclipse to-night!'[1]

But a word is enough to a wise man. None of these, of course, is a fully-developed judgement (ethical *or* scientific) at all. Just as the rhetorical element in ethics can be paralleled in science, so the rational element in science has its analogue in ethics: and it is only the judgements in which the rational element predominates which can be called 'fully-developed'. What exactly are the logical criteria applicable to ethical judgements? In what sense are moral judgements the 'fruit of experience'? How do they 'account for' our actions and responses? What (in short) is the function of ethics? These problems still remain to be solved.

[1] Recall F. P. Ramsey's suggestion that the force of any empirical generalisation or law of nature is at least partly *imperative*; that 'Every O is X' means, among other things, 'When you come across an O, expect it to be an X!'

10

THE FUNCTION AND DEVELOPMENT
OF ETHICS

'THE function of scientific judgements is to alter one's expectations: that of ethical judgements, by contrast, is to alter one's
feelings and behaviour.' If this were the only result of all that we
have gone through, one might justifiably complain of having been
dragged twice round the world only to be left in exactly the same
position as one started from. For the question we posed in the
very first section took all this for granted. Given that 'ethical'
arguments are those designed to influence behaviour, we asked,
to which arguments ('ethical', needless to say) are we to pay
attention, and which are we to reject, when making up our minds
what to do? That 'ethical' arguments are arguments designed to
influence behaviour seems hardly worth mentioning; the real
problem, which (you may protest) remains as unanswered as ever,
is not *whether* but *in what respects* we are to let them influence our
behaviour.

The defence of this is the same as the defence of all round trips:
it broadens the mind. Although, geographically speaking, the
place you come back to is the 'same' place as that you set out
from, you understand it better, feel more at ease in it, and can be
more intelligently critical of the things that go on there.[1] So now,
although all the real work lies ahead of us, we know very much
better what it will involve, what kinds of approach are sure to be
vain, and which are at all likely to be fruitful.

10.1 *The Question at Issue*

The first step towards solving our problem is to set it into its
background; to see what it means in terms of our life and

---

[1] Cf. T. S. Eliot, *Little Gidding*:
　　　'We shall not cease from exploration
　　　And the end of all our exploring
　　　Will be to arrive where we started
　　　And know the place for the first time.'

activities. The key to the logic of ethical arguments and sentences is to be found in the way in which we come to allow reasons to affect our choice of actions. If we are to discover how to select 'valid' ethical arguments from 'invalid' ones, we must first answer the question, 'How is it that we come to let reasoning affect what we do at all?'

Now this question can be interpreted, and so answered, in a number of different ways. All the interpretations and answers are of interest to us, but only one of them is our direct concern. To mention four possibilities:

(i) It might be taken historically, as calling for a description of the course of events by which our ancestors passed from purely impulsive, unreasoning behaviour to the present, limited degree of rational behaviour; for a record of the different kinds of moral code which have existed, of the attitude, at various stages in the development, to conscience, tyranny and the reform of the moral code; and so on.

(ii) It might be taken psychologically, as calling for a description of the course of events accompanying the development of an individual's powers of moral reasoning; for a factual comparison of the different methods of education; for a study of the relation between poverty and vice; and so on.

(iii) It might be taken logically, as an enquiry about the kinds of change in behaviour characteristic of a decision based on 'moral' grounds; about the way in which reasoning must be designed to influence behaviour if it is to be called 'ethical'; and so on.

(iv) It might be interpreted philosophically, as a demand for a 'justification' of ethics; as asking why reasoning should be allowed to influence our behaviour at all.

Neither of the first two interpretations (nor the anthropological one, which can be regarded as a cross between them) is our immediate business. Answers to all these forms of the question will be interesting as illustrating what we are after, but the nature of the logical criteria applicable to ethics is manifestly independent of them. It cannot matter to us exactly what Socrates said, what attitude the sect of Thugs adopts towards ritual murder, how this or that degree of malnutrition affects individual moral standards, or at what age one first sees that there is a difference between 'wrong' and 'what Daddy forbids'.[1] The truth of what we are now after must be independent of whether Socrates even existed. We must therefore concentrate on the third interpretation mentioned—on the kinds of change in behaviour at which reasoning must be aimed, if we are to call it 'moral' or 'ethical'. If this investigation is a success, its results should help us, by the way, to understand and deal with the fourth, philosophical form of the question.

10.2   *The Notion of 'Duty'*

Suppose, then, that two people are arguing about what to do. The one (A) begins by advocating course α; the other (B) rejects α and proposes β instead. They continue to argue, bringing forward all kinds of reasons for and against α and β. Finally, they come to a decision, agreeing that γ and δ are *really* the right things to do. What kinds of reasons would they have to bring for and against α, β, γ and δ in order for us to say that 'ethical' considerations had affected their decisions, and that they had refrained from α and β in favour of γ and δ because they recognised that it would be 'morally wrong' to do otherwise?

The answer to this question must, in the first place, be twofold. Two types of consideration, not at first sight comparable, cry out to be called 'moral':

(i) arguments showing that γ and δ fulfil a 'duty' in the 'moral code' of the community to which A and B belong, whereas α and β contravene this part of the 'code';

(ii) arguments showing that γ and δ will avoid causing to other members of the community some inconvenience, annoyance or suffering which would be caused by α and β.

The second type of consideration suggests that ethics and ethical language can be regarded as part of the process whereby, as members of a community, we moderate our impulses and adjust our demands so as to reconcile them as far as possible with those of our fellows. But what about the first type of consideration—arguments from 'duty'? How far does it falsify our notions to regard these as a part of the same process? And does

---

[1] We may of course be influenced by the results of historical, psychological or anthropological research when discussing whether the moral code needs to be altered; but that is another matter.

it derogate from the 'absoluteness' of 'duty' to characterise it in terms of this process? The answer is that the only context in which the concept of 'duty' is straightforwardly intelligible is one of communal life—it is, indeed, completely bound up with this very feature of communal life, that we learn to renounce our claims and alter our aims where they conflict with those of our fellows. If this is not immediately obvious, it will become clear when we examine our use of the concept of 'duty' in a concrete case.

Suppose, therefore, that someone declares that he has made an 'anthropological discovery'—the discovery that, whereas there is no single 'duty' which is currently accepted in all communities, there is no community in which some 'duties' are not recognised: 'Particular moral principles are Relative', he may say; 'but all communities recognise the Absolute Value of Duty.'[1] What kind of evidence shall we require him to cite, if he is to establish his discovery?

One sort of testimony will be no good at all: namely, the reports of an anthropologist who has asked the members of all the communities he has visited, 'Do you recognise the Absolute Value of Duty?' The majority of them would not speak his language, and could not understand his question. An unavoidable preliminary to asking them about it would therefore be to discover what their word for 'duty' was (if they had one). Now this is not nearly as simple a matter as it may seem. More than mere 'translation' is required, and it is all too easy to overlook the steps involved.

In order to discover what word these people used for 'duty', he would have to watch their behaviour, and identify the word required, if there were one, by reference to the use they made of it in their relations with one another. And, given this, he would hardly need to ask the question. What features of their behaviour would one have to point to, therefore, in order to justify the discovery?

First, one would presumably remark on the fact that, in all the communities visited, some kinds of conduct were rewarded and reprobated respectively: secondly, that the exact kinds of conduct

---

[1] Cf. A. Macbeath's contribution to the symposium on 'Ethics and Anthropology', in *Aristotelian Soc. Suppl. Vol.* xx (1946).

so treated varied from community to community. But one would require more than this. In all communities, there are many types of behaviour which are socially expected and yet which, taken singly, are hardly what we should call 'duties'. I should not say that I was 'morally' bound to wear white flannels for tennis, even though that is the 'expected' thing, and even though I might risk some slight degree of ostracism if I were to wear grey ones at a polite tennis party. Nor should I regard a single public belch, or ignorance of the formal modes of address, as grounds for a 'moral' reproach.

It is true that one does recognise a duty to conform on the whole: a man who always dresses eccentrically, never shows any respect for persons, and habitually belches in public does seem to invite criticism—and 'moral' criticism at that. But, in recognising this, we are concerned less with the eccentric behaviour itself than with the fact that it gives offence to others, and with the inconsiderateness of a man who can consistently ignore that fact.

Suppose, for example, that a Patagonian were giving a list of the 'duties' current among the English. He would not start off his list with points of dress or etiquette: still less would he class our going in for crossword puzzles, and giving a prize to the sender of the first correct solution opened, as a striking example of our recognition of the value of 'duty'. His interest would be more in types of behaviour which, if given up generally, would lead to distress in the society. Further, if winning competitions or wearing the right-coloured trousers were the only type of behaviour he found rewarded or punished among the inhabitants of our island; and if we let murder and rape, robbery and lying go by unnoticed, he would hesitate before saying that we provided a confirming instance of the law at all. But then, if that were the way we carried on, he could hardly call us a 'community' either!

This fact is most important: it shows us the nature of the 'discovery', and (by implication) that of our concept of 'duty', too. For consider what kinds of thing we require before we agree to call any collection of people a 'community'. Suppose, for example, that we visit an island, and find that its inhabitants all habitually avoid types of behaviour particularly liable to inconvenience their fellows: then we shall be prepared to refer to the inhabitants of the island as forming a single 'community'. And we shall also say that the members of the community 'recognise a duty to one another', and 'have a moral code'. But if, instead, we find that we have to divide the inhabitants into two classes, C_1 and C_2—such that members of C_1 are scrupulous only in so far as their conduct affects other members of C_1, but ignore the interests of those of C_2; and those of C_2 respect the interests of other members of C_2, but ignore those of C_1—we shall not be able to call them 'members of a single community' at all. In fact, we shall call the two sets of people, C_1 and C_2, 'separate communities'. Likewise, we shall not be able to say that members of C_1 'recognise any duty' to members of C_2, or vice versa. But we shall have to agree that, within C_1 and C_2, duties are recognised: only in the extreme case, if C_2 consists of one man only, who has 'cut himself off from all communal life', and carries on regardless of anyone else, can we say that there is anyone on the island who 'recognises *no* duties'.[1]

The degree of mutual respect we find between members of the two classes decides the extent to which we can call them parts of 'a single community'. The same degree of mutual respect decides how far we can say that the inhabitants 'recognise common duties'. Only if we found no such respect between any of the people on the island, and so no semblance of a 'community', could we say that there was no recognition of the value of duty.

The 'anthropological discovery' that 'all communities recognise the Absolute Value of Duty' is therefore not a discovery at all, but something which an anthropologist could safely announce before he ever set out: it only explains, in an obscure and roundabout way, part of what we mean by the notion of a 'community'. 'In all "communities" (i.e. groups of people living together, and respecting one another's interests)', our informant is saying, in effect, 'people control their behaviour so as to have regard for one another's interests'. His 'law of human nature' is a truism, admitting of only one possible exception—a 'community' of angels, who always managed to do what was right instinctively and so had no need for a moral code. They might conceivably be said 'not to recognise the Absolute Value of Duty', but this

---

[1] Even he may be described as recognising 'duties towards himself' and, perhaps, 'duties towards his God'—but to say this is to shift our ground somewhat.

would be the case only because they never had cause to stop and 'recognise' it. No less talented 'community' could be so placed.

Even if 5000 supporters of the 'imperative doctrine'—all of them so enlightened as to realise the 'irrational' nature of morality, and all of them vowing to renounce ethical words and arguments as 'mere rationalisation'—even if they tried to live together as a community, they would soon have to adopt rules of behaviour; and, when it came to educating their children, some of their words would perforce become 'ethical'. 'You'll *burn* yourself if you play with fire', uttered as the child was pulled away from it, would acquire the meaning of our own, 'You *mustn't* play with the fire, or you'll *harm* yourself'; 'It's *annoying* of you to cut holes in Daddy's trousers', accompanied by the removal of trousers and scissors, would come to mean, 'It's *naughty* of you to cut holes in Daddy's trousers'; and so on. And, after 20 years, either their 'community' would have ceased to exist, or it would have developed a code as 'moral' as any other—and the fact that the familiar words, 'good', 'bad', 'wicked' and 'virtuous', had been given up would be irrelevant. This sort of thing does happen (I am told) in 'progressive schools', whose products grow up using words like 'co-operative', 'undesirable' and 'anti-social', with all the rhetorical force and emotional associations commonly belonging to 'good', 'wrong' and 'wicked'.

The concept of 'duty', in short, is inextricable from the 'mechanics' of social life, and from the practices adopted by different communities in order to make living together in proximity tolerable or even possible. We need not therefore worry about the apparent duality of ethical arguments—about the contrast between arguments from 'duty' and arguments from the welfare of our fellows. And we can fairly characterise ethics as a part of the process whereby the desires and actions of the members of a community are harmonised.

The central importance of 'disposition' in ethics is now understandable: there would be no use for ethical reasoning, either among people whose feelings were wholly·unalterable (and who would therefore behave exactly the same whether exhorted to change or not) or, on the other hand, among angels, whose dispositions were always of the best (and who would therefore have no need to inquire or discuss what to do).

Further, the analysis of what I have called the 'function' of ethics can now be completed; we can provisionally define it as being 'to correlate our feelings and behaviour in such a way as to make the fulfilment of everyone's aims and desires as far as possible compatible'.

It is in the light of this function, and of its context of communal living, that we must examine

    (i) the development of morality and of ethical reasoning, and

    (ii) the logical rules to be applied to ethical arguments.[1]

10.3   *The Development of Ethics.* (I)

Historically and psychologically alike, the development of ethics is most conveniently described in two contrasted stages. This division we shall find later reflected in the logic of ethics.

The first and most obvious way of preventing conflicts of interest in a community (whether a tribe or a family) is for all its members to have the same aims, the same interests, the same desires, hopes and fears; in fact the same dispositions. In its early stages, therefore, morality boils down to 'doing the done thing': and this is true, both of the way in which a child learns from its parents, and, in social pre-history, of moral codes. Primitive ethics is 'deontological', a matter of rigid duties, taboos, customs and commandments. It prevents conflicts of interest by keeping the dispositions of all concerned aligned, and condemns behaviour directed away from the prescribed aims. Further, these aims are not advocated but imposed, the use of

---

[1] 'Ah!' you may say, 'But compatibility of aims and desires takes one only a certain distance, since it could be achieved on various levels of excellence. Push-pin, to use Bentham's illustration, is as good as poetry, as an example of a non-competitive good.' It is true that we should deplore the taste of a community whose members did not discriminate between poetry and parlour games; but we could not condemn them on *moral* grounds. It is also true that, when discussing the arts, we often say things like, 'You *ought* to hear his violin concerto'; but again the notion of obligation is involved only by transference. So also is it when, in talking to a friend with a busy evening before him, we say, 'You *ought* to have a rest this afternoon'. One would never think of using examples of this kind when teaching anyone the notion of what he 'ought' and 'ought not' to do: the idea of obligation, as it affects our decisions, is primarily moral. In consequence, the present discussion must elucidate the notion of *moral* obligation first: less primitive and transferred uses of the notion will be touched on later—e.g. in §§ 11.8 and 12.1. On Bentham, see § 13.6 below.

ethical language being part of the behaviour adopted by 'those in authority' for enforcing co-operation: so no wonder if ethical utterances are often 'rhetorical'.

Respect for fixed 'social practices' (or 'done things'), though most characteristic of primitive morality, continues throughout the later stages of development, and can be recognised in our own societies. Although 'doing the done thing' may be merely conventionalism, it may equally be anything but that; especially in those situations in which *some* common practice must be adopted and, within limits, it does not matter what.

The Rule of the Road is a good example. By appealing to this practice, the statements, 'It is right to drive on the left in England' and 'You ought to be driving on the left', may be used to alter the hearer's disposition, so that in the future he drives on the left. (The ethical judgements are here used 'persuasively'.) But the same utterances can also be used simply to draw attention to the rule, or to evince the speaker's displeasure.

Now consider two more subtle examples: first, that of the schoolboy who hears that he has been given his cricket colours. His immediate reaction will probably be one of pleasure, and he will cry out, 'Why, that is good news!' But his school-fellows may feel differently about it, especially if they suspect that he has been given them only because the cricket captain is fond of him. Then they will do their best to make him feel that his rejoicing is misplaced, pointing out (for example) that another, better bats- man has had to go without colours as a result. If the schoolboy has a tender conscience, accepts the 'principle' that cricket colours should go to the best cricketers, and not just to the captain's favourites, and admits both that he is rather a friend of the captain's, and that the man who has had to go without has the better batting record and more 1st XI matches to his credit; then he may eventually say, 'Well, naturally I was pleased at the time, but I see now that I *ought not really* to have been given them'.

In this example, several of the most characteristic features of ethics are displayed. To start with, an ethical term is used simply to evince pleasure. Next, contrary feelings are aroused in, and evinced by others. These are concerned at the way in which the schoolboy's award has cut across another's interests—in this case, someone's 'natural right' to colours, based on a generally accepted practice. (The conflict between one schoolboy's winning his colours, and the other's failure to obtain them, is a typically ethical one, in that it is only possible for one of them to have them.) Reasons are advanced for the view that the award was not *really good*. The principle is appealed to as authority. Finally, the schoolboy admits the facts, accepts the principle, and agrees that, though the news originally *seemed* good to him, it was not *really* good.

Again, suppose that I am already rich, and then win £10,000 in a lottery. At first, I may excusably rejoice. But now someone may try to persuade me that I *ought not* to be so glad. He may remind me of all the shillings paid by labourers out of their wages, that went to make up my prize; he may point out that I already have as much money as I have any use for; and he may insist that the prize-money would do more good anywhere but in my bank. In the end, I may come to admit that, however pleased I was to win the prize, it was, all in all, not a good thing that I did. Though it *seemed* good to me at first, it was not *really* good. In this case, a number of 'principles' may be appealed to—for instance, the 'principles' that opportunities for satisfying people's needs should not be neglected; that no one should retain more than he needs of anything while others suffer through going without; and that one should not accept anything which has been got by unnecessary suffering.

Appeal to a 'principle' in ethics is like appeal to a 'law' in science: 'principles' and 'laws of nature' may both be thought of as shorthand summaries of experience—as condensed comparisons. If I explain the 'bending' of a stick in water by reference to the laws of optics, my purpose is to relate the present experience to past observations and experiments; the explanation in terms of 'Snell's Law' is then shorthand for, 'If you had put the stick above a bonfire, you'd have expected it to shimmer in the heated air, wouldn't you? And if.... And if.... So you see, the look of bentness in this case was to be expected.' Likewise, appeal to the 'principle' that you should not accept anything got by unnecessary suffering can be thought of as shorthand for, 'If you found out that your garden was being cultivated by a team of slaves, who were whipped until they produced all the flowers and vegetables you asked for, you wouldn't ask for them any more, would you? And if.... And if.... So you see, winning £10,000 in this lottery was nothing to be so pleased about.'

Like scientific theories again, all principles are not equally well established; some refer to wider, some to narrower ranges of experience. There is an air of conventionality about the principle that the best cricketers shall be given their colours, which is absent from the principles involved in the second example. The principle that all promises ought to be kept may seem less compelling than the principle that unnecessary suffering ought to be prevented; but, equally, it is less conventional than the rules by which colours are distributed. We shall have to return to these differences in discussing the next stage of development.

10.4 *The Development of Ethics.* (II)

In any particular community, certain principles are current— that is to say, attention is paid to certain types of argument, as appealing to accepted criteria of 'real goodness', 'real rightness', 'real obligation', etc. From these, the members of the community are expected to try and regulate their lives and judgements. And such a set of principles, of 'prima facie obligations',[1] of 'categorical imperatives',[2] is what we call the 'moral code' of the community.

At the primitive stage of development, this is something fixed and unalterable.[3] There is no room for criticism of the moral code as a whole, as there is of a particular action, expression of pleasure, or ethical judgement. However, the methods used in primitive communities to harmonise the desires and actions of their members are very crude and, although at first they may do their job, something always happens to throw doubt on them. New opportunities emerge. People discover that different principles of the code conflict. As a result of contact with other

---

[1] W. D. Ross, *The Right and the Good*, p. 19.

[2] Kant, op. cit. p. 37.

[3] As a matter of anthropology, this is not altogether exact: the features characteristic of my 'second phase of development' are probably present to a limited extent in all communities. The division I adopt is, however, an illuminating one; and this inaccuracy is not one which can affect the validity of the logical considerations of Chapter 11, to which we are leading up.

peoples having different codes, or of changes within the community, they begin to question not only the rightness of particular actions but also the standards laid down in the code. They realise that, as a result of these changes, the present code is causing frustration and suffering which, by making a specific alteration in the practices of the community, could be avoided—and avoided without incurring any comparable evil.

The same situation arises within the family, when the growing child, having learnt to accept appeal to a principle as an argument for and against actions, begins to question the need for some of the principles with which he has been brought up, and to argue that they cause needless annoyance. When this happens, he ceases to accept authority as the sole moral argument, and becomes himself a 'responsible being'.

At this stage, there are two possible reactions: either for those in authority—those who enforce the existing 'code'—to assert its absolute rightness, and to attempt to legislate for every possibility; or for them to agree, first to criticism, and eventually to modification of the code, so as to remove its objectionable features. If the first course is adopted, the continual changes in the circumstances of the community tend only to aggravate the situation: the second course, on the other hand, represents a natural extension of the process by which moral codes themselves grow out of conflicts of interest—i.e. it takes account of the function of ethics.

When it is recognised that the members of a community have the right to criticise the existing practices, and to suggest new ones, a new phase in the development of ethics begins. In this phase, it is the *motives* of actions and the *results* of social practices, rather than 'the letter of the law', which are emphasised. The 'deontological'[1] code was at first supreme; the 'teleological'[2] criterion now amplifies it, and provides a standard by which to criticise it. This does not mean that morality becomes wholly

---

[1] 'Deontological theories hold that there are ethical propositions of the form: "Such and such a kind of action would always be right (or wrong) in such and such circumstances, no matter what its consequences might be."' (Broad, *Five Types of Ethical Theory*, p. 206.)

[2] 'Teleological theories hold that the rightness or wrongness of an action is always determined by its tendency to produce certain consequences which are intrinsically good or bad.' (Broad, op. cit. p. 207.)

teleological, as Utilitarianism[1] would suggest. All that happens
is that the initially inflexible system of taboos is transformed into
a *developing* moral code—a code which, in unambiguous cases,
remains mandatory, but whose interpretation in equivocal cases
and whose future development are controlled by appeal to the
function of ethics; that is, to the general requirement that preventable suffering shall be avoided.

The contrast between the two main phases of development is
strikingly reflected in the contrast between the Old and New
Testaments. The moral code of the Israelites—a nomadic tribe
in a hostile environment—was understandably strict; but, in
the more settled atmosphere of Palestine under Roman rule,
anomalies arose in this code. Jesus was therefore able to criticise
contemporary ethical practices in a spirit to which the Pharisees
could hardly take open exception. Whatever form their questions
took, they could not get him to say that his teaching was meant
to *supersede* the Law and the Prophets: in fact, whenever there
was any discussion of the Jewish code, he made it clear that he
took it as his starting-point. Instead, it was his aim throughout
to get the existing code applied in a more intelligent manner:
to point out that the prevention of human suffering is more important than formal respect for obsolete customs. Thus, when
challenged in the Temple about the propriety of healing the sick
on the Sabbath, he asked, 'Whether is it lawful on the sabbath
days to do good or to do evil? to save life or for to destroy it?',[2] and
went on to heal the man with a withered hand. Again, in a phrase
echoed by Kant[3] he declared, 'Whatsoever ye would that men
should do to you, even so do ye to them. This is the law and the
Prophets.'[4] He was ready to criticise the existing code, certainly;
but only by reference to its function—the function which he expressed, in his own way, as the 'New Commandment', to love
one another.

We can trace the beginnings of this new outlook further back:
it is clearly to be seen, breaking through the old, rigid morality,

---

[1] 'The doctrine that it is the duty of each to aim at the maximum happiness of
all, and to subordinate everything else to this end.' (Broad, op. cit. p. 183.)
[2] Luke vi.
[3] Cf. *Fundamental Principles of the Metaphysic of Ethics* (tr. Abbott), p. 66: 'Act
always on such a maxim as thou canst at the same time will to be a universal law.'
[4] Matt. vii.

in the more 'advanced' of the Greek tragedies. Contrast, for example, the approaches which different dramatists adopted towards the same traditional stories, and the lessons which they drew from them. Both Sophocles and Euripides wrote plays, which have survived, using the story of Electra and Orestes as their foundation. Sophocles produced an archaic 'drama of duty'. In his play, the central figures perform their ritual act of vengeance—the murder of their own mother, Clytemnestra—without emotion: 'there is no shrinking back, no question of conscience at all.'[1] Euripides' play is in vivid contrast: it is a psychological 'drama of motive'. After the murder, Orestes and Electra suffer 'a long agony of remorse';[2] and even the gods, through the mouth of Castor, are made to condemn the act. For Euripides, the blood-feud has lost its absolute authority. For Sophocles, however, old ways held good, and there could be no question of blame.

We can now see how it is that different 'moral principles' have such different degrees of 'conventionality'. To return to the three examples discussed before: the 'duty' to give cricket-colours to the best cricketers, the 'duty' to keep a promise, and the 'duty' to prevent avoidable suffering. The reason why the first of these appears comparatively conventional, the last comparatively compelling, is clear, when we bear in mind the overall requirement that, wherever we can, we shall prevent suffering from being inflicted upon others. To abolish the custom of giving cricket-colours would have a trivial effect by these standards; to abandon the social practice of promise-keeping might, by the same standards, be expected to have intolerable results; and the third principle cannot be rejected, without completely abandoning the very ideas of 'duty' and of 'ethics'.

[1] Gilbert Murray, *Euripides and his Age*, p. 154.
[2] Op. cit. p. 156: the whole discussion of the contrast between Sophocles' and Euripides' treatments of the story is well worth study (op. cit. pp. 152–7).

11

THE LOGIC OF MORAL REASONING

Iт is in relation to this background that we have to discuss the logic of ethical reasoning. I do not mean that the validity of our results will depend at all on the truth of any historical and psychological facts that I have quoted: this will not be the case. Such facts will be useful more as illustrating the parts which different kinds of ethical question and statement play in our lives. The only facts, upon which the truth of what we have to say will depend, are those more familiar, unquestionable facts of usage— of the kind that we found obliquely expressed in the 'anthropological law', 'All communities recognise the absolute value of duty'—namely, facts about the ways in which we do recognise a 'duty', a 'community' and so on.

Bearing this background in mind, then, what questions shall we expect to find arising in ethical contexts, and how are they to be answered?

11.1 *Questions about the Rightness of Actions*

Consider, first, the simplest and commonest ethical question, 'Is this the right thing to do?' We are taught when young to behave in ways laid down as appropriate to the situations we are in. Sometimes there is a doubt whether or no a proposed action conforms to the moral code. It is to resolve such doubts that we are taught to use the question, 'Is this the right thing to do?', and, provided the code contains a relevant principle, the answer is 'Yes' or 'No', according as the proposed action does or does not conform. Questions like, 'What is the right thing to do?', 'What ought really to have been done?' and 'Was this the correct decision?' do similar jobs, and can be understood in similar ways.

In consequence, if someone complains, 'That wasn't the thing to do' or 'That was hardly the way of going about things, was it?', his remark may have a genuinely ethical force. And this remains the case, although the only *fact* at issue is whether the action in question belongs to a class of actions generally approved of in the speaker's community. Some people have been misled by this into arguing that many so-called 'ethical' statements are just disguised statements of fact; that 'what seems to be an ethical judgement is very often a factual classification of an action'.[1] But this is a mistake. What makes us call a judgement 'ethical' is the fact that it is used to harmonise people's actions (rather than to give a recognisable description of a state of affairs, for instance); judgements of the kind concerned are unquestionably 'ethical' by this standard; and the fact that the action belongs to a certain class of actions is not so much the 'disguised meaning of' as the 'reason for' the ethical judgement.

Furthermore, the test for answering questions of this simple kind remains the accepted practice, even though the particular action may have unfortunate results. Suppose that I am driving along a winding, country road, and deliberately keep on the left-hand side going round the blind corners. It may happen that a driver going the other way is cutting his corners, so that we collide head-on; but this does not affect the propriety of my driving. My care to keep to the left remains 'right', my decision not to take any risks on the corners remains 'correct', in spite of the fact that the consequences, in the event, were unfortunate. Provided that I had no reason to expect such an upset, provided that I was not to know how the other man was behaving—knowledge which would have made a material difference to my decision, and would have taken my situation out of the straightforward class to which the rule applies—the existence of the Rule of the Road is all that is needed to make my decision 'correct'.

11.2   *Reasoning about the Rightness of Actions*

This brings us to questions about one's 'reasons' for a decision or an action.

If the policeman investigating the accident asks the other driver, 'Why were you driving on the right-hand side of the road?', he will have to produce a long story in order to justify himself. If, however, I am asked why I was driving on the *left*, the only answer I can give is that the left-hand side is the one on

---

[1] Ayer, *Language, Truth and Logic* (2nd ed.), p. 21.

which one *does* drive in England—that the Rule of the Road *is* to drive on the left.

Again, the schoolboy who gets his colours through favouritism may ask, 'And why shouldn't I have been given them?' If he does so, his schoolfellows will point out that it is the practice (and in fact the whole point of colours) for them to go to the best cricketers; and that there were better cricketers to whom they could have been given. And this will be all the justification needed.

Finally, an example in which the logical structure of this type of 'reasoning' is fully set out: suppose that I say, 'I feel that I ought to take this book and give it back to Jones' (so reporting on my feelings). You may ask me, 'But ought you really to do so?' (turning the question into an ethical one), and it is up to me to produce my 'reasons', if I have any. To begin with, then, I may reply that I ought to take it back to him, 'because I promised to let him have it back before midday'—so classifying my position as one of type S_1. 'But ought you *really*?', you may repeat. If you do, I can relate S_1 to a more general S_2, explaining, 'I ought to, because I promised to let him have it back'. And if you continue to ask, 'But why ought you really?', I can answer, in succession, 'Because I ought to do whatever I promise him to do' (S_3), 'Because I ought to do whatever I promise anyone to do' (S_4), and 'Because anyone ought to do whatever he promises anyone else that he will do' or 'Because it was a promise' (S_5). Beyond this point, however, the question cannot arise: there is no more general 'reason' to be given beyond one which relates the action in question to an accepted social practice.

11.3   *Conflicts of Duties*

This straightforward method of answering the questions, 'Is this the right thing to do?' and 'Why ought you to do that?', can apply only in situations to which a rule of action is unambiguously appropriate. The most interesting practical questions, however, always arise in those situations in which one set of facts drives us one way, and another pulls us in the opposite direction.

If the muck-heap at the bottom of my garden bursts into flames in midsummer, and someone says, 'There's nothing to be surprised at in that: it's a simple case of spontaneous combustion. Surely you've heard of ricks burning in the same kind of way?', his explanation may satisfy me: the analogy between the burning of my muck-heap and the spontaneous combustion of a hayrick is close enough for it to be plausible. But, if it is late January, I may reject the explanation, and protest, 'That's all very well in July or August, but not in midwinter: whoever heard of a hayrick catching fire with snow on the ground?', and, unless he can assure me that it does quite frequently happen, I shall continue to hanker after a different explanation.

In much the same way, the fact that I promised to let Jones have his book back will seem to me reason enough for taking it to him on time—if that is all that there is to it. But, if I have a critically ill relative in the house, who cannot be left, the issue is complicated. The situation is not sufficiently unambiguous for reasoning from the practice of promise-keeping to be conclusive: I may therefore argue, 'That's all very well in the ordinary way, but not when I've got my grandmother to look after: whoever heard of risking someone else's life just to return a borrowed book?' Unless evidence is produced that the risks involved in breaking my promise to Jones are even greater than those attending my grandmother, if she is left alone, I shall conclude that it is my duty to remain with her.

Given two conflicting claims, that is to say, one has to weigh up, as well as one can, the risks involved in ignoring either, and choose 'the lesser of the two evils'. Appeal to a single current principle, though the primary test of the rightness of an action, cannot therefore be relied on as a universal test: where this fails, we are driven back upon our estimate of the probable consequences. And this is the case, not only where there is a conflict of duties, but also, for instance, in circumstances in which, although no matter of principle is involved, some action of ours can nevertheless meet another's need. Here again we naturally and rightly conclude that the action is one that we 'ought' to perform, but we record in our usage the difference between such circumstances and those in which a matter of principle *is* involved: although we should say that we 'ought' to perform the action, we should not usually say that we had a 'moral obligation' to perform it, or even that it was our 'duty'. We here appeal to consequences in the absence of a relevant principle, or 'duty'.[1]

So it comes about that we can, in many cases, justify an individual action by reference to its estimated consequences. Such a reference is no substitute for a principle, where any principle is at issue: but moral reasoning is so complex, and has to cover such a variety of types of situation, that no one logical test (such as 'appeal to an accepted principle') can be expected to meet every case.

11.4   *Reasoning about the Justice of Social Practices*

All these types of question are intelligible by reference to the primitive stage in the development of ethics. As soon as we turn to the second stage, however, there is room for questions of a radically different type.

Recall our analysis of 'explanation'. There I pointed out that, although on most occasions the question, 'Is this really straight?', has a use, situations might be encountered in which the question, in its ordinary sense, simply cannot be asked. These occasions were of two kinds:[2]

(i) those on which the criterion of straightness is itself questioned, within the framework of a particular theory, and

(ii) those on which the criteria of straightness used in alternative theories are found to be different.

The same kinds of situation arise (and, indeed, are more familiar) in ethics. To give an example of the first: so long as one confines oneself to a particular moral code, no more general 'reason' can be given for an action than one which relates it to a practice (or principle) within that code. If an astronomer, who is discussing light-rays in outer space in terms of non-Euclidean geometry, is asked what reason he has for saying that they are straight, he can only reply, 'Well, they just *are*': in the same way, if I am asked why one ought to keep a particular promise, all that I can say is, 'Well, one just *ought*'. Within the framework of a particular scientific theory, one can ask of most things,

---

[1] We can, and sometimes do, employ the language of 'duty' in this case also, by treating the reference to consequences as a reference to a completely general 'duty' to help one another when in need. For our present purposes, the difference between these two ways of putting it is purely verbal.

[2] See § 8.5 above.

'Is *this* really straight?', but the *criterion* of straightness cannot be questioned: within the framework of a particular moral code, one can ask of most individual actions, 'Is *this* really right?', but the *standards* of rightness cannot be questioned.

As an example of the second type of situation: the question, 'Which is it really right to do—to have only one wife like a Christian, or to have anything up to four like the Mohammedans?', is odd in the same way as the question, 'Is a light-ray going past the sun really straight, as a non-Euclidean theorist declares, or deflected, as a Euclidean theorist says?' If corresponding standards in two moral codes are found to be different, the question, 'Which of these is really right?', cannot arise. Or rather (to put the same thing in another way), if the question *does* arise, it arises in a very different way, serves a different purpose, and requires an answer of a different sort.

What kind of purpose does it serve, and what kind of answer does it require? In science, if I insist on asking of the standard of straightness, 'But is *it* really straight?', I am going outside the framework of that particular scientific theory. To question the standard is to question the theory—to criticise the theory *as a whole*—not to ask for an explanation of the phenomenon ostensibly under discussion (the properties of light-rays in outer space). So again in ethics: if I ask of the behaviour prescribed in any standard of conduct, 'Is *it* really right?', I am going outside the moral code; and my question is a criticism of the practice *as a practice*, not a request for a justification of a particular case of promise-keeping (or whatever it may be).

To question the rightness of a particular action is one thing: to question the justice of a practice *as a practice* is another. It is this second type of question which becomes intelligible when we turn to the second stage of development. If a society has a developing moral code, changes in the economic, social, political or psychological situation may lead people to regard the existing practices as unnecessarily restrictive, or as dangerously lax. If this happens, they may come to ask, for instance, 'Is it right that women should be debarred from smoking in public?', or 'Would it not be better if there were no mixed bathing after dark?', in each case questioning the practice concerned *as a whole*. The answer to be given will (remembering the function of ethics) be reached by estimating the probable consequences

  (i) of retaining the present practice, and

  (ii) of adopting the suggested alternative.

If, as a matter of fact, there is good reason to suppose that the sole consequences of making the proposed change would be to avoid some existing distresses, then, as a matter of ethics, there is certainly a good reason for making the change. As usual, however, the logically straightforward case is a comparatively uninteresting one: in practice, the interesting problems are those which arise when the happy consequences of the change are not so certain, or when they are likely to be accompanied by new, though perhaps less serious, distresses. And what stake may reasonably be risked for any particular likelihood of gain is something only to be settled with confidence—if then—by appeal to experience.

11.5 *The Two Kinds of Moral Reasoning*

Two cautions are necessary. Although, as a matter of logic, it makes sense to discuss the justice of any social practice, some practices will in fact always remain beyond question. It is inconceivable (for instance) that any practice will ever be suggested, to replace promising and promise-keeping, which would be anything like as effective. Even in the most 'advanced' stages of morality, therefore, promise-keeping will remain right.

Again, the fact that I can discuss the rightness of promise-keeping as a practice, in this way, does not imply that there is any way of calling in question the rightness of keeping individual promises. In arguing that promise-keeping will remain right at all stages, 'because its abolition would lead to suffering', I am doing something different in important respects from what I am doing, if I say that I ought to take this book back to Jones now, 'because I promised to'. I can justify the latter statement by pointing out that I am in any of the situations S_1 to S_5:[1] and such reasons will be acceptable in any community which expects promises to be fulfilled. But I cannot further justify it by saying, 'Because one must not inflict avoidable suffering': this kind of

[1] See § 11.2 above.

reason is appropriate only when discussing whether a social practice should be retained or changed.

The two kinds of moral reasoning which we have encountered are, therefore, distinct. Each provides its own logical criteria—criteria which are appropriate to the criticism of individual actions, or social practices, but not both. It was this distinction between the 'reasons' for an individual action and the 'reasons' for a social practice which Socrates made as he waited for the hemlock: he was ready to die rather than repudiate it—refusing, when given the chance, to escape from the prison and so avoid execution. As an Athenian citizen, he saw that it was his duty (regardless of the actual consequences in his particular case) to respect the verdict and sentence of the court. To have escaped would have been to ignore this duty. By doing so, he would not merely have questioned the justice of the verdict in his case: he would have renounced the Athenian constitution and moral code as a whole. This he was not prepared to do.

The history of Socrates illustrates the nature of the distinction, and the kind of situation in which it is important: the kind of situation in which it ceases to be of value can be seen from the story of Hampden and the 'ship-money'. It is those principles which we recognise as just which we have to respect most scrupulously: if we are prepared to dispute the justice of a principle, everything is altered. One of the most striking ways of disputing the justice of a principle is, indeed, by refusing to conform on a particular occasion: and such refusals give rise, in law and morality alike, to the notion of a 'test case'.

Over 'test cases', the distinction between the two sorts of moral reasoning vanishes. In justifying the action concerned, one no longer refers to the current practice: it is the injustice of the accepted code, or the greater justice of some alternative proposal, which is now important. The justification of the action is made 'a matter of principle' and the change in the logical criteria appropriate follows accordingly. In making an action a test case one must, however, take care that one's intentions are clear. If this is not done, the action may be criticised on the wrong level. It may be condemned, either by reference to the very principle it was intended to dispute, or as self-interested, or both; and the question of principle may go against one by default. There is an element of pathos about a test case which goes wrong for this reason; but those men whose protests are carried off successfully are often remembered as heroes.

11.6 *The Limited Scope of Comparisons between Social Practices*

The scope of ethical reasoning is limited as well as defined by the framework of activities in which it plays its part. We have already encountered one limitation: that, in unequivocal cases, once it has been shown that an action is in accordance with an established practice, there is no further room for the question, 'But is this *really* the right thing to do?' The other questions which we have been discussing are, however, limited in similar ways, which we must now turn and consider.

Consider, first, the kinds of circumstance in which we question the rightness of a social practice. If, for example, it is regarded as disgusting for women to smoke in public, and I ask, 'But ought they really to be debarred from doing so?', the nature of my inquiry is clear: I am suggesting that in future, when a lady lights a cigarette, people need not turn away in disapproval, look horrified, or cut her from their acquaintance. The change I propose is quite sufficiently indicated in my question for us to be able to discuss it as it stands, and even reach a decision about it, on its merits.

If, on the other hand, I ask, 'Is it really right to have only one wife, like the Christians, or would it be better to have anything up to four, according to the old Mohammedan practice?', my question is a good deal less intelligible. In the first place, there seems to be a suggestion that we abandon our present practice in favour of an alternative one; but the exact nature of the change proposed is not clear; so how can one begin to estimate its probable consequences? Secondly, it is questionable whether the practices compared can be regarded as 'alternatives' at all. The ramifications, both in Christian and in Muslim societies, of the institution of marriage, its relations to the institutions of property, of parenthood and so on, are so complex that there is no question of simply replacing the one institution by the other. Such different parts does the institution of 'marriage' play in the ways of life of a Christian society and of a Muslim one that we might even feel it hardly right to describe Christian and

Muslim marriage as being instances of the 'same' institution at all.

The question, 'Which of these institutions is "right"?', is therefore an unreal one, and there is no conceivable way of answering it—as it stands. The only way of understanding it is to regard it as an even more general question, in a disguised form. As we saw, the question, 'Is this the right thing to do?', when persisted in beyond a certain point, has to be understood as an inquiry about the justice of the social practice of which 'this' is an instance—but an inquiry couched in an inappropriate form: so now the question, 'Is it right for me to marry one wife or four?', has to be transformed, first into, 'Is Christian marriage or Muslim marriage the better practice?'; and then again into, 'Is the Christian or the Muslim *way of life* the better?'

When someone asks of two superficially similar institutions, from different ways of life, 'Which is the better?', one may have to say that, by themselves, they are not comparable: all that can be compared are the ways of life *as wholes*. And *this* comparison is, if anything, a private one: which is to say, not that it *cannot* be reasoned about, but that, reason as you may, the final decision is personal. There is no magic wand which will turn the English social system into a Muslim one overnight: the only practical use for the question, 'Which way of life is the better?', is in the service of a personal decision—for example, whether to remain here in our society, such as it is, or to go and live as an Arab tribesman in the desert.

In general, then, if one is to *reason* about social practices, the only occasions on which one can discuss the question which of two practices is the better are those on which they are genuine alternatives: when it would be practicable to change from one to the other *within one society*. Given this, the question, 'Which is the better?', has the force of, 'If we changed from one to the other, would the change have happy or unhappy consequences on the whole?' But, if this condition is not satisfied, there is, morally speaking, *no* reasoning about the question, and pretended arguments about the merits of rival systems—personal preferences apart—are of value only as rhetoric. (More of this later.)[1]

---

[1] See § 13.6 below.

11.7 *The Limits to the Analysis of Ethical Concepts*

Consider, secondly, the musty old conundrum over which moral philosophers have battled for so long: namely, whether the 'real' analysis of 'X is right' is 'X is an instance of a rule of action (or maxim, or prima facie obligation)', or 'X is the alternative which of all those open to us is likely to have the best results'.[1] If the scope of ethical reasoning is limited by its function, does this question fall within or outside the limits?

To begin with, it must be clear from our discussion that, in talking of the 'analysis' of 'X is right', philosophers cannot be referring to the 'meaning' of 'X is right'. The 'meaning' of 'X is right' is certainly neither of the alternatives proposed: it is 'X is the thing to do in these circumstances, to encourage others to do in similar circumstances, etc. etc.' To suppose otherwise is to be trapped into the 'naturalistic fallacy'[2]—that is to say, it is to confuse facts and values (the reasons for an ethical judgement, and the judgement itself), by attempting to express the 'meaning' of an *ethical* judgement in *factual* form. The question which the 'analysis' of 'X is right' *can* answer is the question, 'Which kinds of reason are required in order to show that something is right (i.e. the thing to do, to encourage others to do, etc.)—(i) that it is an instance of a rule of action, or (ii) that it is the alternative likely to have the best results?'

The answer, with comparatively little over-simplification, is that it depends upon the nature of the 'thing'. If it is an action which is an unambiguous instance of a maxim generally accepted in the community concerned, it will be right just because it *is* an instance of such a maxim; but, if it is an action over which there is a 'conflict of duties', or is itself a principle (or social practice) as opposed to a particular action, it will be right or wrong according as its consequences are likely to be good or bad.

When we bear in mind the function of ethics, therefore, we see that the answer to the philosophers' question is, 'Either, depending on the nature of the case'. The question, in other words, falls within the logical limits set by the function of ethics—provided only that you are prepared to accept 'Either' as an answer.

As a matter of history, philosophers have not been so prepared:

---

[1] Cf. Broad, *Five Types of Ethical Theory*, pp. 206–7.   [2] See § 4.5 above.

they have tended to demand an 'unequivocal' answer—'The first' or 'The second', and not 'Either'—and to assume that either the 'deontological' or the 'teleological' answer must be 'true', and the other 'false'.[1] But this is to mistake the nature of the problem. Questions presenting a pair of alternants, 'Which is true—A or B?' are of two kinds: those to which the answer can sensibly be 'Either' or 'Neither', and those to which the only possible answers are 'A' and 'B'. If I report to the police that I have seen a stolen car being driven along the Bath Road, and they ask me, 'In which direction was it going?', the only positive answers I can give are 'Eastwards' and 'Westwards'. I can, of course, say, 'I didn't notice', but I *cannot* say 'Either' or 'Neither': if it was being driven along the Bath Road at all, it *must* have been going in the one direction or the other. This seems to be the kind of model which philosophers have had before them when attempting to answer their question, 'Which is the analysis of "X is right"—A or B?' In any case, they have certainly overlooked the resemblance of their question to the other, verbally-similar type of question, represented in the extreme case by the algebraic query, 'Which is the correct solution of the equation $x^2 - 5x + 6 = 0$, $x = 2$ or $x = 3$?'—the answer to which is, 'Either, depending on the conditions of the particular problem'.

If we must answer the philosophers' question about the 'analysis' of 'X is right', it will be along the lines of the algebraic query, rather than along those of the policeman's enquiry. It is, in fact, only as long as one is prepared to accept this kind of answer that the function of ethics leaves one room to ask the question at all.

11.8   *The Limits to Questions about the Rightness of Actions*

Let us return, next, to the simplest and most primitive types of ethical question, 'Is this the right thing to do?' and 'Which of

---

[1] And the consequences of this demand have been interesting, especially in the cases of the more honest and self-critical philosophers. Notice, for example, the comment made by A. E. Duncan-Jones on the second of the alternatives which I have quoted above (see *Mind*, n.s. XLII, p. 472): 'I believe it in a peculiar way, so that sometimes the theory strikes me as undeniable and sometimes I am sceptical about it.' This seems to me the kind of predicament into which a candid man is bound to find his way, if he demands an 'unambiguous' answer to the present question.

these actions ought I to do?' What limits are there to the circumstances in which we can ask these questions?

Once more we can get some guidance from the parallel between
science and ethics. The question, 'What is the scientific explanation of this?', can be answered in a great variety of circumstances,
but one comes across some situations in which science cannot
help to still the surprise which prompts the question. The instance
I gave as an illustration of this was that of the family all of whom
died on their birthdays.[1] When, after the first two children have
died on their birthdays, the third does also, you may well be
surprised; but the fact that it happens is one to be accepted, not
to be explained. None of the laws of nature, which we have
developed as a summary of experience, could have led you to
anticipate the event: none can now show you that it was to have
been expected. There it is—and the pathologists cannot help you.
The range of things for which it makes sense to talk of a 'scientific explanation' is limited: there is a point up to which science
can take you, but beyond that point it cannot go.

In ethics, too, the range of decisions for which it makes sense
to talk of a 'moral justification' is limited: again there is a point
up to which morality can take you, but beyond which it cannot go.
If you ask me, 'Which of these two courses of action ought I to
choose?', we can see which of the accepted social practices are
relevant and, if no 'matter of principle' is involved, estimate (as
best we can) the effects which either course of action will have on
the other members of the community. These considerations may
lead us to rule out one of the two courses as 'morally wrong'—
that is, as one which, on moral grounds, you ought not to choose.
But they may leave us where we were: no matter of principle may
be involved, and the foreseeable consequences to others may be
neither better nor worse in the one case than in the other. If this
happens, and you persist in asking me, 'But which *ought* I to
choose?', I can only reply, '*Morally* speaking, there's nothing to
choose between them, so there's no "ought" about it. It's entirely up to you now which you do.'

The notions of 'duty', of 'obligation', of 'morality', are
derived from situations in which the conduct of one member of
a community prejudices the interests of another, and are to be

[1] See § 7.5 above.

understood as part of the procedure for minimising the effects of such conflicts. Provided that two courses of action are equally acceptable according to the established code, and their foreseeable effects on others are equally tolerable, the notions of 'duty' and 'obligation' no longer apply in their primitive senses. If one is to choose between the two courses of action, it is on grounds of a different kind, for 'moral grounds' are no longer conclusive.

What kind of grounds will be relevant? It would be going beyond the scope of this book to discuss this question in detail, but we can take a quick look. At any given time, one can answer the question, 'What, at this moment, do you wish to do?', and, if at that instant this wish were granted, one would, for the moment, be satisfied. (You do not have to be a psychologist to know this: it is just in the nature of a 'wish'.) But we soon find out that to get what we wish for each instant, quite apart from its effects on others, may bring no deep or lasting satisfaction. We therefore begin to bend our energies, less towards those things for which we have a momentary desire, and more towards other things—things which we expect to bring deeper and more lasting contentment. In doing so, we develop a 'rule of life', a personal 'code' with the help of which, when moral considerations are no longer relevant, we can choose between different courses of action. In developing this 'rule of life', we have, of course, not only our own experience to guide us; we have the records which others have left of their attempts, failures and successes in the same quest, and the advice of friends and relatives to help us—or confuse us. Given all this mass of experience, we can now 'reason' about proposed courses of action, even when moral considerations are no longer conclusive. At this stage, however, the decision must be a personal one. The argument will be of the form, 'a_1, a_2,... (the reasons): so, if I were you, I should choose this course'; and the test of the argument concerns the future of the person concerned. If the course recommended was, as a matter of fact, likely to lead to his deepest and most permanent happiness, the advice was *good* advice—that is, advice worthy of acceptance: and, if the reasoning was such as to establish the true value of the advice, it was *good* reasoning— that is, reasoning worthy of notice.

Passing beyond the scope of 'morality' means passing out of the reach of those principles which find their rightful place in 'morality'—principles which can be formulated in terms independent of person and occasion. In the new field, every argument depends for its validity on an explicit or implicit 'If I were you'. Here the agent's 'feelings' and 'attitudes' enter in, not as the cardboard creatures of philosophical theory, but as logically indispensable participants. And if there is little space in a book of this kind to discuss this new field of argument, there is no reason to suppose that it is less worth discussing than those to which space has been given. It is simply a field in which less can be formalised; and therefore one in which the logician has less to contribute. Perhaps it is more important. Perhaps the chief value of discovering how much of the logic of ethics can be formalised lies in seeing why so much of it cannot—in seeing how (as E. M. Forster suggests in *Howards End*) the formal world of 'moral principles', of 'telegrams and anger', pales by comparison with the richer world of 'personal relations'. In some respects logic must be content to lag one step behind discovery: 'form', at any rate, is created always after the event. 'Moral principles' carry us only so far: it is only rarely that we can go all the way with their help. And when their job is done, the harder task remains of seeing the right answer to a question beginning 'If you were me...'.

All this, though a matter of logic rather than of 'empirical fact', was seen by Socrates and strikingly expressed by Plato. With his help, we can characterise, figuratively, the formal difference between the two kinds of reasoning relevant to the choice of an action. One is 'reasoning on moral grounds', aimed at the Harmony of Society: the other, to which we turn when reasoning on moral grounds does not lead to a decision by itself, is concerned with each man's own Pursuit of the Good. And the Good?—

The Good differs from everything else in a certain respect.... A creature that possesses it permanently, completely and absolutely, has never any need of anything else; its satisfaction is perfect.[1]

But this is not the end of the matter. The second type of reasoning about the choice of individual actions—that concerned

---

[1] *Philebus*, 60 B-C (tr. Hackforth); see *Plato's Examination of Pleasure*, p. 125.

with Happiness rather than with Harmony—has its counterpart
in social ethics just as much as the first; and it is one which comes
into the picture in similar circumstances. If we took a restricted
view of 'ethics', it might seem to be the case that, when the
existing social practices were causing no positive hardship, so
that people did not actually complain about them, then there was
nothing to be said against them; and that the institutions were
therefore 'perfect'—by definition, as it were. This is a position
which few people would wish to maintain. Over individual
actions, to say that it does not matter what one decides to do, as
long as it is within the moral code, is simply to shirk a proper
decision—for often enough moral considerations do not take us
all the way—and so also is it if one says that it does not matter
what the present institutions and social practices are, as long as
they do not cause positive and avoidable hardship. Certainly this
is the first thing we must ask of our institutions; but, when we
have satisfied ourselves about this, they are not necessarily
exempt from all criticism. We can now inquire whether, if some
specific change were made, the members of our community would
lead fuller and happier lives. And again, if there are reasonable
grounds for believing that they would, the change is surely
justified.

One might naturally and properly argue that our definition of
the 'function' of ethics should take account of these considerations too. And we could extend it to do so, if we chose. It is
important, however, if we are going to do so, to notice one thing:
namely, that this *is* an extension. Our ideas of 'right', of 'justice',
of 'duty', of 'obligation', are manifold: each word covers a genus
of concepts. But some members of each genus are more characteristically ethical than others. 'You ought to rest this afternoon, as
you've a busy evening ahead of you', 'You ought to hear his
violin concerto', 'You ought to visit him, if you promised to':
these remarks all make use of the notion of 'obligation', but only
in the last of the three does it carry its full force. If you used
instances of this last kind to teach someone the notion, you might
expect him to recognise that the other uses were natural exten-
sions of it; but you would never expect him to understand the full
nature of 'moral obligation' if given only instances of the first
and second kinds—instances having hardly more force than that

of 'You'll enjoy his violin concerto if you hear it' and 'If you don't rest this afternoon, you'll regret it later'. The notions of 'obligation', 'right', 'justice', 'duty', and 'ethics' apply in the first place where our actions or institutions may lead to avoidable misery for others; but it is a natural and familiar extension to use them also where the issue concerns the chance of deeper happiness for others, and even for ourselves.

11.9   Is any 'Justification' of Ethics Needed?

In talking about the logic of ethical reasoning in the light of the function of ethics, I have tried to indicate two things:

(i) the different types of question which naturally arise in ethical contexts, and the ways in which they are answered; and

(ii) the limits of ethical reasoning—that is, the kinds of occasion on which questions and considerations of an ethical kind can no longer arise.

So far, however, I have not given an explicit answer to the question from which we set out: namely, 'What is it, in an ethical discussion, that makes a reason a good reason, or an argument a valid argument?'

In previous chapters this question has always caused trouble. When discussing the objective doctrine of ethics, we found it impossible even to reach it without first mastering some highly mysterious arguments about 'non-natural' properties; even more surprisingly, the advocates of the subjective and imperative doctrines tried to dismiss it as vain. But now we are in the opposite position. In this chapter, I have not attempted to give a 'theory of ethics'; I have simply tried to describe the occasions, on which we are in fact prepared to call judgements 'ethical' and decisions 'moral', and the part which reasoning plays on such occasions. This description has led us to see how, in *particular types* of ethical question and argument, good reasoning is distinguished from bad, and valid argument from invalid—to be specific, by applying to individual judgements the test of principle, and to principles the test of general fecundity.

Now we have to ask, 'Is any further answer needed? Given particular rules applicable to different kinds of ethical judgement and question, have we not all we want? And, if any more were needed, could it not be supplied from an account, more detailed and accurate than has been given, but of the same kind?'

I myself do not feel the need for any *general* answer to the question, 'What makes some ethical reasoning "good" and some ethical arguments "valid"?': answers applicable to particular types of argument are enough. In fact, it seems to me that the demand for any such general answer (however it is to be obtained) must lead one to paradox as surely as did the corresponding demand over science.[1] For either such a general answer will, in particular cases, be equivalent to the rules which we have found, or it will contradict them. In the first case, it can do one of two things. Either it can distort our account, so that one of the criteria alone seems important; or else it can point out, in a more or less roundabout way, the advantages—indeed, 'the absolute necessity to the existence of society'[2]—of harmonious co-operation. Instead, however, it may contradict our results. What then? What if we try to adopt the new rules for criticising arguments about conduct, which this general answer lays down?

If we do adopt these new criteria, then it will no longer be 'ethical' reasoning, 'moral' considerations, arguments from 'duty' and questions about what we 'ought' to do that we are criticising: it will be questions, arguments and considerations of another kind—in fact, a different mode of reasoning. This can be shown quite quickly. For suppose that, far from radically changing our criteria, all that the new rules do is to select one of them as the *universal* criterion. If the test of principle is chosen, so that we are never to be allowed to question the pronouncements of those who administer the moral code, then it is not 'morality' to which they apply—it is 'authority', and authority of a kind which may reasonably be expected to develop rapidly into tyranny. And conversely, if the test of principle is itself ruled out in favour of a universal test of consequence (of the estimated effects on others), then we are faced with something which is no more 'morality' than the other—it would now be better described as 'expediency'. But arguments from expediency and arguments from authority are no more 'ethical' than experienced guess-work is 'scientific'. Consequently, even

---

[1] See § 7.6 above.
[2] Hume, *Natural History of Religion*, § XIII, *ad fin.*

if all we do is to give up one or other of our present logical criteria, we turn ethics into something other than it is. And if this is the case there is no need for us to go on and consider more drastic alterations: they can be ruled out at once.

No doubt those philosophers who search for more general rules will not be satisfied. No doubt they will still feel that they want an explicit and unique answer to our central question. And no doubt they will object that, in all this, I have not even 'justified' our using reason in ethics at all. 'It's all very well your laying down the law about particular types of ethical argument', they will say; 'but what is the justification for letting *any* reasoning affect how we decide to behave? Why *ought* one to do what is right, anyway?'

They are sufficiently answered by the peculiarity of their own questions. For let us consider what kind of answer they want when they ask, 'Why ought one to do what is right?' There is no room *within* ethics for such a question. Ethical reasoning may be able to show why we ought to do this action as opposed to that, or advocate this social practice as opposed to that, but it is no help where there can be no choice. And their question does not present us with genuine alternatives at all. For, since the notions of 'right' and of 'obligation' originate in the same situations and serve similar purposes, it is a self-contradiction (taking 'right' and 'ought' in their simplest senses) to suggest that we 'ought' to do anything but what is 'right'. This suggestion is as unintelligible as the suggestion that some emerald objects might not be green, and the philosophers' question is on a level with the question, 'Why are all scarlet things red?' We can therefore parry it only with another question—'What else "ought" one to do?'

Similar oddities are displayed by all their questions—as long as we take them literally. Ethics may be able to 'justify' one of a number of courses of action, or one social practice as opposed to another: but it does not extend to the 'justification' of all reasoning about conduct. One course of action can be opposed to another: one social practice can be opposed to another. But to what are we expected to oppose 'ethics-as-a-whole'? There can be no discussion about the proposition, 'Ethics is ethics'; any argument treating 'ethics' as something other than it is must be false; and, if those who call for a 'justification' of ethics want 'the case for morality', as opposed to 'the case for expediency', etc., then they are giving philosophy a job which is not its own. To show that you ought to choose certain actions is one thing: to make you *want to do* what you ought to do is another, and not a philosopher's task.

11.10 *Reason and Self-Love*

Hume ran sharply into this difficulty. He had, in fact, to confess (of a man in whom self-love overpowered the sense of right), 'It would be a little difficult to find any [reasoning] which will appear to him satisfactory and convincing.'[1] This confession of his was, however, a masterpiece of understatement. The difficulty he speaks of is no 'little' one: indeed, it is an 'absolute and insuperable' one, an 'impossibility'. But note the reason: it is not a *practical* impossibility at all, but a *logical* one. A man's ignoring all ethical arguments is just the kind of thing which would lead us to say that his self-love *had* overpowered his sense of right. As long, and only as long, as he continued to ignore all moral reasoning, we should say that his self-love continued in the ascendant: but once he began to accept such considerations as a guide to action, we should begin to think that 'the sense of right' had won.

It is always possible that, when faced with a man whose self-love initially overpowered his sense of right, we might hit upon some reasoning which appeared to him 'satisfactory and convincing'. The result, however, would not be 'a man in whom self-love was dominant, but who was satisfied and convinced by ethical reasoning' (for this is a contradiction in terms); it would be 'a man in whom self-love was dominant, until reasoning beat it down and reinstated the sense of right'.

There is, in this respect, an interesting parallel to be drawn between the notion of 'rational belief' in science, and that of 'reasonable belief' in ethics. We call the belief that (for instance) sulphonamides will control pneumonia a 'rational belief', because it is arrived at by the procedure found reliable in clinical research. The same applies to any belief held as a result of a series of properly conducted scientific experiments. Any such belief is strengthened as a result of further confirmatory observations.

[1] Hume, *Enquiries* (ed. Selby-Bigge), p. 283.

These observations (we say) increase the 'probability' of any hypothesis with which they are consistent: that is, they increase the degree of confidence with which it is rational to entertain the hypothesis. In practice, of course, we do not always adopt the most reliable methods of argument—we generalise hastily, ignore conflicting evidence, misinterpret ambiguous observations and so on. We know very well that there are reliable standards of evidence to be observed, but we do not always observe them. In other words, we are not always rational; for to be 'rational' is to employ always these reliable, self-consistent methods of forming one's scientific beliefs, and to fail to be 'rational' is to entertain the hypothesis concerned with a degree of confidence out of proportion to its 'probability'.[1]

As with the 'rational' and the 'probable', so with the 'reasonable' and the 'desirable' (the 'desirable', that is, in its usual sense of what ought to be pursued): the belief that I ought to pay the bill which my bookshop has sent me is a 'reasonable' belief, and the bookseller's demand for payment is a 'reasonable' demand, because they represent a practice which has been found acceptable in such circumstances. Any ethical judgement, held as a result of properly interpreted moral experience, is also 'reasonable'. Any such judgement is strengthened by further experiences which confirm the fecundity of the principle from which the judgement derives. Such experiences increase the 'desirability' of the principle: that is, they increase the degree of conviction with which it is reasonable to advocate and act upon the principle. In practice, of course, we do not always adopt the most satisfactory methods of reaching moral decisions—we jump to conclusions, ignore the suffering of 'inferior' people, misinterpret ambiguous experiences, and so on. We know very well that there are reliable standards to be observed in shaping our principles and institutions, but we do not always observe them. That is to say, we are not always reasonable; for to be 'reasonable' is to employ these reliable, self-consistent methods in reaching all our moral decisions, and to fail to be 'reasonable' is to advocate and act upon our principles with a degree of conviction out of proportion to their desirability.

[1] In connection with this discussion, see Ayer (op. cit. pp. 99–102), whose argument I paraphrase.

Consider the light which this parallel throws on Hume's difficulties and on the 'justification' of ethics. It is sometimes suggested that the 'probability' of a hypothesis is just a matter of our confidence in it, as measured by our willingness to rely on it in practice. This account is over-simplified, for it would be completely acceptable only if we always related belief to observation in a 'rational' way. 'Probability' is, rather, a matter of the degree of confidence with which it is rational to adopt a hypothesis. In an analogous way, Hume's theory of ethics makes the 'desirability' of a moral principle a matter of the conviction with which all fully-informed people do hold to it.[1] This likewise would be true—provided that we always related our moral judgements to experience in a 'reasonable' way....

But this clears up the problem. The truth is that, if different people are to agree in their ethical judgements, it is not enough for them all to be fully informed. They must all be *reasonable*, too. (Even this may not be enough: when it comes to controversial questions, they may reasonably differ.) Unfortunately, people are not always reasonable. And this is a sad fact, which philosophers just have to accept. It is absurd and paradoxical of them to suppose that we need produce a 'reasoned argument' capable of convincing the 'wholly unreasonable', for this would be a self-contradiction.[2]

If, therefore, the request for a 'justification' of ethics is equivalent to this demand, there is no room for a 'justification'; and the question used to express this demand, 'Why ought one to do what is right?', has no literal answer. There may yet be room for answers of a *different* kind: but, if there is, it is certainly not the business of a logician, and probably not the business of any kind of philosopher, to give them. (What kinds of answer might be given, and whose business it would be to give them, are questions I shall return to later.)[3]

---

[1] See § 2.5 above.

[2] I should have thought it unnecessary to formulate such an obvious truth, had I not found it overlooked, in practice, by eminent philosophers. For instance, I recall a conversation with Bertrand Russell in which he remarked, as an objection to the present account of ethics, that it would not have convinced Hitler. But whoever supposed that it should? We do not prescribe logic as a treatment for lunacy, or expect philosophers to produce panaceas for psychopaths.

[3] In Chapter 14 below.

ETHICS AND SOCIETY

BEFORE leaving ethics proper, in order to tie up these last threads, I want to comment on a number of more or less isolated topics. These come under two general headings:

(i) the connection between the function of ethics and the nature of ethical concepts, and

(ii) the social character of ethics.

In the following three sections, I shall deal with topics falling within the first set.

12.1 *Ethics and Language*

Ethical words are used, at one extreme, in fully developed, logically complex judgements designed to harmonise the aims and actions of the members of a community. At the other extreme, they appear in unpondered, logically crude interjections —exclamations and commands—which release the emotions of the speaker, or act like goads upon the hearer. These two extreme uses we have discussed in some detail. For every black and white, however, there are several greys and, on the majority of occasions, our use of ethical terms conforms strictly to neither of these extremes. A more comprehensive survey of the logic of ethics would have to treat of these intermediate uses at equal length, but I shall be content to give them the barest mention and outline.

One of the factors which influences the logic of ethical concepts, as it does the logic of scientific concepts, is the need for words to be common to all and constant in application. Quite apart, therefore, from any concern for the suffering of others, we correct the reports of our feelings against a constant standard, simply in order that other people may understand our reactions at all. And in these modified reports of our feelings, as in the more vehement exclamations of horror and delight, we frequently use ethical and ethically-toned words. As Hume pointed out:[1]

---

[1] In the *Treatise* (ed. Selby-Bigge), p. 582.

In general, all sentiments of praise and blame are variable, according to our situation of nearness and remoteness, with regard to the person blam'd or prais'd, and according to the present disposition of the mind. But these variations we regard not in our general decisions, but still apply the terms expressive of our liking or dislike, in the same manner, as if we remain'd in one point of view. Experience soon teaches us this method of correcting our sentiments, or at least, of correcting our language, where the sentiments are more stubborn or inalterable. Our servant, if diligent and faithful, may excite stronger sentiments of love and kindness than Marcus Brutus, as represented in history; but we say not upon that account, that the former character is more laudable than the latter. We know, that were we to approach equally near to that renown'd patriot, he wou'd command a much higher degree of affection and admiration. Such corrections are common with regard to all the senses.

In part, at any rate, the development of ethics and ethical language (like that of science) reflects a desire to replace our unedited and momentary reactions by descriptions in a language independent of the occasion on which the judgement is passed.

And indeed 'twere impossible we cou'd ever make use of language, or communicate our sentiments to one another, did we not correct the momentary appearances of things, and overlook the present situation.

Taking the different uses of ethical language in succession, from the unreasoned to the reasoned extreme, we might characterise them in Hume's terminology, as follows:

(i) The use 'expressive of our momentary liking or dislike'— e.g. 'Good!', and 'How wicked!'

(ii) The use in which we 'correct our language', but do not 'correct our sentiments'—e.g. if I acknowledge Brutus' moral superiority over my butler, while continuing to feel more affection for the latter than for the former.

(iii) The use in which we 'correct our sentiments' as well— e.g. if, as a result of moral reflection, I cease to admire one who has previously been my hero.

(iv) The use in which we 'correct our conduct', in addition to our 'sentiments' and 'language'—e.g. if I change my mind as to which course it would be right for me to pursue.

12.2   *Equity in Moral Reasoning*

In order for a fully-fledged ethical argument to be an instance of 'reasoning', it must be equally 'worthy of acceptance' whoever is considering it. Further, if this argument appeals to principles, fit to be called 'ethical', these must be such as would harmonise the actions of those who accepted them. Taken together, these features of the use of ethical reasoning account for the logical demand for 'equity' in the formulation of moral principles. As ethical judgements become more general, specific references to 'me', 'here' and 'now', 'them', 'there' and 'then' are eliminated, and as long as any such references remain, there is room for an appeal to a more general principle. The point at which the justification of a moral decision must cease is where the action under discussion has been unambiguously related to a current 'moral principle', independent (in its wording) of person, place and time: e.g. where 'I ought to take this book and give it back to Jones at once' has given way to 'Anyone ought always to do anything that he promises anyone else that he will do' or 'It was a promise'. If, in justifying an action, we can carry our reasons back to such universal principles, our justification has some claim to be called 'ethical'. But, if we cannot do so, our appeal is not to 'morality' at all: if, for example, the most general principles to which we can appeal still contain some reference to us, either as individuals or as members of a limited group of people,[1] then our appeal is not to 'morality' but to 'privilege'.

This argument is, of course, purely logical, and can therefore have no immediate empirical consequences. At the same time, if the point is overlooked, the consequences may be important. Suppose, for instance, that one is trying to teach someone the notions of morality: then equity in the formulation and application of the judgements from which he is expected to learn them will surely be essential. It is a recognised fact that 'spoilt' children tend to be those whose upbringing has been markedly vacillating, rather than markedly gentle; that the occasionally strict education ruins more characters than the con-

---

[1] Allowing, of course, for the reservations made in § 11.6, concerning the comparability of similar institutions in different societies.

sistently mild one. Recall the lesson of Jane Austen's *Mansfield Park*:[1]

> Too late he [Sir Thomas Bertram] became aware how unfavourable to the character of any young people must be the totally opposite treatment which Maria and Julia had been always experiencing at home, where the excessive indulgence and flattery of their aunt had been continually contrasted with his own severity. He saw how ill he had judged, in expecting to counteract what was wrong in Mrs Norris [their aunt], by its reverse in himself; clearly saw that he had but increased the evil, by teaching them to repress their spirits in his presence so as to make their real disposition unknown to him, and sending them for all their indulgences to a person who had been able to attach them only by the blindness of her affection, and the excess of her praise.

This result was really to be expected. The child who has a consistent upbringing clearly has a good opportunity to 'get the idea' of ethics; while the child who can find no reason or principle in its upbringing may never do so. And from this example we can see one of the ways in which logic mirrors life— how the logical demand for equity in the formulation of ethical principles is reflected in the need for a just and consistent pattern of behaviour towards moral 'learners'.

12.3 Self-Command in Ethics

In all that I have said so far, I have failed to mention explicitly one important feature of ethics. The nature of its function decides not only the logic of moral reasoning; it also determines the attitude which it is 'right' for us to take up towards the current principles and the feelings of others.

Except when there is reason to believe that an existing principle could be superseded by another involving less suffering and annoyance on the whole, we are 'obliged' to embrace it. And, likewise, only in extraordinary cases can it be 'right' for us to ignore the feelings of others. One might put the point paradoxically by saying, 'Considerateness is not a virtue'— meaning that it is the *essence* of 'virtue', rather than *a* virtue. To quote Democritus (the contemporary of Socrates, and a philosopher of pre-Platonic simplicity), 'To be good means

---

[1] Everyman Edition, pp. 386–7.

to do no wrong; and also, not to *want* to do wrong'.[1] The 'good' is not just that which *is* desired; it is that which is *to be* desired.

This feature of ethics, also, is recognised by Jane Austen:[2]

Julia, whose happy star no longer prevailed, was obliged to keep by the side of Mrs Rushworth, and restrain her impatient feet to that lady's slow pace....The politeness which she had been brought up to practise as a duty made it impossible for her to escape; while the want of that higher species of self-command, that just consideration of others, that knowledge of her own heart, that principle of right, which had not formed any essential part of her education, made her miserable under it.

Reflect on the author's illuminating treatment of 'that higher species of self-command, that just consideration of others, that knowledge of her own heart, that principle of right' as four descriptions of the same thing. It shows how well she understood both the personal and the social function of ethics.

12.4   *Ethics and Social Institutions*

The remaining topics will form something in the nature of a coda: I shall just rough them in, like charcoal drawings, in thick black and white lines, leaving the detailed work and colouring for another time and place. All have to do with the social character of ethics; and the first is the relation between ethics and social institutions.

Since the function of ethics is to reconcile the independent aims and wills of a community of people, the account which I have given could provide the skeleton for an essay in social history. All the principles, which together make up a moral code, can be related to some institution within the society, the code as a whole to the complete social organisation. 'It is wrong to keep this book because it is wrong to break a promise' is accepted as an argument in our society because making and keeping promises is one of the things we do: 'the promise' is one of our institutions. So are 'cricket-colours', 'loans' and 'the Rule of the Road'.

---

[1] See, for instance, Mullach's edition of Democritus (Berlin, 1843), *Fragmenta Moralia*, no. 109: Ἀγαθὸν οὐ τὸ μὴ ἀδικέειν, ἀλλὰ τὸ μηδὲ ἐθέλειν. The source there given for the fragment is Stobaeus, *Florilegium*, IX, 31.

[2] Op. cit. pp. 75–6.

And, conversely, every social institution is built upon a system of duties and privileges: the Member of Parliament has a moral obligation to represent his constituents faithfully, the husband to support his wife and children. 'My station and its duties'[1] is a phrase which summarises fairly the moral obligations arising out of the first stage in the development of ethics.

This, however, is not the end of the story. The development, which first takes us from 'Every man for himself' to 'My station and its duties', leads us later to criticise the 'duties' and 'stations' as at present established, and to suggest changes. When this happens, there are two extreme possibilities. The first is for those in effective control to 'freeze' the moral code and institutions: to assert their absolute authority, to legislate for every possibility, to isolate the community from outside influences, to discourage independent speculation and the airing of grievances, and to provide a communal aim which the citizens must like—or lump.

The second course is to encourage criticism, and to modify the code and institutions, wherever it is reasonable to believe that, by a possible change, unnecessary strains could be removed and new opportunities created or exploited; in fact, so to organise the institutions of the society that they develop naturally in this way, taking into account every citizen's aims and grievances.

The first type of development cannot be justified by any appeal to reason, for it is the outcome of mutually contradictory desires in the rulers. They want to insist on the citizens' fulfilling absolutely a set of 'moral obligations' towards them, which, at the same time, they want to be excused from respecting towards the citizens—thus presenting in the guise of 'morality' a collection of privileges without foundation in ethics.

The second course, on the other hand, is in line with the natural development of ethics. It is in the nature of ethics that changes in the moral code should have as their goal a self-developing, 'open' society—a society in which individuals are free, and encouraged, to make their own moral decisions—rather than the tribal, tyrannical and collectivist, 'closed' society.[2]

---

[1] This is the phrase Bradley used as a title for his fifth essay in *Ethical Studies*.

[2] For the distinction between the 'open' and the 'closed' society, see Popper, *The Open Society and Its Enemies, passim.*

12.5   *Ethics and Engineering*

In a society with a self-developing code and institutions, it is not necessary that every citizen should be himself a politician or a moralist, but he does have to be a 'social engineer'; and the analogy between ethics and engineering can help to elucidate several features of ethics which are at first sight obscure.

Consider, to begin with, an engineer, in the primary sense of the word. He is continually faced with practical problems, which it is his business to solve within the limits laid down by his 'code of standard practice'. This code takes into account the properties of the materials and means open to him, and the conditions to which his creation will be exposed, as far as all these are predictable; and, for the unpredictable factors, it makes allowances which are the result of accumulated experience ('factors of safety').

Suppose, for instance, that an engineer is designing an aeroplane; and that he is trying to decide what material to use for the members of the fuselage. He can solve a large number of his problems immediately, since they will fall directly under one or other of the general cases covered by his code. By application of the code, he will discover what he 'ought' to do: it will tell him, for example, which is the 'right' material—'Use $\frac{1}{2}$-inch angle iron', it will specify, or else, 'Duralumin is the best material in such circumstances'. However, he may find that the requirements he has set out to meet cannot be satisfied within the limits of the code. 'I want this 'plane to have a top speed of 520 miles per hour as 20,000 feet', he may explain, 'and I do not want the all-up weight to exceed 25 tons: but to allow for that speed with the usual factors of safety I shall have to use 1-inch girders, and I cannot do this without exceeding my maximum weight.' In such a case, with the existing code of practice, the demand for high speed and the demand for low weight conflict. The demand for high speed requires him to use 1-inch girders; the demand for low weight to use $\frac{3}{4}$-inch ones. The engineer can now do one of three things:

(i)   abandon the job,

(ii) modify his aims to meet the requirements of the code, or

(iii) take a chance—i.e. reduce the factors of safety and so ignore the code—relying on his special knowledge of the conditions applying to this particular case, and maybe on good fortune, to prevent ill results.

Compare the position of this engineer with that of an individual in society. We are all continually faced with moral problems, which we have to solve within the limits of our moral code. This code takes into account the nature of the men with whom we shall be dealing, the means open to us, and the kinds of situation with which we shall be faced, as far as all these are predictable; and, for the unpredictable, it makes allowances which are the result of accumulated experience.

Suppose, for example, that we are managing a shop, and that we are deciding what prices to charge for our goods. Many of our problems will solve themselves, being covered by statutory orders, or by the conventional retail rates of profit: our code will tell us what prices are 'extortionate', and therefore wrong. However, we may find that our aims conflict, with each other or with those of our customers. We may find that, in order to make a clear profit of £20 a week (as we want to do), we can only afford to employ three shop assistants, whereas to prevent queues (which will annoy our customers) we shall have to have four. Here the demand for high profit and the demand for quick service lead to conflicting obligations—the demand for high profit requires us to use three assistants, the demand for quick service to use four. In such a case we, too, have three possible courses of action:

(i) we may close the shop;

(ii) we may modify our aims to meet our customers' demands; or

(iii) we may take a chance—i.e. ignore our customers' convenience, and so the moral code—relying on special knowledge of local shopping habits, and on good fortune, to prevent ill results.

In this example, the analogy is particularly close, since the considerations involved are almost entirely ones of economics. In most of the situations we encounter, however, there are non-economic factors, which weaken the analogy in three ways:

(i) We cannot usually solve our moral problems by abandoning them—in most ethical situations there is no 'safe' course open to us, as there is to the engineer or the shop-keeper.

(ii) The unpredictable element may be of extreme importance —we have to allow for possible changes in the dispositions of the other people concerned, and these changes will have an effect analogous to changes in the specification of the aeroplane after it has been built.

(iii) Our own futures are bound up in our ethical situation, in a way in which the future of the engineer is not involved in his aeroplane—it is as though he himself, his friends, relations and fellow-citizens were the 'members' out of which the body of the aeroplane was to be constructed!

The combined effect of these three factors is to put the problem more directly upon the individual, and to remove it further from the sphere of authority, than it is in engineering and economics. The possibility of changing one's attitude, 'that higher species of self-command, that knowledge of one's own heart', as Jane Austen called it, simplifies the problem for the individual, and the special knowledge we acquire about our families and friends adds a finesse and flexibility to our decisions which would be absent if we acted only 'upon authority'. At the same time, they complicate the statistical approach and, except in purely economic cases, take away from a centralised authority much of its power to predict what will be 'for the best'. Ethics is more a matter of conscience, less of authority, than engineering and economics.

12.6   *Ethics and Psychology*

The analogy between ethics and engineering may suggest to us another question. In ethics and in engineering alike, there is a code of rules which is used to meet certain practical needs. The rules of engineering have a certain theoretical backing: many of the rules used by mechanical and electrical engineers can be explained in terms of physics, and many of the rules of chemical engineering in terms of chemistry. Now can we extend our parallel this far? Do the rules of ethics have any similar backing? If mechanical engineering is to be called 'applied physics' and chemical engineering 'applied chemistry', what are we to call ethics? The answer, to be taken with a pinch of salt, is easy— 'applied psychology'.

This answer must be treated with caution for a number of reasons. First, it suggests (misleadingly) that psychology must come before ethics *in time*—that there cannot be any ethics until there is some psychology to be 'applied'—and, if this were so, we should expect morality to be a recent growth, instead of one of the oldest things in human history. However, the form of the question is responsible for this impression: to call mechanical engineering 'applied physics' is misleading in the same way. Atomic and nuclear physics may have been a prelude, without which there would have been no electronic engineering and no atomic bomb, but cooking came before chemistry, and the Pyramids before there was anything worth calling 'physics'.

A second impulse to protest arises from the feeling that there are plenty of good people who do not know any psychology, and that psychologists are not always the best of men. But this too is beside the point. The talents needed by an outstanding physicist, to conduct a detailed experimental investigation, differ from those which make up the fine craftsman or engineer, the man who provides immediate solutions to practical problems. This difference does not affect the point of calling mechanical engineering 'applied physics'. Likewise, although the qualities which make a good psychologist on the one hand, and a good man on the other, are very different, there is still a logical connection worth indicating between psychology and ethics.

To begin with, then, both subjects have the same 'raw material': they are both concerned, from their own points of view, with our behaviour. It may also be said that ethics and psychology have a common ideal—complete confidence about the ways in which all our actions will be received by others—and in a sense this, too, is true. But in its partial truth lies a danger: that of overlooking the radical differences between the aims and methods of the two subjects. Indeed, supporters of the subjective and imperative doctrines have been deceived into arguing that, in so far as ethics is logically a respectable subject at all, it is a branch of psychology. For example, Schlick, convinced that ethics must be either 'science' or 'nonsense', wrote, 'In so far as ethical questions have any meaning, and can therefore be answered, ethics is a science....The central problem of ethics is a pure question of psychology.'[1] And Ayer follows in his footsteps, saying: 'Ethics, as a branch of

[1] Moritz Schlick, *Fragen der Ethik* (tr. S. E. T.), pp. 1, 21.

knowledge, is nothing more than a department of psychology and sociology.'[1]

Notice, therefore, the differences as well as the similarities between the subjects. The physicist and the experimental psychologist begin their experiments by selecting and arranging their material: their first care is to obtain a characteristic specimen in a reproducible situation. It is on this specimen (X) in this situation (S) that they work, and to the combination (X, S) that their results apply, whether S is a cloud-chamber or a class-room, and X a piece of aluminium foil or a set of 9-year-old, Welsh, primary schoolchildren. By contrast, the engineer in his work and the 'responsible citizen', faced with a moral decision, have to make the best of things as they are: they cannot choose or arrange their material. Instead of a specimen X (guaranteed 99·99 % aluminium or Welsh 9-year-old), about which much is already known or can be predicted with confidence, they are presented with incompletely specified material in an incompletely known situation. Both their aims and their modes of reasoning differ from those of a scientist. The scientist's aim is to formulate a law, 'For every X in S, developments D may be expected', a law taking the form of a factual proposition: the engineer is content with a law, 'When faced with X in S, do Y (or, Y is the right thing to do)', a law taking the form of a rule which he can use to meet a practical demand.

In saying, therefore, that ethics and psychology have, as a common ideal, complete knowledge of the ways in which our actions will be received by others, this is all I have in mind—that, supposing that we had such knowledge, and that it were common property, then to every moral principle would correspond a law of psychology. To the moral principle:

'When faced with X in S, D_1 is the right and D_2 is the wrong thing to aim at';

would correspond the factual law:

'For every X in S, D_1 may be expected to lead to general happiness, D_2 to general misery.'

However, in so far as our psychology is imperfect, our morality has to develop independently of it; and their union

_____
[1] Ayer, *Language, Truth and Logic* (2nd ed.), p. 112.

remains an ideal towards which, like tunnellers under the Alps, the moralist struggles in one direction, the psychologist in another.

12.7 *The Task of the Moralist*

I have written the word 'moralist', and I cannot let it go without comment. The traditional notion of a moralist is that of a 'person given to moralizing'[1]—addicted to it, rather—and it calls to mind the image of an armchair critic, secure from the need to strive for material things, and free to pass gratuitous and unfavourable moral judgements upon the conduct of the less fortunate. When I used the word, I was thinking of someone quite unlike this traditional picture; and I only referred to him as a 'moralist' for lack of a better word. There is, however, a certain virtue in the choice of this word; for my picture is the one upon which these armchair moralists seek (as hopelessly as the Frog emulating the Ox) to model themselves. Maybe, therefore, I can be excused for using it in this short, concluding section, instead of resorting to such tendentious phrases as 'ideal moralist', 'ethical reformer' and the like.

Here is the problem that I had at the back of my mind. It is one thing to recognise the logical criteria appropriate to moral decisions, and another to apply them. In our day-to-day judgements, we can all rely on the existing code as a guide; but to criticise the code, and to recognise in which directions it needs changing, are jobs in which we cannot all be equally expert, and for which very marked qualifications are needed. As a matter of logic, it is easy enough to define the criteria to be used: as a matter of practice, their application becomes increasingly difficult, the more we leave behind the elementary daily decisions, and try instead to judge the worth of existing institutions, and the desirability of particular reforms. We must, therefore, not only answer the question, 'What kinds of reasoning is it proper to accept in support of an ethical judgement?'; we must also ask, 'What kinds of qualification should be required of a man, if his judgement about the reform of the moral code and institutions is to be trusted?'

It is not enough to think of such a man as a psychologist, for, although his understanding of human nature must be as deep as

---

[1] *Pocket Oxford Dictionary*, entry against 'moralist'.

any psychologist's, his point of view is different. He has a more practical aim than the experimental psychologist, and is bound to work on a larger scale, thus resembling an engineer. But it is not enough to think of him as an engineer, either. If we regard ethics as 'applied psychology', then we are all 'moral engineers': every time we come to a moral decision, we apply the moral code (the code of standard practice) which we have been taught. The moralist's task is not just to apply present principles to day-to-day problems. He must also be able to recognise when a principle or institution has outlived its usefulness, and when, to make the most of altered conditions and new opportunities, something fresh is needed—a new pattern of behaviour, new rules of conduct, a new social institution—and in this respect he resembles more the research engineer than the journeyman. But even more than the research engineer, who has opportunities to *experiment* where the moralist can only *observe*, he is like an artist, who has, from a study of the examples which have gone before, to envisage what could be done and needs doing now, and then has to work out a way of putting his conception into effect.

We might say of the moralist that in him the psychologist, the engineer and the artist meet. The psychologist in him must be knowledgeable about the ways in which people may be expected to feel in different circumstances; the engineer in him must be used to handling the full-scale, practical situations of life, to estimating the 'factors of safety' to be applied, over and above the limits found in the laboratory and the consulting-room; and the artist in him must be sensitive enough to recognise those crucial moments when particular rules of conduct must be super-seded, and to trace out 'the features of the soul'[1] in the new stage of its growth. The moralist must study the institutions and practices of society, not simply for what they do, but for what they could be made to do. And this means, at any rate in a time like ours, that he must have a grounding in economics; unless he has this, the eternal miseries of hunger, unemployment and homelessness will return and wash away his reforms like sand-castles.

This, however, is only a beginning; solving the Economic

---

[1] Goldsworthy Lowes Dickinson, *The Meaning of Good* (1901), pp. 86–7; cf. Epilogue, below, *ad fin.*

Problem is only a preparation for more positive achievements. It is not enough for the moralist to be familiar with those inevitable features of the social metabolism to which the calculus of economics can be applied—those commodities, like food, shelter, work and leisure, which meet fixed interests and un-alterable aspects of our dispositions. He must also under-stand the greater goods which—unlike Christmas-cake or the sugar ration—we can both 'eat' and 'have'.[1] He must know how people feel and what they want, certainly; but even more he must know how they *could* feel and what they are *capable of* enjoying. And he must learn to show them the things which could most deeply satisfy them, in such a way that they will take to them.

But there is a danger in this kind of talk: the danger of suggest-ing that there is a superior class of persons, worthy of special respect, who are alone entitled to criticise the moral practices of society. In talking of the 'moralist', however, I have not been meaning to assume the existence of such a privileged class. The title of 'moralist' can be thought of as something to be earned, rather than as the name of a caste or profession. The notion is akin more to that of a 'citizen' than to that of a 'surgeon'—certainly it cannot be anybody's *job* to be a moralist. In fact, of course, social institutions develop to a great extent without the need for people with special vision: it is not the ideas of Great Men, but the refusal of ordinary people in their day-to-day be-haviour to conform to an out-of-date code which produces the changes required. But this is not to discredit my notion of a 'moralist': it is to say rather that we are all moralists in a limited way, and that this refusal to conform is often based on protest against the rule, whether or no one can see how a better rule could be introduced.

There remain those stages in the development of society when private protests are not enough, or when public opinion gets too far left behind—the advantages of privilege blinding those who could help to the sufferings of the remainder. At such stages, we often find an outstanding figure succeeding in the task of the moralist. But, in the nature of the case, he who is to do so must live, not as an isolated figure, an oracle, a heroic 'world-historical personality' in the mad, romantic, Hegelian mould; but among

[1] On this point, see A. C. Pigou, *The Economics of Welfare* (2nd ed.), pt. 1, ch. v.

his fellows, learning from his contacts with them, putting his policies continually to the test of their criticism, shaping his proposals to their capabilities and desires, and remembering always what Pericles insisted on, that, though he may be one of the few who can originate a policy, 'We are all able to judge it'.[1]

It is too much to ask that all the qualities and qualifications required should be embodied in one man. There are not many, indeed, who care sufficiently about the inequities of the current institutions to take an interest at all; and, in those who do, indignation too often extinguishes the light of reason.

It is only a few rare and exceptional men who have that kind of love towards mankind at large that makes them unable to endure patiently the general mass of evil and suffering, regardless of any relation it may have to their own lives; [and who] will seek, first in thought and then in action, for some way of escape, some new system of society by which life may become richer, more full of joy and less full of preventable evils than it is at present.[2]

Still fewer combine with indignation and reason the clarity of conception and vision needed if the right change is to be proposed at the right moment. There need be no surprise or shame, therefore, at the discovery that, measured against this standard, even the greatest are only partly successful, and even the best fall short in one direction or another.

On the one plane, there are the great religious teachers; but they (perhaps wisely) did not tackle the economic problems of their times. On another, there are men like Pericles and Socrates, but their work could not stand against the whirlwind. On a third, we can put those of our contemporaries who have come nearest to the ideal; men such as Roosevelt, Keynes, Shaw and Sidney Webb.

Even when one considers men like these, one finds, in Roosevelt and Pericles, maybe too much of the engineer, and, in Socrates, maybe too little. The spectacle of balance, in the qualities which I have tried to analyse, is indeed the rarest thing of all; and for this balance, whatever magnitude he comes to assume from a distance, Keynes must be remembered. He had not only the vision of what was desirable and the knowledge of what was

---

[1] Recall the famous oration on the Athenians fallen in the war against Sparta, in which he set out the principles of Athenian democracy; cf. Thucydides, II, 37-41.

[2] Bertrand Russell, *Roads to Freedom*, p. 10.

practicable, but a patience with details of technique worthy of Leonardo. And it will always add to his stature that he saw the limits to the fiction of 'economic man', as a creature of constant needs, disposition and capacity; and that, while being himself an economist, his chief hope was for the day

when the Economic Problem will take the back seat where it belongs, and the arena of the heart and head will be occupied, or reoccupied, by our real problems—the problems of life. and of human relations, of creation and behaviour and religion.[1]

At any rate, he understood the nature of the problem.

[1] J. M. Keynes, *Essays in Persuasion* (Preface), p. vii.

PART IV

THE BOUNDARIES OF REASON

13

PHILOSOPHICAL ETHICS

The Valais is an incomparable country; at first I did not understand the truth of this because I compared it...with the most significant things in my memory, with Spain, with Provence (with which it is indeed, via the Rhône, related by blood), but only since I admired it for its own sake has it revealed itself in all its grandeur.

RAINER MARIA RILKE

13.1 *Stocktaking*

Throughout the argument which I have been presenting, I have (apart from a few deliberate and well-marked lapses) remained strenuously literal. I have tried to write nothing which could not be interpreted strictly literally, and I have dismissed everything not so intelligible as out of my scope. Such care, though it would be excessive for any other purpose, is proper in a logician; even when, in consequence, we have done less than justice to the doctrine under consideration. Up to now the policy has been justified by its fruitfulness: but now it is time to relax this severity, and to look with a more liberal eye at some of the things which we have dismissed.

Only a few of the uses of ethical concepts which we commonly encounter have passed the test:

(i) Their use to express (or give vent to) our feelings.

(ii) Their use in coming to a decision about an individual action.

(iii) Their use in criticising and modifying our social practices.

This leaves a number of notable omissions, omissions which fall into three categories:

(*a*) Their use in discussing such straightforwardly ethical matters as the value of personal characteristics (say, whether or no meekness is good), the propriety of motives (say, how one ought to feel about lads who, never having had a happy home, steal simply in order to win the admiration of their friends), and the moral characters of men (say, whether or no Jones is a better man than Smith).

(*b*) Their use in questions which, though asked in a seemingly 'ethical' way, and similar in form to those 'ethical' questions that we have been discussing, arise in situations which leave no logical room for such questions: as when someone insists on an un-ambiguous answer to the question, 'Which ought I *really* to do, *A* or *B*?', there being morally nothing to choose between them, and no 'ethical' answer but, 'Make up your own mind!'; or when someone persists in asking, 'Why ought one to do *anything* which is right?', and is not satisfied with the reply, 'What else "ought" one to do, pray?'

(*c*) Their use in abstract questions, such as one encounters in philosophical ethics, questions of a form quite unlike those which arise in typically ethical situations: for example, 'Is goodness subjective or objective?', and 'What is the real analysis of "right"?'

There is no need to discuss at any length the questions falling into the first class. Their meaning requires no elucidation, and the way of answering them is sufficiently obvious from what has already been said. And the same is true of all the other, more complex moral questions which may crop up in situations of the kind we have discussed.

Now this shows the chief source of trouble that I am likely to encounter. My account is most seriously inaccurate and defective, where it is too *cursory*. Few things in real life are quite as straight-forward as I have made out: in consequence, there is hardly a point over which one might not argue that my account is over-simpli-fied. My only justification for leaving it so is my desire to keep the most general features of the logic of ethics clear. It is worth while for once to draw a small-scale map, showing the position of ethics relative to other subjects, instead of plunging straight away into the detailed problems of the subject itself. And, if you feel like rejecting such a map, because of the inaccuracies and omissions which it cannot help containing, remember the alterna-tives: a picture as complicated and finely shaded as observation and craftsmanship can provide, which, for fear of drawing a line through anything, would make nothing clear; or a map like the Bellman's—that is to say, 'a perfect and absolute blank!'

The second class of questions will lead us to explore the borderland between Reason and Faith, between religion and ethics: I shall consider them in the next (and final) chapter. For the rest of this chapter, I want to return and reconsider the last category—made up of the theories of philosophical ethics, which we discussed and dismissed in the first part of the book.

13.2   *Return to Philosophical Ethics*

When we discussed the traditional theories of philosophical ethics, we divided them for convenience of analysis into three categories, according to their general approach: these we referred to, respectively, as the 'objective', 'subjective' and 'imperative' categories. At the time, we took the theories completely at their word, and were forced to abandon them all as false, in one respect or another. But it is possible that, in so doing, we were missing the point of them and, now that we have satisfied ourselves about the central problem, we must go back and see whether we can find this point. Suppose, therefore, that advocates of each of these three lines of approach were to read the account we have given: what kinds of reaction should we expect them to show?

To begin with, the advocate of the imperative doctrine might say: 'I am prepared to accept quite a lot of your account —especially the parts about the way in which ethical language is used to give vent to our feelings. This seems to me important, because it brings out the ways in which the objective and subjective doctrines fail. To accept the former is to be deceived by the forms of words we use in ethics. To accept the latter, on the other hand, is to mistake an exclamation of pleasure for the assertion that one is pleased.... As for my own position, it seems to me to have been strengthened rather than weakened by your account. Admittedly you have brought out more explicitly than I did the ways in which other people's ethical feelings influence our own, but this only gives my theory a greater degree of generality. My position remains much as before. I hold to the imperative doctrine: not, perhaps, to the over-simplified theory I started with, but to an imperative one none the less—in short, one with a more sophisticated logic of exclamation.[1] Ethical

[1] This phrase I borrow from John Wisdom's lectures on 'Verification', Cambridge, May 1946.

utterances do evince our feelings, but they are feelings which have been shaped and modified by all our dealings with our fellow-men.'

To this, I can imagine the supporter of the objective doctrine replying: 'No, that isn't the lesson of the discussion at all. It is this question of *generality* that matters: any argument which shows that the truth of fully-fledged ethical judgements is independent of the speaker (that they are *objective*, in other words) tends to confirm rather than to refute my theory. I am, of course, glad to have the relation between values and our feelings more accurately expressed. One has always had to admit that there was some such relation: even if we hold that the developed moral judgement is not the outcome of emotion but of rational insight, there is still the important fact to be considered, that emotions tend to be related to moral judgements as they are not related to purely scientific judgements.[1] But this part of the account is quite compatible with my own view. Our feelings of satisfaction and obligation play the part of a "moral sense", by which we detect the non-natural properties of goodness and rightness. My theory may have to be slightly amplified, but you have scarcely brought any grounds for throwing it away.'

And, in his turn, the advocate of the subjective doctrine might well say to the 'objectivist': 'It's no good playing down the importance of our feelings in ethics: even the imperative doctrine does more justice to them than yours. Nor is the variability of our dispositions, which wrecked the analogy between science and ethics, a mere sideline: in fact, of course, it's essential to the idea of "conscience". No, to my mind it is this which is the most important feature of the present account of ethics: it shows that the "good" is that of which all reasonable and fully informed men will *approve*—it shows, that is to say, the *subjective* nature of ethical concepts. Nothing in it fundamentally contradicts the subjective doctrine—if anything it enhances its importance.'

This is at first sight a surprising situation. The objective, subjective and imperative approaches have always been con-

[1] See the review by L. A. Reid in *Mind*, n.s., XLII, p. 90: the strange thing is that the author never pauses to consider whether it might not be the 'outcome' (delightfully vague word!) of both emotion *and* rational insight.

sidered as *rivals*; but now they begin to seem less incompatible with one another. We must clearly take a second look at their arguments.

13.3 *The Compatibility of Opposed 'Ethical Theories'*

If we do so, the solution of this paradox is easily found. The supporter of the imperative doctrine approves of our account as drawing attention to the *rhetorical force* of moral judgements—to the difference between values, on the one hand, and properties and subjective relations, on the other. The supporter of the subjective doctrine approves of it as drawing attention to the way in which ethical judgements *express our feelings*—to the difference between ethical judgements, on the one hand, and exclamations and statements about properties, on the other. The advocate of the objective doctrine welcomes the attention our account pays to the *generality* of ethical judgements—a characteristic they share with judgements about properties.

The advocate of each approach, that is to say, is struck by those features of our ethical concepts which favour his own theory and discredit the others. But when, for example, the 'subjectivist' contends that values are, logically, the same as what we have called 'subjective relations', what he says is quite uninformative: and it is no more helpful and just as misleading of the 'objectivist' to insist that values are *not* the same as subjective relations. It would be more helpful of them if they showed in what ways values are *like* subjective relations, and in what ways they are unlike them. And the same goes for the theories that ethics has to do with 'properties' and 'exclamations'.

The 'imperativist' is prepared to consider the present account because it represents for him a sophisticated imperative theory: the 'objectivist' likes to think of it as a modified objective theory: the 'subjectivist' regards it as a form of subjective theory. And, of course, it could be regarded as any of those—or none. If you modify a philosophical theory enough, you will have to give it a new name—not because of any marvellous metaphysical metamorphosis, but because you are now impressed by the resemblances between your subject-matter and a new class of concepts. But before you reach this stage there will come a point, at which you can argue until Doomsday what it should be called.

And you will not get anywhere if you do, for you will be arguing at cross-purposes.

The opposition between the advocates of the objective, subjective and imperative doctrines reflects no more material a difference than the 'opposition' between the 'deontologists' and the 'teleologists'. For (if you remember)[1] these two groups of philosophers, in discussing what we mean by 'right', are preoccupied with different sets of logical criteria—the first with those appropriate to individual moral decisions, the second with those appropriate to the criticism of institutions. As a result of this, and since they both believe that one or the other set of criteria must represent the only *true* meaning of 'right' (in the way that a car travelling along the Bath Road 'must' be going *either* east *or* west), they differ as to what 'right' *really* means: and, in so doing, resemble two algebraists arguing as to whether $x = 2$ or $x = 3$ is the *real* solution of $x^2 - 5x + 6 = 0$.

Our three philosophers are in a like position. 'Ethical terms are. *really* used to give vent to our feelings', declares the 'imperativist' (if we have taken his point correctly). 'No!', replies the 'objectivist', 'The truth of *real* ethical judgements is independent of the speaker.' 'You're both wrong', retorts the 'subjectivist', '*In reality*, ethical judgements are equivalent to declarations of our feelings.' Each of these utterances reveals the speaker's preoccupations and, on many occasions, what each of them says is obviously true. Nevertheless, they still hanker after a decision between the three approaches—a demand which is quite unnecessary, since the doctrines are not mutually exclusive; but one in which they are encouraged by their idea that, if 'value' is to be a genuine concept at all, it must reside either 'in' the object or 'in' the speaker. Once again, the search for a 'really real' answer, a 'truly true' theory, prompted by the misunderstanding of a spatial metaphor, ends in a wild-goose chase.

13.4 *Ethical Theories as Disguised Comparisons*

Even after we have pointed this out, our philosophers may remain attached to their theories. And, if they do, there is no harm in that. Let them advocate a 'sophisticated imperative

---

[1] See § 11.7 above.

theory', a 'modified objective theory' or a 'kind of subjective theory', to their hearts' content—provided that they remain *true to the facts of our usage*. But, equally, let them not imagine that their theories are mutually exclusive. Is Wrynose in Lancashire, in Westmorland or in Cumberland? What you choose to answer depends largely on the direction from which you approach it: you may say any or all or none. But, whichever you say, make no mistake when you get there: it is the glorious scenery that counts.[1]

Or again, to adopt a metaphor which allots to ethics a fairer share of the map: if you go to Switzerland, you may on arrival be impressed by those features of the country which it shares with the region through which you have been travelling. 'Why!', you may exclaim, 'It's the Bavarian Alps all over again!', or, 'Properly speaking, I suppose it's an extension of the Dolomites', or, 'Just a grander and more rugged Haute Savoie!'—and, whichever you say, there will be some justice in your remark. The only danger is this: that you may be led to pay insufficient attention to the country itself, to its individual character and merits; and to imagine that you who admire one aspect are in real disagreement with those who are struck by other features of the country.

This illustration brings out one of the uses which the philosophical theories of ethics certainly do have: namely, their use as *disguised comparisons*. One can imagine two naturalists comparing elephants, cats and men. 'To my mind', the one might say, 'an elephant is like a cat rather than like a man.' 'I'm surprised to hear you say that', the other might reply, 'for I should have said an elephant was like a man rather than like a cat.' And no one will suppose that there is any material opposition—any contradiction—between their remarks: for one presumably means, 'An elephant is like a cat rather than like a man (in posture, structure, etc.)', and the other, 'An elephant is like a man rather than like a cat (in sagacity, length of life, etc.)'.

There will be no confusion, as long as their remarks are *openly* comparative. But suppose, now, that they become epigrammatic; and try to express the same thing in the words, 'An

---

[1] Cf. John Wisdom's review of C. H. Waddington's book, *Science and Ethics*, in *Mind*, n.s., LII (1943), pp. 275 ff.

elephant *is* a cat', and 'An elephant *is* a man', instead—so disguising the comparative nature of their remarks. If we discount the paradox of calling an elephant a 'cat' or a 'man' at all, we shall have to admit that there is a much greater appearance of contradiction. And if we get rid of the paradox, by replacing 'elephant', 'cat' and 'man', in our example, by 'virus', 'living creature' and 'non-living creature', we shall have an even better analogy. The unreal question, 'Is an elephant a cat or a man?', is transformed into the genuinely philosophical puzzle, 'Is a virus a living creature or not?', the answers to which ('A virus is a living creature' and 'A virus is a non-living creature') are 'disguised comparisons', standing for 'A virus is like a typical "living creature" (in some respects)' and 'A virus is like a typical "non-living creature" (in other respects)'. And the 'philosophical' nature of the type of question becomes still more marked when, for example, the straightforward inquiry, 'In what respects are flowers like those objects to which psychological terms (such as "feelings") are most naturally applied, and in what respects are they unlike them?', is expressed in the puzzling and seemingly scientific form, 'Do flowers have feelings?'[1]

To be honest, these examples are now too good for our immediate purpose. The problem, 'Is a virus a living creature or not?', is a genuine problem in a way in which the problem, 'Is goodness objective or subjective?', is not. The notions of a 'living creature' and of a 'non-living creature', unlike those of a 'cat' and a 'man', are used in such a way as to cover, between them, all material objects (including viruses): the problem is therefore to specify the grounds which would lead us to include 'viruses' in the one category or the other. The notions of 'objectivity' and 'subjectivity', on the other hand, do not form an equally exhaustive pair—however much they may seem

---

[1] Cf. John Wisdom's articles on 'Other Minds', in *Mind*, n.s., vols. XLIX–LII. What makes such borderline examples as these so puzzling is the fact that, while none of the resemblances we have noticed is a *crucial* one, there is yet no specifiable investigation which can be relied on to decide the matter. Possibly, in such a case, future experimental observations will indicate a crucial resemblance in one direction or the other (e.g. between a virus and a living cell), but we cannot be sure that this will ever happen, and until it does the question must remain open. If it does, of course, the example will cease to be a borderline one, and the remarks about it in the text will cease to apply.

to, when we write 'in the object' for 'objective' and 'in the speaker' for 'subjective'. To this extent, the question, 'Is goodness objective or subjective?', and others like it, are less genuine: but they can still do duty as 'diguised comparisons' standing, for example, in place of the longer question, 'Is "goodness" (like or unlike) a "property of the object", or (like or unlike) a "response of the speaker" (and in what respects)?'

13.5 Theory and Description in Philosophical Ethics

An ethical theory is, therefore, not just a paradox. If we reject it out of hand, on the grounds that, when taken literally, it is false, we misunderstand what its advocates are getting at. Such a theory has a certain positive value, which it would be wrong to ignore, as expressing, in its own paradoxical way, a comparison between concepts of two different kinds. This value is, however, limited: a single comparison tells one very little. A description of Switzerland as 'the Bavarian Alps all over again', as 'an extension of the Dolomites', or as 'a grander and more rugged Haute Savoie' is no substitute for a good guidebook: and an ethical theory of the traditional kind is no substitute for a descriptive account of the function of ethical concepts—an account of the kind that I have tried to give.

We may agree with the 'objectivist' that ethical words are 'like' words for properties—but they are not *just* like them: in some respects, they are *unlike* them also, and his description of 'value' as a 'property of the object' is therefore only partially acceptable. They are also like, *and* unlike, words for subjective relations; and passing an ethical judgement is like, *and* unlike, exclaiming: so the other doctrines are equally unhelpful. And this is what is to be expected, if they are 'disguised comparisons'. The disguised comparison, 'An elephant "is" a cat', is much less informative than the open assertion, 'Cats and elephants alike have four legs, are vertebrate, etc. etc.'; and it is no use expecting the philosophical theories to be any more specific—to tell us *in what respects* ethical concepts are unique, or *in what ways* the different types of concept resemble and differ from each other.[1]

---

[1] Cf. John Wisdom, 'Metaphysics and Verification', in *Mind*, n.s., XLVII (1938), p. 492: 'When we have an X sentence used in that way with which you are familiar, is there some combination of Y sentences used in that manner with

Ethical notions, like properties, do indeed have a certain generality; but it is a generality all their own:

We understand this generality through itself, and not through looking at something else. And understanding it through itself is a question of considering facts... which illustrate the rules for the use of ethical words, 'good', 'right', etc.[1]

And what is true of their generality applies equally to their rhetorical force, their expressiveness and their other logical characteristics. Each is understood best 'through itself', by looking at it directly, and refusing to be beguiled by any particular analogy—coming to it *by air*, as it were, instead of through a different but distractingly similar country.

If this lesson is taken to heart, one's interest in the philosophical theories of ethics is likely to diminish. Instead of appearing as possible sources of wonderful new knowledge— after the manner of scientific theories—their characteristic doctrines begin to look more like partisan slogans. 'Goodness is a non-natural, unanalysable, objective quality', 'Judgements of value are expressions of the speaker's attitude', 'Ethical utterances are merely ejaculations': such doctrines are tendentious truisms, or 'persuasive definitions',[2] rather than helpful analyses —they start off promisingly enough, but the amendments necessary to overcome their deficiencies only make them more complicated and less informative, while bringing them gradually nearer to the ideal of a description.

As soon as the truth of this is recognised, the desire for a *theory* vanishes. A *descriptive* account of our ethical concepts is what we need; a less cursory one than I have given, perhaps, but a descriptive account nevertheless. 'What is wanted' (to adapt something John Wisdom wrote in another context), 'is some device for bringing out the relation between the manner in which ethical sentences are used and the manners in which

which you are familiar, which serves the same purpose?...We have only to put the question in the plural, "Which of the purposes served by an X does a Y serve?", to see that the answer is a matter of describing these, and if after this it is asked, "Well, does it serve the same purpose?", the question is now obviously, "Shall we say, 'It serves the same purpose', or shall we choose not to?"'

[1] Mrs Helen Knight, *Aristotelian Soc. Suppl. Vol.* XVII (1938), p. 192.

[2] Stevenson's term; see *Ethics and Language*, ch. IX, and *Mind*, n.s., XLVII (1938).

others are used—so as to give their place on the language-map.'[1]
It will be from such a description, or 'language-map', rather than
from a one-sided and disguised comparison, that we shall obtain
the understanding that we seek—whether of the generality of
ethical judgements, their expressiveness and rhetorical force,
the function and importance of moral principles, the place of the
moralist, or the principles of the 'open society'; or, most important, what it is that makes an ethical argument a valid
argument, and what things are *good reasons* for ethical judgements. Furthermore, such an account, free from the distractions
of any particularly beguiling analogy, will suggest to us all the
comparisons we want: and enable us to display the distinctions
between concepts of different kinds without falsifying our usage.

13.6 *Ethical Theories as Rhetoric*

To describe the philosophical theories of ethics as 'disguised
comparisons' may, however, be to tell only a part of the story.
No doubt there are many philosophers in whom the sole motive
for the pursuit of such theories is the disinterested desire for
truth; who accept this theory rather than that because it seems
to them to express a particularly important feature of our ethical
notions, a feature they like to regard as the 'real' essence of
these notions. But there are some in whom the search also has
an extraneous, political aim. For them, the disguised comparison
is valuable, not just as the expression of an important truth, but
also because, being tendentious and persuasive, and harping
without seeming to on one aspect of our notions at the expense
of others, it has a rhetorical force useful in forwarding their
particular policies. This class of philosophers includes Bentham,
Hobbes, Hegel and Marx: according to K. R. Popper, we should
add Plato to the list.[2]

As a philosopher, Bentham was the father of Utilitarianism—
the doctrine that nothing is 'good' or 'right' unless it leads to
'the greatest happiness of the greatest number'. And this
doctrine is like every such philosophical doctrine: unquestionably
true in some situations, but equally false in others.

---

[1] See his paper on 'Philosophical Perplexity', in *Proc. Aristotelian Soc.* xxxvii
(1936–7), p. 87.
[2] Popper, *The Open Society and its Enemies*, vol. i.

As a politician, Bentham's aim was the reform of the English law, his enemies Blackstone and authority. And, by teaching people to inquire about the 'use' of every law, instead of regarding the existing statutes as sacred and unalterable, he and his followers were able to achieve this aim.

What is the connection between Bentham the philosopher and Bentham the politician? As a matter of logic, the utilitarian criteria which he used in his attack on the existing laws were near enough correct. But they were correct in their own right, and did not need the 'justification' he sought to give them, by explaining all 'value' in terms of the 'greatest happiness principle'. It is only in the criticism of institutions that this principle provides the uniquely important standard: if we exalt it into a universal definition of 'value', it leads to paradox in other contexts. Of course, if we grant Bentham his identification of 'value' with 'the greatest happiness of the greatest number', his criteria follow directly from it: but so also do his utilitarian standards of literary merit, which require us to rate *Christmas Day in the Workhouse* as a finer epic than *Paradise Lost*—and this alone is enough to show that he has falsified our notion of 'value'.

Indeed, the kernel of the problem is to discover why, if his criteria were correct and his 'justification' was (logically speaking) unsound and unnecessary, he bothered to 'justify' his criteria at all. The answer is to be found in history and psychology, rather than in logic. The circumstances of his time were such as to encourage an exaggerated respect for the existing laws and authorities. It was not enough, therefore, to criticise the law, and to point out the appropriate standards of criticism. It was necessary also to counterbalance the existing prejudices by some kind of rhetoric: to find some argument which would replace the current feelings against reform by others in favour of it. This was the function of Bentham's 'justification'. By exaggerating the generality of the 'greatest happiness principle', he persuaded people to accept it in the field to which it belonged. But in other fields, such as aesthetics and literary criticism, he was less interested, and his doctrines had correspondingly little effect.

These important features emerge clearly from any historical

account of his work. Here, for example, is that given by G. M. Trevelyan, in his book, *English Social History*:

This high conception of the supremacy of law was popularised by Blackstone's *Commentaries on the Laws of England* (1765), a book widely read by educated people in England and America, for it was a legally-minded age. The fault was that the law thus idealized was regarded too much as static, as a thing given once for all; whereas, if law is indeed to be the permanent rule of life to a nation, it must be apt to change with the changing needs and circumstances of society. In the Eighteenth Century, Parliament showed little legislative activity, except in private acts for enclosure of land, for turnpike roads, or other economic measures. In administrative matters there was a lag in legislation, at a time when great industrial developments were every year changing social conditions, and adding to the needs of a growing population.

Therefore Jeremy Bentham, the father of English law reform, regarded Blackstone as the arch-enemy, who stood in the way of change by teaching people to make a fetish of the laws of England in the form which they actually bore at the moment, a form dictated by the needs not of the present age but of ages long past.

The first blast against Blackstone was blown by young Bentham in his *Fragment on Government* in 1776.... When the octogenarian Bentham died in 1832, the laws of England had only just begun to be altered from what they had been when he first denounced them in Blackstone's day. Yet his prolonged efforts had not been in vain, for he had converted the rising generation. Onwards from that time our laws were rapidly changed in accordance with the commonsense, utilitarian principles that Bentham had laid down.

Reform was to be the specific work of the Nineteenth Century. The specific work of the earlier Hanoverian epoch was the establishment of the rule of law; and that law, with all its grave faults, was at least a law of freedom. On that solid foundation all our subsequent reforms were built. If the eighteenth century had not established the law of freedom, the nineteenth century in England would have proceeded by revolutionary violence, instead of by Parliamentary modification of the law.[1]

In the new Age of Reform...every institution, from the 'rotten borough' to the Church benefice, was subjected to the rude Benthamite enquiry: 'What is the use of it?'[2]

As for Hobbes, Hegel and Marx, the ethical conclusions they advocated were, on the whole, less acceptable than those of Bentham. The status of their arguments is, however, much

---

[1] G. M. Trevelyan, *English Social History*, pp. 350–1.   [2] Op. cit. p. 511.

the same: each presents us with philosophical reasoning falsifying our notions in a direction favouring his political aims.
Hobbes' theory of the State, for example, idealises such notions
as 'monarchy', 'sovereignty', and 'fear', in a way which is
subtly false to our actual usage; but in each case the distortion
is of such a kind as to favour unconditional submission to the
King's will—the political course he was concerned to advocate.[1]
The relation between Hegel's ethical and political theory, and his
financial and academic dependence on the Prussian State, is more
flagrant, and has been thoroughly exposed by Popper:[2] so also
have the motives and weaknesses of Marx's arguments for a pro-
letarian revolution. In all these philosophers, we find arguments
which remain obscure or paradoxical so long as they are taken
literally, but which are immediately intelligible by reference
to their political aims. Not that there is any serious evidence
of their insincerity, except in the case of Hegel—they all seem
to have believed in the soundness of their arguments, and of
their conclusions—but they all to some extent display, in their
fallacies, Marx's own self-confessed desire not so much to *understand* the world as to *change* it.[3]

It is possible to argue, of course, that men of this kind, in their
political work, are not really being 'philosophers' at all. And,
in support of this, one could point to Marx's own denunciations
of 'philosophy'.[4] But this would be to misunderstand what
I have been meaning by the 'philosophical' theories of ethics.
Consider a parallel, but simpler case, expressed in the manner
of a late-nineteenth-century *Punch* joke:

VICAR (observing Jenkins the grocer, bent over the counter,
alternately chewing the end of his pencil and scrawling illegibly on
a flour-bag): 'Ah, Jenkins! Engaged on a complex arithmetical
computation, I see!'

JENKINS (straightening up and scratching the back of his head):
'No, y'r Rev'rence, 't bain't anything loike thet. Oi be jest reck'ning
Mrs Will'ms's groc'ry bill.'

VICAR (exploding with laughter and leaving the shop in a hurry):!!!!

[1] How else are we to understand the things he writes, for example, in the
Leviathan?

[2] In op. cit. vol. II.

[3] 'The philosophers have only interpreted the world in various ways; the point
however is to *change* it' (*Theses on Feuerbach*, no. 11, 1845).

[4] Cf. his polemical treatise entitled *The Poverty of Philosophy*.

What makes Jenkins' scrawling an 'arithmetical computation' is the way in which he manipulates the symbols, not the purpose for which he does so; and what makes the writings of Bentham, Hobbes, Hegel and Marx 'philosophical', in our sense, is the logical characteristics of their statements, not the special purpose for which they make them. Since their central doctrines are false if taken literally, but can be made true if we are prepared to falsify our notions a little, they can be put into the same logical category as arguments about the 'objective' or 'subjective' nature of 'goodness', or about 'non-natural properties' and 'attitudes'. As such, they are unquestionably 'philosophical', and like their prototypes they are, if true at all, true by definition—tendentious truisms. However, they are interesting on their own account as a reminder that such tendentiousness may have several functions: it may reflect a purely intellectual preoccupation with one logical feature of a concept at the expense of the others, but it may reflect a more practical aim.

13.7 *Ethical Theories: Rhetoric and Reason*

As compared with straightforward ethics, with its definite criteria of truth and falsity, of validity and fallaciousness, of 'good' and 'bad' reasoning, philosophical ethics—as used politically—looks very like pure persuasion. Apart from the elementary rules of deductive and inductive inference, no fixed logical criteria can be applied to it; and even those that do apply help us only to tell arguments which *appear* to be valid from those which do not even appear to be. The notion of 'logical validity' itself can hardly be applied: the only test by which to decide whether or not a particular argument is appropriate in a given situation lies *outside* the mode of 'reasoning'—if the philosophical argument lends colour to an ethical conclusion which is itself a just one, then, as a matter of *ethics*, it can be accepted: if not, we ought to reject it. In fact, I went so far as to describe Bentham's philosophical ethics as having been required in order to 'counterbalance the existing prejudices by rhetoric', and to 'replace the current feelings against reform by others in favour of it'. But to give the impression that such arguments are concerned with the emotions alone, completely divorced from reason, would be to misrepresent them; and, in so far as I have done this, I must make amends.

Certainly this use of philosophical ethics is less characteristic an instance of 'reasoning' than ordinary ethics; but that does not make it pure 'persuasion'. This will be obvious when we compare it, instead, with a 'hell-fire' sermon, lovers' chatter, or a suffragette oration. There is such a thing as a *direct* appeal to the emotions, as arguments designed to act—and acting—on the heart alone, arousing fear and submission, affection or sympathy, with the minimum of reasoning. Such arguments are as effective in moving the stupid or uneducated as they are in moving the sophisticated and intelligent. But a peculiarity of philosophical arguments is that they act more strongly on the intelligent and sophisticated than on the under-educated or stupid: they rely for their effect on familiarity with quite advanced types of reasoning, rather than on a simple-hearted response; and the simple are less prone to be dazzled into accepting them as the literal truth than are the educated, for they just miss the point. There is therefore something to be said for regarding this type of argument as a form of 'reasoning'—as appealing to a kind of reason, rather than to pure emotion: but it is a type of reasoning logically less typical and more complex than those which we have considered so far.

There are some simpler uses of language which share with this one many of its characteristic features. Consider, for example, the kinds of slogan which are put out in Road Safety Campaigns. These also act rhetorically; may take the form of 'tendentious truisms'; may appear to be mutually contradictory without inconsistency; and yet can frequently be defended by reasoning. In a recent campaign in Cambridge, for instance, the same organisation was putting out at the same time two slogans, the one reading, 'You Never Know What May Happen!', and the other, 'Accidents Never Happen—They Are *Caused*!' If we took these slogans (mistakenly, of course) as assertions of fact, we should have to conclude that they were both false. Quite often we *do* know everything that can happen; and quite often accidents *do* happen—otherwise there would be no call for a Road Safety Campaign. Again, if the slogans were taken as assertions of fact, it would be inconsistent for them both to be used in the

same campaign—the truth of one would make the other unnecessary: if it were true that accidents never happened, the fact
that we do not always know what may happen next would not
matter at all.

In fact, of course, to treat them as assertions is to misunderstand them. Taken literally, they are no doubt false. No doubt
also we could make them true, by small changes in our usage.
And in this form they could be defended philosophically, in the
way in which the sentences, 'One can never really know anything
about the future' and 'Every event must have a cause', can be
defended. But even to take them like this would be to misunderstand them, for their tendentiousness is not meant intellectually, as a matter of logic—to underline the differences
between knowledge of the future and knowledge of the present,
or to liken all phenomena to those involved in a typical causal
sequence. It is meant rhetorically—to remind us, as a matter of
practical importance, first of the need, when driving, to allow
for unexpected developments, such as a child running out from
behind a stationary motor car; and secondly of the high proportion of accidents for which one of the parties involved can
fairly be held responsible. It would be stupid to say that the
slogans were paradoxical, untrue or inconsistent; for *in use* they
serve a definite purpose, and serve it successfully. Both draw
our attention to similarities and differences which remind us to
take care on the road; and no one is bothered by the fact that the
slogans are 'literally' ridiculous.

A speech for the defence in a Paris murder trial, a road-safety
slogan, Hobbes' political theory; each appeals to reason *of a kind,*
but it remains an oblique and rhetorical kind. Each relies on
comparisons rather than on direct statements, and none can over-
ride or supersede the conclusions of ethical reasoning proper.
Nevertheless, just as slogans may do more for road safety than
the mere recital of accident statistics, or of the evidence given at
coroners' inquests, so the arguments of a Hobbes or a Bentham
may be of greater practical effect than the assertion of genuinely
ethical or political statements, however true and relevant these
may be.

14

REASON AND FAITH

It is the heart which is conscious of God, not the reason. This is faith—God evident to the heart and not to the reason....Faith is within the heart, and makes us say not 'Scio', but 'Credo'.

PASCAL[1]

14.1 *The Finite Scope of Reasoning*

In all the modes of reasoning analysed so far, we found that the 'reasons' which could logically be given in support of any statement formed a finite chain. In every case, a point was reached beyond which it was no longer possible to give 'reasons' of the kind given until then; and eventually there came a stage beyond which it seemed that no 'reason' of any kind could be given. As a reminder of what I mean: the question, 'Why ought I not to have two wives?', calls to begin with for reasons referring to the existing institutions; secondly, may raise the more general question whether our institution of 'marriage' could be improved by altering it in the direction of polygamy; thirdly, transforms itself into a question about the kind of community in which one would personally prefer to live; and beyond that cannot be reasoned about at all.[2] Now we have been interested throughout in *literal* answers only: so, when faced with requests for reasons of any kind beyond the point at which these ceased to be appropriate we dismissed them as illogical.

In doing so, we were acting on the same principle as the father who, when his child goes on asking, 'Why?', parrot-wise, stops answering its questions and checks him instead. Thus:

CHILD. 'Why are you putting your coat on, Daddy?'
FATHER. 'Because I'm going out.'
C. 'Why are you going out, Daddy?'
F. 'I'm going to see Aunt Matilda.'

---

[1] *Les Pensées de Pascal, disposées suivant l'ordre du cahier autographique*, ed. G. Michaut, Fribourg (1896), no. 13, p. 11, and no. 58, p. 25; tr. Rawlings, in *Selected Thoughts* (The Scott Library), VIII, p. 10 and XXXIV, p. 20.
[2] See §11.6 above.

C. 'Why?'

F. 'Because she isn't very well to-day.'

C. 'Why?'

F. 'Because she ate something which disagreed with her.'

C. 'Why?'

F. 'Well, I suppose she was hungry, and didn't realise the food was bad.'

C. 'Why?'

F. 'How should I know?'

C. 'But why, Daddy?'

F. 'Oh, don't ask silly questions!'

There are four particularly interesting situations on which we have to adopt this course:

(i) When someone asks, 'How do you explain that?', of something which there is no question of 'explaining', such as the deaths on their birthdays of three children in one family.[1]

(ii) When someone asks, 'But which ought I to do?', of two courses of action between which, morally, there is nothing to choose, and insists on an answer independent of his personal preferences.[2]

(iii) When someone asks, not just 'What reason is there for accepting this explanation?'—meaning 'this' one rather than 'that'—but also, 'What reason is there for accepting any scientific explanation?'[3]

(iv) When someone asks, not just 'Why ought I to do this?' —meaning 'this' course of action rather than 'that' one—but also, 'And why ought I to do anything that is right?'[4]

In each of these situations, no literal question framed in those particular words can arise. And I mean by this more than that such a question does not happen to arise, or that it happens not to be able to arise. I mean that, as a consequence of the ways in which we employ the words concerned, and of the purpose which questions of this form serve, there is logically no place in such a situation for this question—taken literally. And, since we have confined ourselves strictly to literal interpretations up till now, that means no place at all of the kinds that we have been considering.

[1] See § 7.5 above.   [2] See § 11.8 above.
[3] See § 7.6 above.   [4] See § 11.9 above.

14.2 'Limiting' Questions

Nevertheless, one often wants to go on asking such questions, even when there is no literal, rational sense in them. The fact that one does so may be a sign of confusion—a sign that one has just not got the hang of questions of the type concerned—or it may not. For example, you may use the 'scientific' questions, 'Why does this happen?' and 'How is that to be explained?', as expressions of surprise; and then you will probably be satisfied by a genuinely scientific explanation. Or you may go on asking them after they have ceased to be appropriate, through failing to realise that there is no further room for a scientific explanation; and then you will be satisfied when this fact is pointed out. But you may use the same questions as expressions, not merely of surprise at the unexpected, but also of wonder that there should be any phenomenon of this sort. If you do, then when all possible scientific explanations have been exhausted, when it has been shown that things always happen so, and that the phenomenon about which you are asking is paralleled by familiar phenomena in other fields, you may still feel that your desire for an 'explanation' remains unsatisfied; and, when someone points out that no further scientific explanation can be given, you may come to the conclusion that these things are so wonderful as to be 'beyond human understanding'.

Surprise and curiosity at the antics of the wagtail, or at the winged seeds of the sycamore, may be satisfied by the study of botany or ornithology. No amount of scientific knowledge, however, will still the feeling that birds and trees are *wonderful* things; it will probably only enhance it. And if this is the feeling which prompts your request for an explanation, it will arise again even when science has done all that can be asked of it.

Other feelings may find expression in the same way. The sad deaths of the Jones children may occasion in us both surprise and distress. We soon come to recognise that the question, 'Why did they have to die so young; and all on their birthdays, too?', cannot arise, as a matter of science—that science can do nothing for us in such a situation. And in the absence of a murderer (about whose motives for killing them we might be enquiring) the question cannot arise in *any* form to which there is a literal answer. All the same, we may still want to ask it, and still feel the need of an answer, as an expression of our distress, rather than of our surprise; and indeed, in such a context, it is in this sense that one would most naturally interpret the question.

It is questions of this kind with which I am concerned in the present chapter—questions expressed in a form borrowed from a familiar mode of reasoning, but not doing the job which they normally do within that mode of reasoning. It is characteristic of them that only a small change is required, either in the form of the question, or in the context in which it is asked, in order to bring it unquestionably back into the scope of its apparent mode of reasoning. But it is equally characteristic of them that the way of answering suggested by the form of words employed will never completely satisfy the questioner, so that he continues to ask the question even after the resources of the apparent mode of reasoning have been exhausted. Questions of this kind I shall refer to as 'limiting questions': they are of particular interest when one is examining the limits and boundaries of any mode of reasoning—and of ethical reasoning in particular.

14.3 The Peculiarities of 'Limiting Questions'

I want to point out three peculiarities of questions of this type, which make the ways of answering them quite different from the ways of answering more literal questions. These peculiarities I shall then illustrate in two instances:

(i) Our usage provides no standard interpretation of such questions. Their form suggests a meaning of a familiar kind, but the situations in which they are asked are such that they cannot have that meaning. The form of words may therefore express any of a varied selection of personal predicaments, and we can only find out as we go along what is 'behind' the question.

(ii) If the question were to be interpreted literally—that is, by reference to its apparent logical form—we should expect there to be genuinely alternative answers, each applicable over a limited range of cases. Within the apparent mode of reasoning, all questions require a definite choice to be made—e.g. between two theories or social practices, between one moral decision and another, or between one scientific prediction and another. A 'limiting question', however, does not present us with genuine alternatives to choose between: it is expressed in such a way that the only reply within the apparent mode of reasoning is (for instance), 'Well, isn't the "right" just what one "ought" to do?'

(iii) Finally, a 'limiting question' is not flagrantly 'extra-rational' in its form. It is not like the questions in Blake's *Tyger*, which no one would ever dream of trying to answer literally:

> What the hammer? What the chain?
> In what furnace was thy brain?
> What the anvil? What dread grasp
> Dare its deadly terrors clasp?

There is therefore always the urge to give it the kind of answer which its form appears to demand. However, either to answer or to refuse to answer in this way will leave the questioner equally dissatisfied. If you refuse, his desire for such an answer remains unstilled: if you answer, there is nothing to stop the question from arising again about your reply.

Consider a familiar instance. One learns to ask the questions, 'How is it supported?' and 'What does it rest on?', in all kinds of everyday situations; for instance, when talking to a gardener about his peach-tree, or to an engineer about some piece of machinery. In these familiar situations, there is always the possibility that the object referred to might collapse if there were nothing to support it, nothing for it to rest on: or, at any rate, in all these instances we can understand what it would mean to say that it had 'collapsed'. But, if you start with a familiar object and ask, 'What does it rest on?', and continue to ask of each new object mentioned, 'And what does that rest on?', you will eventually reach the answer, 'The solid earth', and after that you cannot ask the question any more—in that sense anyway.

In the everyday sense, the question, 'What holds the earth up?',[1] is a 'limiting question', having all the peculiarities I have referred to:

(i) If someone does ask it, it is not at all clear what he wants to know, in the way it is if he asks, 'What holds your peach-tree

---

[1] I recall Wittgenstein's likening the problem of induction to this question; and saying that those philosophers who asked for a 'justification' of science were like the Ancients, who felt there must be an Atlas to support the Earth on his shoulders (Cambridge University Moral Science Club: 14 November 1946).

up?' In ordinary cases, the form of the question and the nature of the situation between them determine the meaning of the question: here they cannot do so, and one can only guess at what is prompting it.

(ii) The different answers to the question, 'What holds your peach-tree up?', are intelligible enough, and one can imagine a peach-tree's 'falling down': but neither of these things is the case when someone asks, 'What holds the earth up?'

(iii) Still, there is a strong desire to take the question literally, in a way in which one would never take Blake's questions literally. But, if we do, it will get us nowhere. If we answer 'An elephant', the questioner can ask, 'And what holds the elephant up?'; if we now answer 'A tortoise', the question arises again; and there is no way of stopping its recurrence this side of infinity.

We might of course answer, 'Nothing', and, when the questioner protested, 'Nothing? But it must be held up by something', we might explain to him his error, pointing out that he was misunderstanding the nature of questions of the form, 'What holds it up?', and failing to see that this form of question cannot be asked of 'the earth' at all. If the question had arisen from such a misunderstanding, the questioner would be satisfied by this; and, to the extent that it did satisfy him, we could conclude that the enquiry had arisen in this way, that the motive prompting the question had been the perplexity of misunderstanding. But he might not be so easily satisfied. The question might be a 'cover' for some other feeling; say, for an hysterical apprehensiveness about the future. This could not be settled by any literal answer to his question, or by any rational analysis of the question itself: in fact, the only type of reasoning likely to make any impression on him would be psychoanalytic reasoning.

As a second instance, the question, 'Why ought one to do what is right?', shares these same peculiarities:

(i) The form of the question and the situation in which it is asked do not determine the meaning of the question, in the way in which they determine the meaning of a question like, 'Why ought I to give this book back to Jones?'

(ii) There are no 'alternative answers', in the way in which there are to a typically ethical question.

(iii) Still, the question does seem to call for an ethical answer —even though whatever you say can be queried in its turn, and so *ad infinitum*.

Once again we might explain to the questioner how the notions of 'right' and 'obligation' arise, pointing out that their origins are such as to make the sentence, 'One ought to do what is right', a truism. And again this might satisfy him, showing that it had been the perplexity born of misunderstanding which had prompted his question. But again our answer might leave him unmoved: and, when this happened, we should have to conclude that the motive behind this question was only being obliquely expressed.

Since, when one is faced with a 'limiting question', there is this additional uncertainty about the way in which it is to be interpreted—since the possible concealed motives for asking a 'limiting question' are many and varied—one cannot help being at a loss to begin with. The fact that such questions have no fixed, literal meaning means that there is no fixed, literal way of answering them, and one just has to wait and see what it is the questioner wants. If, for example, someone asks, 'Why ought one to do what is right?', the answers which can be given are of two kinds. Either they must be tailor-made to fit the questioner—in which case they have no universal application— or they must abandon all pretence of literalness, and take on the elusive, allusive quality of poetry. In the first case, they can at the best take account of the questioner's professional preoccupations, drawing attention (for instance) to analogies between ethical and biological concepts, if he is a biologist, to analogies between ethical and psychological concepts, if he is a psychologist, and so on.[1] In the second, they are to be judged less like the questions in the mode of reasoning whose form they have borrowed, than like Blake's poems—by their impact, that is, and not by excessively intellectual standards.

If the questioner insists on having an answer which is at the same time literal and unique, there is nothing further one can do. The question, 'What is the intellectual basis of ethics?', posed by Dr C. H. Waddington in the introduction to his symposium,

----

[1] This would be the peg on which to hang a discussion of the so-called 'scientific' theories of ethics, but this would be too much of a digression.

Science and Ethics,[1] is a good example. In substance, this question is similar to 'Why ought one to do what is right?', but the use of the word 'intellectual' reinforces the demand for a rational, literal answer—and the whole of the discussion which follows makes it clear that the questioner wants a straightforward answer to an oblique question. And, faced with this demand, we can only answer as Wittgenstein answered, 'This is a terrible business—just terrible! You can at best stammer when you talk of it.'[2]

14.4 *The Importance of 'Limiting Questions'*

Some philosophers argue that all utterances which cannot be taken literally ought to be done away with; as though everything which is 'nonsense' to them were also, necessarily, dangerous nonsense. And no doubt, where 'limiting questions' arise solely out of logical confusions, there are some grounds for wishing them out of existence. In other cases, however, they are not to be argued away. That one should learn to tell such limiting questions from questions in the mode of reasoning whose form they borrow, may well be desirable. But that we should be exhorted to stop asking them altogether, is ridiculous. The feeling of urgency behind so many of them, the insistence with which they recur, itself suggests that no good is done by bottling them up; and, provided that one recognises them for what they are, what can there be against our asking them?

Indeed, such questions have a positive value, as both psychology and history show. Psychologically, they help us to *accept* the world, just as the explanations of science help us to *understand* it. We recognise that the question, 'Why did they have to die so young?', may be hardly more than a cry of distress arising from the desire to reject an unpleasant fact; and, if this is the case, are not Pascal's 'limiting questions' the expression of distress also, even though of a distress which is at once more general and deeply rooted?—

When I consider the briefness of my life, swallowed up in the eternity before and behind it, the small space I fill, or even see,

---

[1] Op. cit. p. 7.
[2] Waddington himself quotes this remark (loc. cit.) but he has evidently not appreciated its full force.

engulfed in the infinite immensity of spaces which I know not, and which know not me, I am afraid. . . . Who has set me here? By whose order and arrangement have this place and this time been allotted me? . . . [1]

Again, the example recorded by Dostoevsky in *The Brothers Karamazov*—as Dmitri's dream—shows how importunately such questioning may arise:

He was driving somewhere in the steppes. . . . Not far off was a village, he could see the black huts, and half the huts were burnt down, there were only the charred beams sticking up. As they drove in, there were peasant women drawn up along the road. . . .
'Why are they crying? Why are they crying?', Mitya [Dmitri] asked, as they dashed gaily by.
'It's the babe', answered the driver, 'the babe weeping.'
And Mitya was struck by his saying, in his peasant way, 'the babe', and he liked the peasant's calling it a 'babe'. There seemed more pity in it.
'But why is it weeping?' Mitya persisted stupidly, 'why are its little arms bare? Why don't they wrap it up?'
'The babe's cold, its little clothes are frozen and don't warm it.'
'But why is it? Why?' foolish Mitya still persisted.
'Why, they're poor people, burnt out. They've no bread. They're begging because they've been burnt out.'
'No, no,' Mitya, as it were, still did not understand. 'Tell me why it is those poor mothers stand there? Why are people poor? Why is the babe poor? Why is the steppe barren? Why don't they hug each other and kiss? Why don't they sing songs of joy? Why are they so dark from black misery? Why don't they feed the babe?'
And he felt that, though his questions were unreasonable and senseless, yet he wanted to ask just that; and he had to ask it just in that way. And he felt that a passion of pity, such as he had never known before, was rising in his heart, that he wanted to cry, that he wanted to do something for them all, so that the babe should weep no more, so that the dark-faced, dried-up mother should not weep, that no one should shed tears again from that moment. . . .
'I've had a good dream, gentlemen,' he said in a strange voice, with a new light, as of joy, in his face. [2]

The importance of such questions can also be seen from history. Had we never asked questions extra-rationally, we

---

[1] Op. cit. no. 188, p. 70; Rawlings, xcv, p. 48.
[2] Dostoevsky, *The Brothers Karamazov*, tr. Garnett (1912), pp. 546–8.

should never have come to ask them rationally. All our typically rational methods of argument have developed out of less typically rational prototypes—science, for instance, grew out of magic and primitive religion—and it is illuminating to contrast the undeveloped prototype with its descendant, the developed mode of reasoning.

There are many grounds for uncertainty about the future; and this 'uncertainty' may be of several kinds. It may be an inability to predict particular phenomena correctly: it may be 'an anxious fear of future events'[1] (which is how Hume described the source of the 'primary religion of mankind'). At first, these types of uncertainty are treated alike. The same men, methods and notions are expected to be able to deal with them all; and are used to allay the uncertainty, whether it is the outcome of surprise and curiosity, or of fear and wonder. At this stage, the same questions are asked and the same answers are given, whether it is exact knowledge of the future or reassurance that is wanted.

It is only recently that there has been a special, separate and differentiated way of dealing with requests for exact knowledge; and this has to be remembered, for instance, when we are trying to understand the writings of the Greeks. Much of what seems to us obscure or confused is clarified when we recognise that it is intended, not as pure 'logic', pure 'science', pure 'ethics', or pure 'theology' (as we know these subjects), but as an amalgam, doing as far as it can the jobs of all its descendants.[2]

By the present time, matters of science have become almost wholly divorced from the religious questions of which they were originally a part: we have a special means of obtaining exact knowledge about the future. But that does not mean that the desire for *reassurance* has gone. Indeed, it certainly remains, especially over events like the deaths of the Jones children; and all who have not taken the rationalist vow of silence will continue to ask some (at any rate) of these 'limiting questions'.

---

[1] Hume, *The Natural History of Religion*, § xiii, beginning.
[2] This is especially the case when we are trying to understand the pre-Socratic philosophers.

14.5   *Matters of Faith*

Not only shall we continue to ask these questions, but we shall genuinely want answers to them. And, of the answers which are given to us, we shall regard some as being better than others. And some of them, no doubt, will really be better than others. Some, that is to say, will give us a reassurance which will not be disappointed; will allay our fear of 'the eternity before and behind the brief span'[1] of our lives, and of 'the infinite immensity' of space; will provide comfort in the face of distress; and will answer our questions in a way which will not seem in retrospect to have missed their point.

Now, provided that the answers given are good answers, by this sort of standard, what logical justification can there be for dismissing them? Of course 'theological' arguments, and 'religious' questions and answers—those with which we are concerned here—are on quite a different footing, as a matter of logic, from scientific and ethical arguments, questions and answers. But it is only if we suppose that religious arguments pretend (say) to provide exact knowledge of the future—so competing with science on its own ground—that we can be justified in attempting to apply to them the logical criteria appropriate to scientific explanations; and only if we do this that we have any grounds for concluding (with Ayer) that 'all utterances about the nature of God are nonsensical',[2] or (with Freud) that religion is 'an illusion'.[3] Provided that we remember that religion has functions other than that of competing with science and ethics on their own grounds, we shall understand that to reject all religious arguments for this reason is to make a serious logical blunder—an error as great as that of taking figurative phrases literally, or of supposing that the mathematical theory of numbers (say) has any deep, religious significance. There are two such errors, as Pascal points out—'first, to take everything literally; secondly, to take everything spiritually'[4]—and it is asking for trouble if one ignores the

---

[1] Pascal, loc. cit.

[2] Ayer, *Language, Truth and Logic* (2nd ed.), p. 115.

[3] Freud, *The Future of an Illusion, passim.*

[4] Op. cit. no. 78, p. 31; Rawlings, XL, p. 22; note also his remarks about 'the secret of figures' in no. 87, p. 36; Rawlings, XLII, p. 24.

difference between questions of science and ethics, which are matters of *reason*, and things like the existence of God, which are matters of *faith*.

What is the nature of this distinction between 'faith' and 'reason'? To begin with, it is essential to rule out of account those things which are often called 'matters of faith' or 'articles of faith', by transference: things which are really only matters of fact about which the evidence is inconclusive, but over which one holds a dogmatic opinion out of pride. Examples of this kind—such as, 'It was for him an article of faith that any one Englishman was a match for any ten Frenchmen'—only confuse the issue. Again, not all 'limiting questions' are 'religious',[1] and not all 'religious' questions are 'limiting': it is only over those on the boundaries between religion, science and ethics that real difficulties arise, and it is on these that I shall concentrate.

If one is discussing genuine 'matters of faith' (like the sacredness, for the Cambodians, of white elephants), then there is no question of advancing 'reasons' for individual assertions, of weighing the evidence for different hypotheses, and so on. To talk of bringing evidence of this kind for 'matters of faith' does not make sense. Over matters of faith, one does not 'believe' or 'disbelieve' individual propositions: one 'accepts' or 'rejects' complete notions. Indeed, we might describe the distinction between 'faith' and 'reason' in these terms—belief as a matter of reason is *belief of* a proposition of some kind: belief as a matter of faith is *belief in* a notion of some kind.

Furthermore, since those questions of religion which make use of everyday, scientific or ethical notions are 'limiting questions', this use can only be *figurative* (or, to use Pascal's alternative term, 'spiritual'). The question of God's existence is often discussed by philosophers in a way which would only be appropriate, if it were the literal counterpart of the question, 'Are there any one-eyed cats?'; and, no doubt, anyone who does

---

[1] The questions Dmitri Karamazov asks in his dream (cf. § 14.4 above) are in some ways not typically religious: the very fact that he himself thinks of them as 'unreasonable and senseless' marks them off from the typically religious class of questions. It is natural for anyone who asks 'limiting questions' in a religious manner, by contrast, to emphasise the continuity of his questions with, say, ethical and scientific questions, and to treat theology as a kind of 'super-science' having 'super-ethical' implications.

this will be forced to conclude that the Argument from Design, as given (say) in Paley's *Natural Theology,* is unconvincing. But this is to misapprehend its function: to overlook the radical differences between the kinds of answer the two questions require. The inference from 'appearances of design in nature' to the existence of an 'omnipotent, omniscient and omni-present Deity' is not an argument for the existence of an especially powerful and knowing animal, liable to turn up anywhere at any moment. It consists (and we can quote Paley's own sub-title to illustrate this) in accumulating 'evidences of the existence and attributes of the Deity from the appearances of Nature'. The existence of God, one might argue (though here I doubt whether Paley would follow us), is not something to demand *evidence for*; nor is the sentence, 'God exists', one to be believed if, and only if, the evidence for its truth is good enough. The very last question to ask about God is *whether* He exists. Rather, we must first accept the notion of 'God': and then we shall be in a position to point to *evidences of* His existence.

How uncomfortable Paley seems when he is trying to refute by pure argument the astronomical account of the solar system! How much more at home he is when, instead of tinkering inexpertly with science, he expresses his wonder at the marvels of nature!

Were there no example in the world of contrivance except that of the *eye*, it would be alone sufficient to support the conclusion which we draw from it, as to the necessity of an intelligent Creator.... Its coats and humours, constructed, as the lenses of a telescope are constructed, for the refraction of rays of light to a point, which forms the proper action of the organs; [etc., etc.]......compose altogether an apparatus, a system of parts, a preparation of means, so manifest in their design, so exquisite in their contrivance, so successful in their issue, so precious and so infinitely beneficial in their use, as, in my opinion, to bear down all doubt that can be raised upon the subject.[1]

Once more, Dostoevsky has given us, in *The Brothers Kara-mazov*—to be exact, in Ivan's confession of faith to his saintly brother, Alyosha—the classic expression of these facts:

What's strange, what would be marvellous, is not that God should really exist; the marvel is that such an idea, the idea of the necessity

[1] Paley, *Natural Theology,* ch. VI (opening).

of God, should enter the head of such a savage, vicious beast as man. So holy is it, so touching, so wise and so great a credit it does to man. As for me, I've long resolved not to think whether man created God or God man.... And so I omit all the hypotheses. For what are we aiming at now? I am trying to explain as quickly as possible my essential nature, that is what manner of man I am, what I believe in, and for what I hope, that's it, isn't it? And therefore I tell you that I accept God simply.... I can't expect to understand about God. I acknowledge humbly that I have no faculty for settling such questions.... And I advise you never to think about it either, my dear Alyosha, especially about God, whether He exists or not. All such questions are utterly inappropriate.... I accept God and am glad to, and what's more, I accept His wisdom, His purpose—which are utterly beyond our ken; I believe in the eternal harmony in which they say we shall one day be blended.... [1]

14.6 *Spiritual and Literal Interpretations*

In this passage, Dostoevsky not only shows his grasp of the differences between factual and religious 'belief': he also gives us—in Ivan's references to 'God's purpose'—a perfect example of a concept used 'spiritually', as opposed to 'literally'.

If, through a window, we see a man going through an extraordinary sequence of acrobatics, crawling around with his head on the floor, peering behind the cupboards and so on, we may want to inquire whether there is any 'purpose' in his actions or not. And, if we are told that he is looking for his front stud, we shall be able to 'understand' his previous antics, and anticipate his future ones—for instance, his giving up the search and picking a new one out of the stud-box on his dressing-table. Again, if we are shown the pieces of antler found in the neolithic workings at Grime's Graves in Norfolk, we may ask what their 'purpose' was; and again, by pointing to the finger-marks and worn areas on the antlers, an archaeologist may indicate the kinds of operation for which they were used, and so enable us to reconstruct a picture of the neolithic miner, lying in the mine, with his tallow lamp burning beside him, gripping the antler 'pick' with his left hand, and hammering it into the wall of chalk and flint with the stone held in his right.[2]

---

[1] Dostoevsky, op. cit. pp. 246–7; I have omitted certain irrelevant Kantianisms standing in the text.
[2] See Grahame Clark, *Prehistoric Britain*, pp. 56–60 and figs. 52–6.

These two examples illustrate the literal use of the notion of 'purpose'. In each case, our understanding of the concept depends on there being a certain human background, a situation in which people are doing things that satisfy some recognisable need. In each case, the recognition of the human need met by the actions is the means of answering our questions about 'purpose'.

It is quite otherwise with questions about the 'purpose' of the universe. The ordinary procedure for answering questions about 'purpose' is no longer applicable: questions about the 'purpose' of the universe are therefore 'limiting questions'. And the literal sense of 'purpose' is even less appropriate in discussions of 'God's purpose'. In such cases, the notion of 'purpose' has to be understood 'spiritually'. Such questions are expressions, not of any desire for exact knowledge, or for the ability to anticipate and predict particular future events; they show, rather, a desire for reassurance, for a general confidence about the future. In consequence, the answers to all such questions are necessarily 'spiritual' rather than 'literal', matters of faith, not matters of reason. Reason, through science, tells us what is to be expected. Faith, as the author of the Epistle to the Hebrews puts it, is concerned with 'the confidence of things which are hoped for, and the certainty of things which are not seen'[1]—where of course 'things not seen' has a 'spiritual' meaning also, and does not mean 'things that one cannot see because they are so small, or because they are transparent, like glass'.

All this is not to say that there is no 'reasoning' to be done in theology and religion—it would be highly paradoxical to declare that the writings of Augustine and Aquinas (for example) were not 'reasoned'. It is only to mark the differences between the kinds of 'reasoning' one can sensibly call for, in science and ethics, on the one hand, and in religion, on the other. Pascal remarked, as acutely as anyone, on the nature of these distinctions. He was so struck by them, in fact, that he went too far in the direction of 'fideism': he wished to deny to all religious arguments the title of 'reasoning', on the same grounds as those which prompt the 'imperativists' to deny that title to ethical

[1] Heb. xi.

arguments. 'Who then shall blame Christians', he wrote,[1] 'who confess a religion for which they cannot give reasons, for being unable to give reasons for their belief?. . . If they proved it, they would belie their words; it is the lack of proofs which shows that they do not lack understanding'—and, if by 'proofs' and 'reasons' we understand 'scientific proofs and reasons' (for instance) how true, how necessarily true, this is! He is nearer the mark, and more helpful, when he writes, 'against the objection that the Scripture has no method':

The heart and the mind both have their method. That of the mind is according to principle and demonstration; that of the heart is otherwise. One does not show that one ought to be loved by setting forth in order the causes of love: that would be ridiculous.

Jesus Christ and St Paul have the method of charity, not of the intellect; for they wished to enkindle, not to instruct. So also with St Augustine. This method consists chiefly in enlarging on every point which bears on the end, so as to keep this end constantly in view.[2]

By this he reminds us that, when we are discussing matters of religion, we must seek less for a rational demonstration than for *evidences of* their truth; and that it would be misunderstanding the purpose of religion and the nature of religious 'truth'—and so in a sense self-contradictory—to demand an answer obtained literally, by 'the method of the intellect', to a question meant spiritually, and calling for 'the method of the heart'.

14.7   *Faith and Reason in Ethics*

These remarks about faith and reason have been very general, and we must not leave the subject without returning to our proper field. Let us therefore examine the boundary between religion and ethics—so as to see how, in this sphere, reason marches upon faith.

We encountered 'limiting questions' in three kinds of ethical situation:

(i) When it has been pointed out that an action conforms unambiguously to a recognised social practice, there is no more room for the justification of the action through ethical reasoning: if someone asks, 'Why ought I to give this book back to Jones

---

[1] Op. cit. no. 6, p. 6; Rawlings, III, p. 4.
[2] Op. cit. no. 156, p. 62; Rawlings, LXXV, p. 43.

to-day?', and is given the answer, 'Because you promised to', there is no room within the ethical mode of reasoning for him to ask, 'But why ought I to *really*?'—this question is a 'limiting question'.

(ii) When there is nothing to choose on moral grounds between two courses of action, the only reasoned answer which can be given to the question, 'Which ought I to do?', is one taking account of the agent's own preferences—'If you do *A*, then so-and-so, if you do *B*, then such-and-such: and it's up to you to decide which you prefer'—and if someone now insists on a unique answer, independent of his preferences, his question is again 'limiting'.

(iii) When someone asks, perfectly generally, 'Why ought one do what is right?', and is not satisfied with the answer that the sentence, 'You ought to do what is right', expresses a truism, his question is also a 'limiting' one.

In each of these cases, the logical pattern is similar. In each, ethical reasoning first does for the questioner all that can be asked of it, exhausting the literal answers to his question, and making it clear how far there is any literal sense in his asking what he 'ought' to do. In each case, when this is finished, it is clear that something remains to be done: that moral reasoning, while showing what ought (literally) to be done, has failed to satisfy the questioner. Although he may come to recognise intellectually what he 'ought' to do, he does not feel like doing it—his heart is not in it.

This conflict is manifested in his use of 'limiting questions'. As long as these are taken literally, they seem nonsensical: whether he says, 'I know I promised to, but ought I to, *really*?', or 'Yes, yes; but which ought I *really* to do, *A* or *B*?', or 'But why ought one to do *anything* that is right?', he is ostensibly querying something which it makes no sense to question—literally.

In each case, however, his question comes alive again as soon as one takes it 'spiritually', as a religious question. Over those matters of fact which are not to be 'explained' scientifically, like the deaths in the Jones family, the function of religion is to help us resign ourselves to them—and so feel like accepting them. Likewise, over matters of duty which are not to be justified further in ethical terms, it is for religion to help us embrace them—and so feel like accepting them. In all the three situations referred to, therefore, religious answers may still be appropriate, even when the resources of ethical reasoning are exhausted:

(i) 'Why ought I to give back this book?'
'Because you promised.'
'But why ought I to, *really*?'
'Because it would be sinful not to.'
'And what if I were to commit such a sin?'
'That would be to cut yourself off from God', etc.

(ii) 'Which ought I to do, *A* or *B*?'
'There's nothing to choose between them, morally speaking; it's up to you, but if I were you I should do *B*.'
'But which ought I *really* to do?'
'You ought to do *B*: that is the course more pleasing to God, and will bring you the truest happiness in the end.'

(iii) 'Why ought one to do what is right, anyway?'
'That is a question which cannot arise, for it is to query the very definition of "right" and "ought".'
'But why *ought* one to?'
'Because it is God's will.'
'And why should one do His will?'
'Because it is in the nature of a created being to do the will of its Creator', etc.

14.8   *The Independence of Ethics and Religion*

This kind of thing is familiar enough, and only needs to be pointed out. Where there is a good moral reason for choosing one course of action rather than another, morality is not to be contradicted by religion. Ethics provides the *reasons* for choosing the 'right' course: religion helps us to put our *hearts* into it. There is no more need for religion to compete with ethics on its own ground than with science on its: all three have their hands full doing their own jobs without poaching. In this respect, we can take over into the discussion of ethics Pascal's remarks about the relations between faith and reason in science:

Faith indeed says that which the senses do not say, but not the contrary of that which they say: faith is above the senses, not counter to them.[1]

---

[1] Op. cit. no. 650, p. 312; Rawlings, cccxxvi, p. 178.

This point is sometimes expressed by saying, 'We believe God's will to be good, not because it happens to be *His* will, but because it *is* good'; and it only reflects the difference between the functions of ethics and religion. If an action were not right, it would not be 'God's will' that we should do it. Or again, if an action were not right, it would not be for religion to make us feel like doing it.

Such a non-aggression pact between religion, science and ethics may seem to restrict the scope of religion. But it is a self-denying ordinance rather than an external restriction; and it is to be wished for, not just as a matter of logic, but also as being of eventual advantage to religion itself. For the success of morality in its own task, unhampered by religious irrelevances, will leave us less preoccupied with 'merely material' ends, less circumscribed by the need for taboos and conventions, and therefore freer to concentrate on the choice of our ways of life. And this means more scope for faith in the very spheres in which it is most important—greater freedom for us to try and live 'the life of the saints'—remembering, with Pascal, that

Man's ordinary life is like that of the saints. Both seek satisfaction, and they differ only in the object in which they set it.[1]

One last comment: you are, of course, at liberty to argue that, while religion and religious considerations may be of help to those who feel a need for them, they can be dispensed with by those who do not; that, though religion may help some people to put their hearts into virtue, many people can do so without religion; and that the more people who can the better. But this last is an ethical reflection, not a logical one; and you are not entitled in consequence to rule out all religious and theological judgements as logically improper.

There are many people who do not play bridge, and who in fact consider it a shameful waste of time and energy; but they do not conclude, either that all solutions of bridge problems are therefore invalid, or that it is nonsense to talk of them as 'valid' or 'invalid'. There are some lightning calculators who have no use for the ordinary methods of arithmetic, since they get to the answer more quickly without them—and how much easier our

[1] Op. cit. no. 140, p. 40; Rawlings, XLVIII, p. 27.

schooldays would be if we could all do the same!—but they do not claim that their talents are enough to invalidate all arithmetical proofs. There are some people, for that matter, whose characters are angelic—who hardly seem to need to consider what they ought to do, since they do this instinctively; these people do not feel that same need as the rest of us for ethics and ethical reasoning; and the more of them, also, the better. But we should not allow their existence as an argument against the logical propriety of all ethical arguments: it is simply irrelevant.

In this last chapter, I have been examining the logical characteristics of certain types of religious argument: namely, those which are most intimately related to our earlier discussions about ethics. This I am entitled to do whatever my personal views about the importance or unimportance of religion. The propriety of particular arguments within a mode of reasoning is one thing: the value of the mode of reasoning as a whole is another. And while a discussion of the first can properly appear in a book of logic, one's views on the second would be out of place, and belong rather in an autobiography.

^{1}5

SUMMARY AND EPILOGUE

THE time has come—before the last page is turned, and the book closed—to take a final look round. What, then, was it our aim to do, and how much of this aim has been achieved?

The problem we set ourselves was that of examining the place of reason in ethics. Faced with the recurrent need for moral decisions, and surrounded by a Babel of advisers, we had to discover a means of sifting the conflicting arguments and injunctions presented to us; of deciding which of them were to be regarded and which rejected, which were straightforward and to-the-point, which well-meaning but figurative, which misguided, and which plausible but false.

This was, of course, no virgin field, and plenty of philosophers presented themselves as guides as soon as we set foot in it. It would have been both stupid and churlish to ignore them completely, so, before deciding to set off alone, we examined their credentials. It was this preliminary examination which occupied us for the first quarter of our journey;[1] and it was only after we had cross-questioned them, and compared their evidences with care, that we dismissed them all equally as misleading and unhelpful. Each of the theories of ethics which they put forward as a basis for our itinerary—if interpreted literally—misrepresented our concepts in a way which could not be overlooked: each, at the best, pointed only to a limited comparison, a single facet of ethics and ethical concepts, and had nothing to offer to Everyman in his everyday problems but confusion. We therefore took note of those genuine features of ethics to which they drew our attention incidentally, and then abandoned the philosophical theories of ethics to 'those people who like that sort of thing'.[2]

The common weakness of all these theories was in their treatment of the very problem we were studying: none of them

---

[1] See Part I, Chapters 2–4 above.
[2] Broad, *Five Types of Ethical Theory*, p. 285.

gave any adequate account of the nature of ethical reasoning. In the second part of our journey,[1] therefore, we tried to discover a fresh approach to this problem, a highway avoiding the fens and marshes into which all the other approaches led. This, we decided, must begin with an examination of the *function* of ethics, and of the part which ethical judgements and concepts play in our lives.

In the third part,[2] therefore, we discussed the origin, nature and function of ethical concepts and judgements; and the results of this discussion provided material for an answer to our central question. Ethics is concerned with the harmonious satisfaction of desires and interests. On most occasions it is a good reason for choosing or approving of an action that it is in accordance with an established maxim of conduct, for the existing moral code, and the current institutions and laws, provide the most reliable guide as to which decisions will be happy—in the same kind of way as codes of standard practice in engineering.

At the same time, it is not right to accept the present institutions uncritically—they must evolve, along with the situations to which they apply. There is, therefore, always a place in society for the 'moralist', the man who criticises the current morality and institutions, and advocates practices nearer to an ideal. And the ideal he must keep before him is that of a society in which no misery or frustration is tolerated within the existing resources and state of knowledge. It is for those who are expert in the natural sciences to discover the means of reducing the amount of misery in the world, and so to provide fresh channels for satisfaction and fulfilment: but the evidence of science remains evidence about what is practicable, and so about facts—what *is* or *could be*, not what *ought to be*. It is in the hands of the moralist that possibility becomes policy, what *can* be done becomes what *ought* to be done. All his experience and wisdom are needed to bridge the gap between facts and values. But the gap can be bridged.

Our discussion of the function of ethics led us on to a critique of moral judgement, but the two remained clearly distinguishable. And, by preserving this distinction, which our

---

[1] See Part II, Chapters 6–8 above.
[2] See Part III, Chapters 10–12 above.

self-appointed guides tended to overlook, we were able to keep the chief problem in the centre of our vision. Of course, 'This practice would involve the least conflict of interests attainable under the circumstances' does not *mean* the same as 'This would be the right practice'; nor does 'This way of life would be more harmoniously satisfying' *mean* the same as 'This would be better'. But in each case, the first statement is *a good reason* for the second: the 'ethically neutral' fact is *a good reason* for the 'gerundive' moral judgement. If the adoption of the practice would genuinely reduce conflicts of interest, it is a practice *worthy of adoption*, and if the way of life would genuinely lead to deeper and more consistent happiness, it is one *worthy of pursuit*. And this seems so natural and intelligible, when one bears in mind the function of ethical judgements, that, if anyone asks me *why* they are 'good reasons', I can only reply by asking in return, 'What better kinds of reason could you want?'

This part of the journey gave us the main outlines for an accurate picture of the country: the details we left for others to fill in. In the last part of our exploration[1] we went on to examine the *limits* of ethical reasoning, mapping the boundaries of our territory at those points where straightforward ethical arguments merge into arguments of other kinds. First, we looked again at the philosophical theories of ethics, and were able, in the light of our discoveries, to see the kinds of preoccupation which led their authors astray; and, by relaxing our demand for literal truth, we also came to understand how, as disguised comparisons, such theories could serve either intellectual or rhetorical purposes. Secondly, we followed familiar ethical arguments past the point at which reason must abandon all attempts to assist; and found ourselves in a land of figurative, rather than literal interpretations, and of religious, rather than straightforwardly ethical statements—statements whose function is to 'enkindle', not to 'instruct'.[2]

And this is as far as we need to go. The questions we set ourselves at the beginning have been answered: we can now see how to decide which ethical arguments should be accepted, what reasons for moral decisions are good reasons, how far one

---

[1] See Part IV, Chapters 13–14 above.
[2] Pascal, *Pensées*, ed. Michaut, no. 156, p. 62; Rawlings, LXXV, p. 43.

can rely on reason in coming to moral decisions, and when the giving of more reasons would become supererogatory. And if, in conclusion, you want a summary of the place of reason in ethics, let me refer you to one which has been given already— by Goldsworthy Lowes Dickinson, in his dialogue, *The Meaning of Good*.[1] It is in the figurative language which inevitably accompanies any talk about the 'moral sense'; but, now that we understand the elliptical nature of the language of philosophical ethics, we need no longer let this worry us. If we accept this summary for what it is, we shall find in it a vivid and illuminating expression of all the most important features of ethics:

It is the part of Reason, on my hypothesis, to tabulate and compare results. She does not determine directly what is good, but works, as in all the sciences, upon given data...noticing what kinds of activity satisfy, and to what degree, the expanding nature of this soul that seeks Good, and deducing therefrom, so far as may be, temporary rules of conduct....Temporary rules, I say, because, by the nature of the case, they can have in them nothing absolute and final, inasmuch as they are mere deductions from a process which is always developing and transforming itself. Systems of morals, maxims of conduct are so many landmarks left to show the route by which the soul is marching; casts, as it were, of her features at various stages of her growth, but never the final record of her perfect countenance. And that is why the current morality, the positive institutions and laws...both have and have not the value [sometimes claimed for them]. They are in truth invaluable records of experience, and he is rash who attacks them without understanding; and yet, in a sense, they are only to be understood in order to be superseded, because the experience they resume is not final, but partial and incomplete.

[1] (1901), pp. 86–7.

INDEX

(Subjects listed in the table of Contents are not included)

Generality of ethical judgements, 146, 168, 188, 189, 194
Geometry, Cartesian, 91–2
   non-Euclidean, 94–5, 108, 111, 148–9
Gerundives, 70–4
   and subjective relations, 71–2
Goodness, 'intrinsic', 18

Haldane, J. S., 115–16
Hampden, 151
Hegel, G. W. F., 195, 197–8
History and ethics, 131, 170
Hobbes, Thomas, 195, 197–8, 201
Hume, David, 2, 21, 54, 161, 163, 165, 166–7, 211
Huxley, J. S., 33

Imperative doctrine, 187 ff.
   apparent cynicism of, 48–9, 57 ff.
   a reaction against other doctrines, 47–8, 56–7
Induction, problem of, 99–101
Inference, evaluative, 55–6
   evaluative and validity, 38–41, 51–2, 59
   inductive, 55
'Intuition' in ethics, 18, 25

Kant, Immanuel, 26, 128, 140, 142
Keynes, J. M., 180–1
Knight, Helen, 194

Laplace, 55
Laws and institutions, criticism of, 141–2, 159, 171, 196–7, 223–4
Leonardo da Vinci, 181
Logic, and ethics, 71, 131, 158, 220–1
   and the function of sentences, 84

MacBeath, A., 133
Malcolm, Norman, 25
Marx, Karl, 195, 197–8
Metaphors, 22
   spatial, 43–5, 48, 73, 115–17, 190, 193
Milton, John, 86, 88, 196
Moore, G. E., 5, 18, 19, 22, 55
Murray, Gilbert, 143

Objective doctrine, 47–8, 187 ff.
   sources of, 25 ff., 41 ff.

Paley, Archdeacon William, 214
Paradoxes, philosophical, 24–5, 39, 51–2, 100, 161, 192–3, 201

Pericles, 180
Pascal, Blaise, 202, 209–10, 212, 216–17, 219, 220, 224
Pictograms, 75–6, 80
Pigou, A. C., 179
Plato, 5, 158, 195
Politics and philosophy, 198–9
Popper, K. R., 16, 171, 195, 198
Preaching, 163
Pre-Socratic philosophers, 211
Principles, moral, 138–40, 143, 147–8, 156, 158, 164, 168, 176
Privilege and morality, 168, 171
Probability, 164
Projection, 25
Promises, 140, 143, 146, 150, 170
Properties, 9 ff., 43–4
   analysable, 9
   and ethical concepts, 193
   directly perceived, 9, 10 ff.
   multiple criteria for, 89–91
   non-natural, 9, 21 ff., 47, 62, 160
   unanalysable, 9, 19
Psychology and ethics, 125, 131, 168–9, 174–7, 178, 208
'Purpose', notion of, 215–16

Qualities, complex, 11, 16 ff., 89
   scientific, 11, 91 ff., 107 ff.
   simple, 10, 13 ff., 89
Quantum mechanics, 94

Ramsey, F. P., 129
Reasoning, definition of, 69 ff., 83
   ethical, 68–9
      and the imperative approach, 46, 52–7, 59–60, 61, 63
      and the objective approach, 28, 61, 63
      and the subjective approach, 29, 37 ff., 61, 63
      problem of, 61 ff., 72, 84–5
   nature of, 67 ff.
   scientific, 68
   scientific, logic of, 84–5
   scope of, 54–6, 82–3
Reassurance and religion, 211
Recognition and description, 79
Refractive index, 88, 91
Reid, L. A., 188
Relativity, ethical, 33–5
   theory of, 94
Rhetoric, in ethics, 137–8, 189, 196
   in ethics and science, 129